Global Christianity and the Early Letters of Horace G. Underwood

Global Christianity
and the **Early Letters** of
Horace G. Underwood

James Jinhong Kim

PICKWICK *Publications* · Eugene, Oregon

Pickwick Publications
An Imprint of Wipf and Stock Publishers
199 W. 8th Ave., Suite 3
Eugene, OR 97401

www.wipfandstock.com

PAPERBACK ISBN: 978-1-6667-1571-2
HARDCOVER ISBN: 978-1-6667-1572-9
EBOOK ISBN: 978-1-6667-1573-6

Cataloguing-in-Publication data:

Names: Kim, James Jinhong, author.

Title: Global christianity and the early letters of Horace G. Underwood / by James Jinhong Kim.

Description: Eugene, OR : Pickwick Publications, 2022 | Includes bibliographical references.

Identifiers: ISBN 978-1-6667-1571-2 (paperback) | ISBN 978-1-6667-1572-9 (hardcover) | ISBN 978-1-6667-1573-6 (ebook)

Subjects: LCSH: Underwood, Horace Grant, 1859–1916. | Missions, American—Korea—History.

Classification: BV3462.U6 K56 2022 (print) | BV3462.U6 K56 (ebook)

03/29/22

To

the Underwoods,

Horace & Lillias, Thomas,
Frederick, and Helen

I have a vision of Christian homes, Christian villages, Christian rulers, and a Christian government; and guiding and influencing it all, I see an organized Church, with a competent, well-trained, thoroughly consecrated native ministry

—a united, non-sectarian Church of Christ, where there are neither Methodists, Presbyterians, Episcopalians, Jew nor Greek, Barbarian, Scythian, bond nor free, circumcised nor uncircumcised, but Christ is all in all.

* * * * *

I see this nation, reaching out strong, glad arms of influence—to China on the one hand and to Japan on the other, softening the prejudices and conservatism of the one, and steadying the faith of the other; the three joining the great circle of Christian nations who praise the Lamb for ever and ever, and hail Jesus King of Kings and Lord of Lords.

Horace G. Underwood

Contents

List of Illustrations

Preface and Acknowledgments

THERE ARE THREE THINGS for which I would like to apologize regarding this book. Two are about its title, *Global Christianity and the Early Letters of Horace G. Underwood*. There were suggestions to replace "Global" with "World," now that "global" has become so ubiquitous as to be almost meaningless. Others suggested staying away from mention of "global Christianity" altogether so that the appeal would be more for Underwood's letters themselves. But the appropriateness of using the word "global" with respect to Underwood is, I believe, twofold. Korea at the end of the nineteenth century was literally thought to be "the end of the earth" "where tigers still ate men," the "hermit kingdom" last to open its doors to the world. Underwood's choosing to go there, instead of to China or India as he had envisioned since childhood and where he was in fact initially commissioned, reflects the depths with which he took up the vision of the Protestant mission movements led by such giants of the period as George Müller and Arthur T. Pierson, to become arguably their most beautiful fruit. In short, I felt it was time to bring Underwood out from the confines of the last hermit kingdom *to* the global community, not so much to make him better known worldwide, but to *connect* him via a reverse journey of sorts to the global Christianity in the making today.

This leads to my second reason for titling the book as I have, to examine the journey it takes to go from "global" to "glocal." Underwood's mission in Korea—and more importantly the *spirit* with which he undertook it—marked the peak of the great century of Protestant missions, a century celebrated in 1910 with the convening of the World Missionary Conference, fittingly in Edinburgh, Scotland. Shortly afterward, Pierson himself would make a trip to Korea at Underwood's invitation, and decide on the basis of what he saw on that trip to found the Pierson Institute in Korea rather than in Japan or India as he had originally planned. Then in 1916, Underwood died. I mark the close succession of these three events because they lie at a most interesting juncture in the history of modern Christian missions, a juncture in which the *seeds of* interculturation *were laid as new basis for mission*, but did not get cultivated afterward. Those seeds were lost from history due to global events in the years immediately following—the First and Second World Wars, the Cold War, and the politics of neo-colonialism; and within Korea itself the systemic and calculated erasure of history and culture first under decades of Japanese rule and later under the totalizing impact of the Cold War on the vulnerable only just liberated country, of which the devastations of the Korean War, continued division of its people into North and South, and fragmented political leadership are only a small part. What subsequently arose was a historiography of global missions that continues to be in some sense paralyzed from post-colonial criticism without a viable way forward. I believe Underwood's journey—*to* Korea, but also and perhaps even more importantly "*from*" it—offers vital insights into the nature of that way forward. If my focus in the book seems at times to be too narrowly on Underwood, or the Scottish Enlightenment, or Neo-Confucian Korea, it is not to extol any of them as such in relation to the gospel or the mission. After all, single happenstance events, however extraordinary its fruits, can only be of limited historical interest. Rather, it is my hope that the example of their happy convergence will inspire thoughts—and questions— not only concerning what are the essential qualities and ingredients of interculturation more generally, but also by what means of pedagogy Christians as a collective community might approach newly *glocal* Christianity. These are, I believe, especially timely issues today for and from the perspective of emergent Christians from the global South.

My third apology has to do with the length of time it has taken to get this book published. When in 2013 the Underwood Family came to New Brunswick Theological Seminary (NBTS) with the idea of entrusting to us the body of these previously completely unknown private letters by Underwood, the eventual plan came to be for me to get the letters transcribed, add a short biographical sketch, and publish with the focus very much on the letters. Indeed, just on hearing the news of the project I received emails from several scholars in Korea conveying their eagerness to consult the letters as part of their research interests. That was already several years ago, and I am truly in their debt for their patience! Initially, the transcription of especially the handwritten letters (comprising thirteen of the twenty-four letters) took over a year to complete. But in the course of that year I came to realize more and more what rich repository these letters were, offering new perspectives as well as details on everything from Korean culture and politics of the period, to interpersonal dynamics between Underwood and his fellow missionaries and its impact on the mission, and much more that is not found in his public writings or official mission reports. Alongside my growing concern for how best to present this enormous wealth of materials to the world, a number of events also occurred that both slowed my work on the project and enriched it. In 2014, a generous grant from the Luce Foundation to NBTS led to the opening of the Underwood Center for Global Christianity, and with it my being appointed the Center's Director. The flurry of new responsibilities in its early years took much time, with projects as various as creating and orchestrating annual lectureships, student pilgrimage seminars overseas, and international symposia to build global connections for the Center, hosting the many guests from abroad wishing to visit the Underwood Memorial, and even becoming consultant for the making several TV documentaries about Underwood and the history of missions in Korea. Around that time, though I had finished writing the book's manuscript, the original plan to publish the work as part of the RCA History Series came to naught for reasons beyond anyone's control, and it took time—compounded by the restrictions posed by Covid 19—to arrive at the happy meeting with Wipf and Stock as the work's new publisher.

So it is with enormous sense of gratitude that I acknowledge even just a few people among the many whose guidance and support throughout the past eight years have been instrumental to bringing this project to fruition. Foremost among them I would like to thank John Coakley (NBTS). For his involvement with the project from its very beginning he truly deserves to be recognized as its unnamed second author, not only for his invaluable advice at every turn, but closely reading my numerous manuscript drafts with unflagging graciousness as well as immense scholarship. I would also like to thank Joseph Lee (Pace U) for his critical reading of the manuscript and many key suggestions. Whatever errors and other faults remain in the work in spite of their advice belong to me alone.

Among the NBTS community, while my heartfelt thanks go to all the faculty, students, and staff, especially to the librarians and the NBTS/RCA Archives crew at the Sage Library, I would like to single out the late Dr. Gregg Mast, whose enthusiastic support for the work to be a part of the RCA History Series helped launch the project initially, and President Micah McCreary with his commitment and vision for greater diversity at NBTS in the twenty-first century, who together perhaps represent the two undercurrents—historical and future-oriented—in the present work. I would also like to thank James Brumm for his continued encouragement and support for the project even after its departure from the RCA History Series.

In the years since the project began I have had many opportunities to work with scholars whose works and/or collegial discussions with me have either inspired or helped shape my own. While there are too many of them to mention by name, concerning the rather lengthy section on essentials of Neo-Confucian philosophy I am greatly indebted to the late Dr. Wm. Theodore de Bary, my longtime teacher, as well as colleagues from the Neo-Confucian Regional Seminar and the editorial team of the Sources books series for their insights spanning many years. Given that this is a work of mission historiography I did my best to keep that side of the book as simple and short as possible, assuming readers with little or no prior knowledge of Neo-Confucianism; if in the process I have grossly overlooked certain aspects or subtleties of the vast Neo-Confucian universe, I ask for their indulgent understanding. I am also particularly indebted to the Eastern Fellowship of Professors of Mission at American Society of Missiology for continually energizing and publishing my works in missiology, especially Dana Robert (Boston U), Daryl Ireland (Boston U), Thomas Hastings (OMSC), Dan Nicholas and Craig A. Noll (IBMR); also Bill Burrows (Orbis)—and Robert Hunt (SMU)—for generously laying the bridge connecting this project to Matthew Wimer of Pickwick Publications.

My directorship at the Underwood Center afforded me the pleasure and privilege of working closely also with many scholars outside the field of missiology. I'd like to mention in particular Sarah Coakley (U of Cambridge), Miroslav Volf (Yale), and Nicholas Wolterstorff (Yale) whose conversations, in addition to their contributions as Keynote Speakers at the International Underwood Symposia, not only further affirmed the intimate connection between missiology and theology, but also suggested interesting directions for future work. I am also grateful to the late Dr. Samuel Moffett, my long time mentor, and Mrs. Moffett, as well as Kyung-Bae Min (Yonsei U.), Scott W. Sunquist (Gordon-Conwell Theological), Elizabeth Underwood (Eastern Kentucky U), Sung-Deuk Oak (UCLA), Timothy Kiho Park (Fuller Theological), Loida I. Martell (Palmer Theological), and David E. Goatley (Duke/Lott Carey Mission) for the perspectives they contributed as speakers at the Annual Underwood Symposia at New Brunswick. With the recent surge of interest in Underwood in Korea, among Christians and non-Christians alike, led by academics but increasingly also by specialists working in mass media, the present volume is moreover indebted to the foundational studies done by them. Even the fact that I had the freedom to approach the project as historiography more than a traditional biography is in large measure due to their having paved the way.

My perspective on this project has also been further expanded by activities in partnerships spanning the many affiliated institutions of NBTS around globe; among them I want to especially acknowledge those institutions either founded by or tracing their inspiration to Underwood, who have continuously worked to bring Underwood to light. And so, to Saemoonan Church, Yonsei University, Presbyterian University & Theological Seminary, Seoul Jangsin University, the Association of Underwood Sister Churches, the Underwood Symphony Orchestra in Metro New York, and others too many to mention, I am in debt not only for their encouragement throughout this project, but for their standing in demonstration of the power of one person's interculturation to inspire such tremendous and lasting change.

Last but in many ways the most of all, I am deeply indebted to the Underwood Family, especially Laurel, John, and Peter, for entrusting me with their precious family legacy so wholeheartedly and with undoubting faith all these years. May the spirit of your great-grandparents Horace and Lillias, live on and live strong in you and in the generations yet to come!

From the Sage Library, NBTS, where Underwood used to study,

James Jinhong Kim

Introduction

Re-evaluating Underwood's Significance in Context of Global Christianity

THIS BOOK CULMINATES IN the examination and analysis of previously unknown private letters of Horace Grant Underwood (1859–1916), arguably the most historically significant yet under-recognized Protestant missionary of the nineteenth century. I say "culminates," because in order to convey some sense of the significance of these letters for rethinking the future direction of Christian missiology in the twenty-first century, it was necessary first to establish the different early formative influences that helped shape Underwood's basic missiology, but then also to bring to light the Neo-Confucian ethos of "rightness" he encountered in Chosŏn Korea, which was to subtly yet so fundamentally change the nature and color of his later missional activities. In a sense, what I want to point to with this book is the presence and nature of this *change in the missionary's own conception of the gospel* through his encounter. It is well known that in evangelizing Asia Minor, Apostle Paul "Hellenized" what had been largely a Judaic Messianic event, in effect *expanding* Christianity—not just regionally but *theologically*. Presumably this had not been his design when leaving for Asia Minor; he could not have planned in advance for such an approach in his mission, just as it is doubtful he would have had reason to insist on a Christ who transcends circumcision and kosher laws if he had not been sent to live and work among people to whom his being an upright Pharisee had no meaning. Similarly, Apostle John could hardly have re-configured Jesus as "the Word" (or "*logos*") if he had not recognized in the Greek idea of divine reason implicit in the cosmos a *further clarification of* the Christ he himself knew and experienced. In other words, his reference to "*logos*," far from being an imperfect "translation" or a spiritual/cultural "compromise" to Hellenistic contexts, signified a meaningful *expansion* of his earlier, culturally limited understandings or articulation of Christ

1

one step closer to a fuller, more universal intuiting of him. This *mutuality* of conceptual expansion between the missionary and "missionee" is the essence of what I mean by "interculturation," and contra our general picture of missionaries as those sent to bring change *to* others, history has shown that the most significant, peaceful, and foundational missions have been those where a dynamic of interculturation was most effectively at work. The fact that Underwood embodied this spirit of interculturation in his person and his mission, and did so through his encounter with Neo-Confucian Korea, in East Asia, despite having been born in Great Britain and raised in America during the height of Western imperialism in the nineteenth century—there is great significance, and much we can learn, for the future of global Christianity in his example.

So who was Horace G. Underwood? As the first Protestant missionary to set foot in Korea, and the architect behind much of the early work that took place there, Underwood is regularly credited with Christianity's unparalleled success and fervent presence in Korea to this day. Among the many countries introduced to Christianity by Protestant missionaries since the early nineteenth century, only Korea currently boasts a 30 percent Christian population (as of 2010); among Koreans living in America that number is as high as 71 percent. Perhaps even more surprisingly, South Korea today has over twenty-five thousand full-time missionaries in 170 countries around globe,[1] making it second only to the U.S. in the number of missionaries it sends to foreign lands.[2] For this singular state of affairs alone Underwood ought to be the subject of much study. Yet except for the two books written about him by his wife Lillias Horton Underwood a century ago, and barely

---

1. According to the Korea World Mission Association (KWMA)'s 2013 Year-end Report. See also Timothy Park, "The Missionary Movement of the Korean Church," 19.

2. Moll, "Missions Incredible," 28–34. In making "Missions Incredible" about the Korean mission movement its cover story for the issue, *Christianity Today* expressed surprised admiration that "South Korea is on its way to sending out more missionaries than any other country on earth," with an ambitious vision of sending one hundred thousand full-time missionaries to all over the world by 2030. The article went on to note that whereas only about 10 percent of the world's Christian missionaries are willing to go to the very marginalized regions where the gospel has never yet been heard, a much higher 34 percent of Korean missionaries do not hesitate to go to such regions. Despite such passion in the service of the gospel, however, the article also cited frequent "lone-ranger complex" among Korean missionaries as inconducive to coordinated teamwork and harmonious relations with natives. See Moll, "Missions Incredible," 28–34. Professor of missiology at Fuller Theological Seminary Dr. Timothy Kiho Park, in his Keynote Speech for the 5th Annual Underwood Conference, shared a similar analysis and overview of the situation. Timothy Park, "Korean Christian World Mission."

a handful of articles in English, he remains relatively little known outside of Korea and the few scholars studying Korean Christianity.[3]

It may be that twentieth century ambivalence toward the frequent "marriage" of Christian missions with Western cultural and political imperialism has discouraged "yet another" extolling of a seemingly traditional nineteenth century missionary. John Coakley has written that although "the formation of Underwood [and his Methodist colleague Henry Appenzeller (1858–1902)] for their calling as missionaries . . . was partly an expression of the missionary spirit of their times, the spirit embodied in the notion of a 'crisis of missions' and the vision of an evangelized world within a generation," was the same spirit that, decades later, "in the aftermath of the First World War, had come under criticism in America and elsewhere—for allying itself too easily with American culture, on the one hand, or, on the other hand, *for not adapting its theology adequately to the modern world*."[4] This is in important ways a fair and valid assessment. Underwood's writings about Korea, for example, are not free of elements that to readers today may sound patronizing and presumptuous. But even where clearly encased in outdated modes of language and thought, in Underwood's case I would argue it is also possible to see well defined foundations of entirely different missiological principles at work, which as I hope to show in this book ultimately rests on his openness to *inter*culturation rather than simply inculturation. It must be remembered, too, that his public writings, such as his many mission reports and *The Call to Korea, Political, Social, Religious* (1908), were styled for the broad audience of his time and for the purpose of soliciting more support from them for the mission in Korea. The point, then, is not to discount or gloss over the imperialist cultural context to which he had been born and under which he fashioned his mission, but rather to not let it detract from identifying, inquiring after, and ultimately further building on those other principles at work in his ministry that provide valuable insights for how to approach issues today in the globalization *of Christianity* (as distinct from mere globalization of Western Christianity's outreach).

By happy coincidence, Rev. Laurel Underwood Brundage, a great-granddaughter of Horace Underwood, recently brought to light a previously

3. Lillias Horton Underwood (1851–1921) wrote *Fifteen Years among the Top-Knots, or Life in Korea* (1904) and *Underwood of Korea: Being an Intimate Record of the Life and Work of the Rev. H. G. Underwood, D.D., LL.D., for Thirty-One Years a Missionary of the Presbyterian Board in Korea* (1918).

4. Coakley, "The Seminary Years of the Missionaries Horace G. Underwood and Henry Appenzeller," 79; emphasis added. For an account of how the phrase "Evangelization of the world in this generation" or the origin of "watchword" came to be, see Robert, "The Origin of the Student Volunteer Watchword," 146–49.

unknown body of his letters to his family from the early years of his mission in Korea. Written mostly to his brothers John Thomas (1857–1937) and Frederick (1858–91), these letters illuminate Underwood's understanding of the mission and of Korea at its most frank, intimate, and unguarded. His family were in many ways the most important and constant supporters of his mission, not only spiritually and emotionally but financially as well. Although Frederick—the "saintliest" of the Underwood brothers, according to Lillias (Horton Underwood)—would die at the young age of thirty-three, merely six years after Underwood's departure for Korea, Thomas would continue for the remainder of his life, and even beyond Horace's death, to be the mainstay of his brother's many mission projects, including the founding of Yonsei University. Only two years apart in age, the two were not only close as brothers, but also shared an intimate understanding of the lifelong faith that had led Underwood to Korea as well as what he proposed to do there. These letters therefore carry a very different tone from Underwood's other, more official writings. As I have shown elsewhere, Underwood's Korean mission had its unparalleled success in large part because he (1) insightfully separated the empowering message of the gospel from the "guns" of imperialism—and this in spite of his personal entrepreneurial background; (2) proactively engaged in inter-denominational cooperation on both institutional and personal levels; and (3) committed himself to a long term vision of a Christian *Korea*, as distinct from churches or Christians *in* Korea.[5] Each of these elements is present in these newly discovered letters to family. Indeed they saturate the letters, not as anything of note or new to the brothers, but as principles in which both of them are entirely at home and which they take for granted.

But more than that, Underwood also presages some of the most significant contemporary debates surrounding missiology today, and not necessarily as a negative example. As indicated earlier, this is not to say Underwood's understanding of the mission was free from the limitations and presumptions of the Western worldview of his time (or for that matter that subsequent developments in Korean Christianity have been free of problems). But if questions concerning the theological as well as political implications of separating the gospel from its historical encasing in Western cultural and political imperialism continue to be central to current debates about the dynamics of missions; if the meaning and/or possibility of unity across the many denominations attesting to the enormous variety of cultural and contextual transformations of Christian faith is central to

5. See James Kim, "Bible versus Guns," 33–37; see also James Kim, "A Copernican Re-Evaluation of Appenzeller and Underwood's Mission in Korea," 211–34.

the debates concerning "Global Christianity"; if the Church's relation to the structural imbalances in the world's socio-economic and political policies pose a fundamental challenge to the very ontology as well as function of religion in the world, then there, too, Underwood's example offers a relevant and thought-provoking case study for the building of a new, viably global missiology to be applied for the future.

It is neither the ambition nor the scope of this book, however, to analyze what relationship might exist between Underwood and contemporary missiologies. Instead, the aim here is simply to introduce the newly discovered early Underwood letters to his family, and to do so by way of providing an in-depth examination of key elements that would have played a critical role in his formation *and transformation* as a missionary, followed by a discussion of the historical and missiologial points of interest raised by the letters themselves. As John Coakley has so astutely pointed out, Underwood was a particular product of his disposition, education, and his time.[6] Of these, I focus on the different elements of his education—here broadly defined to include his family heritage as well as the formal schooling/training, the socio-dynamic experiences he had in America, and—not least—the deeply saturated Neo-Confucian culture and ethos with which he came into contact and learned from during his time in Korea, as most germane to and as yet absent from the study of Underwood as a missionary, and as central to the study of interculturation as a new model for missiology.

Chapter 1 will consist of a brief overview of Underwood's life, after which chapter 2 will examine certain formative aspects of his education divided into three sections, each by coincidence spanning roughly thirteen years of his life: (1) his boyhood years in England and France where, in addition to early formal schooling, he absorbed from his family a deeply evangelical, mission-oriented, yet ecumenical social consciousness, as well as lively entrepreneurial mindedness; (2) his American years during which he gained equally from the unmediated personal encounters he had with wide swaths of immigrant population through his passionate if youthful evangelism, as from the training he received from some of the country's elite educational institutions; and (3) the years in Korea covered by the letters in which he encountered the Neo-Confucian culture and ethos that deeply saturated its people and that in many ways not only both echoed and complemented Underwood's Christian spirituality, but in turn ultimately also transformed Underwood's own understanding of the gospel and mission. An important implication for missiology in taking this approach—i.e., taking into account the broad idealisms of both the sending and receiving

6. Coakley, "The Seminary Years."

civilizations as mediating the dynamic and fundamental transformation of *both the missionary as well as the mission field*—is the idea of interculturation, emphasizing the *mutuality* of enlargement as the path for the future of Global Christianity and its missiology.[7]

Chapter 3 is an analysis of Underwood's letters themselves with particular attention to this perspective of mutual interculturation. Chapter 4 provides a transcription of the letters themselves.

7. In that sense I use the term "interculturation" as distinct from both "inculturation" and "intercultural." Inculturation speaks primarily to the kind of contextualization of an idea such that it enables an organic renaissance of the receiving culture from within. While it recognizes the transformative energy within the receiving culture, it nevertheless continues to dichotomize the giver and receiver dynamic. See Schineller, *Handbook on Inculturation*, esp. 6–7, 16–20; Shorter, *Toward a Theology of Inculturation*, esp. 4–16. "Intercultural" is a much broader (and more recent), general term referring to any interaction pertaining to or taking place between two or more cultures, as for example between theology and culture. Intercultural theology has been described as "a domain of theology that pays particular attention to the identity of non-western forms of Christianity in dialogue with western forms." See Cartledge and Cheetham, *Intercultural Theology*.

Underwood at 15 years old

As a 25 year old / 1884 / graduating
from seminary

In his 30's / in Korea

In his 50's / 1910's

Underwood with his wife Lillias
and son Horton, in 1892

Chapter 1

A Brief Outline of the Life
of Horace G. Underwood

UNDERWOOD'S IMMEDIATE ANCESTRY WAS rich in both entrepreneurial and religious spirit. His paternal grandfather, Thomas Underwood (1795–18??) worked in publishing at London's Fleet Street, mostly in medical texts. Though a layman he was apparently known as a man of great faith, and married Mary Easton Waugh (1792–1866), daughter of Alexander Waugh, on February 6, 1817, in Marylebone, Westminster, London.[1] The Waughs were well known as a family of Scottish Presbyterians, tracing their family at least as far back as Adam Waugh (c. 1670–1732) of East Gordon, Berwick, Scotland, where both his son Thomas (1706–83) and grandson Alexander (1754–1827) were born and raised. As the youngest in the family Alexander followed his father's wishes to become a "man of profession" by graduating from the Universities of Edinburgh (1774) and Aberdeen (1777)—both leading centers of the Scottish Enlightenment—before receiving ordination in the Scottish Presbyterian Church of Edinburgh in 1779, and taking up the post of pastor in Newton.[2] In 1782, as a relatively young man of twenty-eight, he was invited by the important Scottish Presbyterian congregation

---

1. Marylebone is an area of central London located within the City of Westminster and part of the West End. Very much an affluent neighborhood today roughly bounded by Oxford Street to the south, Marylebone Road to the north, Edgware Road to the west and Great Portland Street to the east, historically it also encompassed Regent's Park and Doset Square, Baker Street, Wimpole Street, and Harley Street, as well as the neighborhood known as Lisson Grove.

2. The University of Edinburgh was founded in 1583; University of Aberdeen was even older, having been founded in 1495, although it did not offer classes until ten years later, in 1505. As two of four oldest universities in Scotland, by the eighteenth century both had become leading centers of the Scottish Enlightenment alongside the University of Glasgow (founded in 1451), and produced such thinkers as David Hume (1711–76) and Charles Darwin (1809–92).

at Wells Street in London to become their second ever pastor, and went on to become well known throughout the city for his sermons as well as for his strong interest in foreign missions. By all accounts he was a charismatic and eminent leader of ministry whose biography, written shortly after his death, was popular enough to warrant a third printing.[3] It is recorded that in 1815 Rev. Waugh spoke at many pulpits throughout Scotland, raising some £1420 for the cause in the process while his "rival" Rev. Broadfoot of the Oxendon Church is supposed to have raised only £750 for the same cause in the same way.[4] When Thomas Underwood married his daughter, Rev. Waugh enjoyed long amiable relations with his daughter's family, and each of the eight children born to the Underwoods were baptized at his Scottish Presbyterian church on Wells Street. More will be said about Alexander Waugh's influence on Horace Underwood in chapter 2.

Underwood's father, John Underwood (1827–81), was the seventh child and youngest of five sons born to Thomas Underwood and Mary Waugh Underwood. An admirer of the great English scientist Michael Faraday (1791–1867)[5] even as a boy, John eventually studied chemistry under Faraday, and—perhaps from his familiarity with the publishing industry through his father—soon made a name for himself by developing new types of ink that greatly eased printing as well as writing. In 1855, at age twenty-eight, John married Elizabeth Grant Mair (1828–65), a woman also of Marylebone, well educated enough to be listed in the *1851 Census for England and Wales* as a teacher of German and French.[6] If she was remembered

3. The *Memoir of the Rev. Alexander Waugh, D.D., with Selections from His Epistolary Correspondence*, by James Hay and Henry Belfrage was first published in Edinburgh by William Oliphant & Sons and in London by Hamilton, Adams & Co. in 1830, then again in 1838. It was published once more, this time in New York, by R. Carter & Brothers in 1851.

4. The Church at Wells Street, together with the congregation at Oxendon Street, represented the Burgher and Anti-Burgher branches of the Scottish Presbyterian with respect to the Burgess Oath in Scotland. That schism occurred in 1746. For a lively description of Waugh's ministry at the Wells Church and for the London Missionary Society, see Black, *The Scots Churches in England*, 208–10. More will be said on this point later in this chapter, as part of discussions of Underwood's vocational education. Black wrote, "Scotland has the name of being the mother of innumerable sects and denominations, yet it must be borne in mind that she has also seen a great many religious and denominational unions." Black, *The Scots Churches in England*, 14–15.

5. More is discussed about Faraday in relation to the Underwoods later in chapter 2.

6. "Elizabeth Grant Mair, July 26th, 1855" in *Church of England Marriages and Banns, 1754–1921*. Born on February 11, 1828 to John and Helen Mair, Elizabeth was baptized into the Church of England at St. Olave's Hart Street, the small but historically important church where Queen Elizabeth I held service of thanksgiving upon her release from the Tower of London in 1554, and was the beloved resting place of the essayist Samuel Pepys (1633–1703). See *Church of England Births and Baptisms, 1813–1917*. Elizabeth's father John Mair was also a native of Marylebone.

by the family as a gentle woman who "never showed anger or raised her voice to the children," her husband John was both an intellectual grounded in the sciences and a man of devout faith, strong in expectations of the Second Coming of Christ.[7] He was also a sincere and generous supporter of Christian charitable institutions, including those run by his fellow premillennialist George Müller (1805–98), the Christian evangelist and highly respected Director of the Ashley Down orphanage in Bristol, England.[8] It is perhaps not all that surprising that Horace Grant Underwood, born on July 19, 1859, as the fourth of their six children and youngest of three sons, declared his vocation for the ministry at the age of only four years.[9]

In 1865, when Horace was barely six, he suffered the deaths of his mother, his newborn sister Mary, and his paternal grandmother Mary Waugh Underwood. This was followed the following year by his father going bankrupt from the misdeeds of a business partner, leaving the family in difficult circumstances. Within a few years his father remarried, to Caroline Nunn (c. 1830–??), a widow with two daughters of her own, of whom the younger, Ann—some seven years older than Horace—would eventually move to America with the Underwood family. Not much is known about Caroline, but in late 1869, shortly after his father's remarriage, Horace and his brother Frederick (1858–91) were sent to the Catholic boarding school of Ecole Dié in Boulogne-sur-Mer, the French port city just across the English Channel from London. Then in 1872, their father set out for America to have a fresh start after the troubles of his bankruptcy, and by 1873 had reunited his family in New Durham, New Jersey.[10] It was here on December 5, 1874, that the Underwoods including Horace were registered into the Dutch Reformed Church by "profession of faith" and became very active in the life of the community.[11]

7. Lillias Underwood, *Underwood of Korea*, 19.

8. Lillias goes so far as to describe George Müller as having been one of her father-in-law's "closest and most intimate friends." See Lillias Underwood, *Underwood of Korea*, 25. More will be discussed about George Müller in relation to the Underwoods later in chapter 2.

9. Lillias Underwood, *Underwood of Korea*, 30.

10. *Passenger Lists of Vessels Arriving at New York, 1820–1897*: Microfilm Serial: M237, 1820–1897; Microfilm Roll: Roll 372, Line 5, List Number 156.

11. Those registered as official members of the Church at this time were John Underwood, his three sons John Thomas, Frederick, and Horace Underwood, and their sister Helen Evelyn. Their elder sister Hannah Elizabeth's name does not appear in the registry, and it is possible that she did not actually emigrate to America with the rest of her family. Their stepmother Caroline Nunn Underwood and her daughter Anne do not appear in the registry either; however, nor would Caroline be buried in the Underwood family plot in the cemetery of the New Grove Church at her death. This

The pastor at the Dutch Reformed Church of New Grove, Rev. William Augustus van Vranken Mabon (1822–92), would especially exert long and important influence on the young Horace Underwood—as "beloved" pastor, private tutor for college entrance examinations, Professor of Theology at Seminary, and model of pastoral leadership. But whereas all the Underwood children participated actively in the life of their new church community in America, as a family of newly arrived immigrants it would appear only Horace was singled out by his father to continue his education at the elite Hasbrouck Institute, while John Thomas (usually called Thomas) and Frederick—older than Horace by two and one years only respectively—worked. This was followed by matriculation at New York University (1877–81) and the New Brunswick Theological Seminary (1881–84). It was while a student at the latter, in October, 1883, that Underwood attended the annual convention of the Inter-Seminary Missionary Alliance. A precursor to the Student Volunteer Movement (for Foreign Missions) soon to begin in 1886, the Inter-Seminary Missionary Alliance had been founded in 1880 by a group of students from twelve different seminaries and was one of the first ecumenical organizations of its kind in America. In fact, the organization's first meeting had taken place at New Brunswick of that year.[12] In 1883, however, its annual convention was held in Hartford, Connecticut, and it was here, among the 345 young men gathered from thirty-one seminaries around the country, that Underwood for the first time (or the second time–if we count the "Altman account" mentioned in Underwood's 1909 reminiscences)[13] heard mention of "Corea, the last of the hermit nations" that had just opened its doors to the West under conditions set by the Shufeldt treaty.[14]

fact has contributed to the conjecture that she might have been Catholic and remained one even after her second marriage. See Hyoung-Woo Park, "A Study on the Coming to Korea," 53–83.

12. One of the speakers at this first meeting in New Brunswick was Arthur Tappan Pierson (1837–1911) who later deeply influenced and supported Underwood's mission to Korea from the beginning. Coakley, "The Seminary Years," 73–74. More will be said about Pierson in section II of this chapter.

13. There is some confusion regarding the exact dating of the steps by which he arrived at his decision to go to Korea. For an outline of the confusion see Coakley, "The Seminary Years," 78.

14. The speaker who mentioned "Corea, the last of hermit nations" was Archibald Alexander Hodge (1823–86), then principal of Princeton Seminary, in his address titled, *The Call to Foreign Missions.* See George F. Moore, "Report of the Fourth Annual Convention of the American Inter-Seminary Missionary Alliance," 93; see also Coakley, "The Seminary Years," 75–76.

The Shufeldt Treaty was a fourteen-article treaty between U.S. and Chosŏn Korea signed in 1882. Besides establishing mutual friendship and mutual assistance in case of attack, the treaty covered such issues as U.S. extraterritorial jurisdiction, prohibition of the import or export of opium, regulations concerning trade, and student exchanges.

Although Underwood had long assumed he would become a missionary to India, he found himself troubled throughout all of the next year that no one was forthcoming to go to Korea. He later recalled that, when despite several applications he found no commission that would allow him to go to Korea and was literally on the verge of mailing in his acceptance of the position of pastor at the prestigious First Reformed Church instead, something about Korea stayed his hand. The very next day he received an offer of a commission to Korea, albeit from the Presbyterian and not the Dutch Reformed mission board, which he readily accepted.[15]

As becoming a missionary in "the hermit kingdom" was considered tantamount to going to one's death,[16] Underwood followed the Presbyterian Mission's as well as his brothers' advice to go to England to take final leave of family remaining there, then took the train for San Francisco—his brother Thomas accompanying him as far as Chicago—to take his passage across the Pacific.[17] Then, during the several months stay in Japan Underwood was introduced to the basics of Korean language and culture by none other than Yi Sujŏng himself (1842–86). Sometimes known by his Japanese name Rijutei, Yi was none other than the Korean Christian whose letter of appeal for missionaries to be sent to Korea was said to have touched and inspired Underwood during his student days.[18] Yi Sujŏng's story of conversion while in Japan had first appeared in the November 1883 issue of the *Missionary Review*, with account of a dream he had right before his conversion: "Soon he had a dream that two men, one tall and the other short in stature, came to him with a basketfull [*sic*] of books; and to his inquiry what the books

---

15. Lillias Underwood, *Underwood of Korea*, 33–36. Lillias quotes at length from Underwood's own account, as given to the Quarto Centennial of the Presbyterian Board in 1909, of the events that led to his going to Korea. Coakley, while recognizing the weight of Underwood's accounting, also points to some inconsistencies in the matter of dating. See Coakley, "The Seminary Years," 78.

16. "We had been told before we went out to work in other lands that Korea was a land into which it was almost death to go. It was the last country to break the seal." H. G. Underwood, "Address," 53–54.

17. Lillias Underwood, *Underwood of Korea*, 36–37. See also Underwood's letter to Helen, December 22, 1884. Until recently, scholarship had accepted Lark-June George Paik's early claim that Underwood "sailed from San Francisco for Japan on December 16th [1884]." Paik, "The History of Protestant Missions in Korea, 1832–1910," 116b. This misinformation was recently overturned by Woonhyung Jung's painstaking research establishing beyond all doubt that the actual date of departure had been December 31, 1884, which is supported also by the first of the Underwood letters in this collection. See Jung's article, "Horace G. Underwood's Decision and Departure for the Mission Field."

18. Lillias Underwood, *Underwood of Korea*, 38.

were, they replied, 'These books are the most important of all books for your country.' He then said, 'What book is it?' and was answered, 'It is the Bible.'"[19] On December 13, 1883, from Yokohama, Japan, Yi Sujŏng penned a letter titled "A Christian Corean's Appeal" to the brethren and sisters of the churches in the United States, which was published in various mission journals such as the *Friend's Review: A Religious, Literary and Miscellaneous Journal* and the *Missionary Review* in early 1884. The letter read in part,

> Your country is well known to us as a Christian land; but if you do not send the Gospel to us, I am afraid other nations will hasten to send their teachers, and I fear that such teachings are not in accordance with the will of the Lord. Although I am a man of no influence I will do my utmost to aid such missionaries as you may send. I beg most earnestly that you will send some one to Japan at once who can consult with those who are laboring here, and prepare himself for work. This, I think, is the best and safest plan.[20]

It would seem that after coming across this letter,[21] Underwood twice applied to the Reformed Church in American Board of Foreign Missions to go to Korea, but they replied in March-April 1884 to decline his application "owing to the exigencies of the work already in hand."[22] Then Underwood wrote to the Presbyterian Board, writing on July 10, 1884,

> I had not decided which field I ought to enter until some months after I read the earnest appeal of Rijutei for missionaries among the Coreans. My heart was stirred by the appeal and I anxiously watched to see what would be done. For some time nothing was

19. Griffis, "Corea: the Hermit Nation," 417–18, citing Henry Loomis' (1839–1920) letter about Rijutei. It may be possible to speculate the short man in the dream to have been Underwood, and Appenzeller who accompanied him the tall man.

20. Yi, "A Christian Corean's Appeal," 401–2.

21. It could also have been initially shortly before; see Coakley, "Seminary Years," 77–79.

22. The report of the Board from that time reads: "In response to the appeal of Rijutei, the converted Corean nobleman now resident in Japan, for Missionaries to be sent to his countrymen from the American Churches, the Board received an application in February, from a student in the Theological Seminary at New Brunswick, to be appointed and sent as a Missionary of the Reformed Church to Corea. Owing to the exigencies of its position, and the demands of the work already in hand, the Board felt compelled to decline the proffered service, and leave to others the honor and labor of introducing into the 'Hermit Kingdom' the gospel of salvation." *The Fifty-Second Annual Report of the Board of Foreign Missions of the Reformed Church in America*, 13.

done & I felt forced to ask my own Board to send me to Corea.
This they felt they could not do.[23]

This time, he was accepted. In October 1884, at the annual Inter-Seminary Missionary Alliance held in Princeton, where Robert P. Wilder (1863–1938), a future leader of the Student Volunteer movement (of Foreign Missions), was also in attendance as a student of Princeton University, Underwood was formally introduced as "Missionary for Corea."[24]

Underwood arrived at the port of Chemulp'o on the outskirts of Seoul, on Easter Day, April 5, 1885. He, together with Henry G. Appenzeller (1858–1902) from Drew Seminary, were the first Protestant missionaries to set foot in the country,[25] and aside from three visits back to America to raise support for the mission while also recuperating from illnesses, he would spend the next thirty years of his life in Korea and wish to get back to Korea even on his deathbed.

Chosŏn Korea at the time of Underwood's arrival was increasingly becoming embroiled in international politics it did not understand. Founded in 1392, Chosŏn Dynasty had the unusual distinction in world history of having been founded expressly for the purpose of realizing an ideological and socio-cultural vision—that of Neo-Confucian idealism emphasizing meritocracy and social mobility rooted in universal education of humaneness. Perhaps because of that early vision—antedating England's Glorious Revolution by nearly three hundred years—the dynasty had enjoyed a longevity far outlasting any other in modern world history.[26] But over the course of the nearly five hundred years since the largely non-violent transfer of power from Koryŏ (918–1392) aristocracy to Neo-Confucian scholarly elite, the idealism and vision had slowly become depleted, and by the time of Underwood's arrival the country had been suffering from a widespread

---

23. Underwood, *Letter to the Board of Foreign Missions of the Presbyterian Church.*

24. Inter-Seminary Missionary Alliance, *Report of the Fifth Annual Convention of the American Inter-Seminary Missionary Alliance, Princeton New Jersey, Oct. 24th, 25th, and 26th, 1884*, 5, cited in Coakley, "The Seminary Years," 79.

25. While Appenzeller did set foot on Chemulp'o, it was Underwood alone who went on to Seoul at this time. Appenzeller, whose recently married wife, Ella, was pregnant, decided to heed the warning of the American Consul and returned to Japan for a time; they then returned with other missionaries on June 20. Lillias Underwood, *Underwood of Korea*, 40.

26. There are mixed views about the significance or effect of this longevity. Some scholars argue the stability is testament to Chosŏn dynasty's commitment to Neo-Confucian egalitarian values, at least as compared to many similar states of its time. Even for the wealthiest aristocrats, for example, there were strict limits set on how large one's place of residence could be. Others have interpreted the longevity more negatively as lethargy leading to lost opportunity for periodic renewal.

spiritual vacuum. Beset by internal factionalism, moribund rituals that had hardened into mere shells of their former meaning, and widespread poverty, the court and governing bureaucracy were moreover surrounded on all sides by the imperial ambitions of Japan and Russia, a China on the brink of demise, and an unknown world order from the West eager to establish their own stakes in the fallout. Korea's fragility at the time was such that some Protestant missionaries regarded the country as something of a provincial outpost to the more established missions in Japan and China. Even Underwood himself seems to have considered Japan as the place to replenish both his spiritual and physical strength, at first and for a time.

As he got to know and understand the history and culture of Korea better, however, and began himself to be changed by that understanding, he increasingly held to a long-term vision of an independent Korea. Often, this could not be expressed in terms of direct opposition toward the Japanese—indeed his very standing as a commissioned member of the Presbyterian Mission required that he maintain a position of political neutrality at all times. Early on he seems to have applied the principles of Nevius' "Self-Church Method" to the whole of Korea itself. In June, 1890, the group of mostly young Presbyterian missionaries led by Underwood invited to Korea John Livingstone Nevius (1829–93), the veteran Northern Presbyterian missionary who had been serving in Shanghai, Hangzhou, Shandong, and other regions of China since 1854, to give a series of seminars. Over the course of two weeks Nevius gave lectures based on works he had previously published in the *Chinese Recorder* such as the "Planting and Development of Missionary Churches" and "Methods of Mission Work," the basic principles of which Underwood and his cohort of Presbyterian missionaries then used to articulate their own mission policies in 1891. Although what they drafted was a Policy of the Presbyterian Mission in Chosŏn Korea, which out of convenience later came to be called simply the *Nevius Plan*, it in fact went on to have tremendous influence on the work of other missions in Korea as well.[27] That is, Underwood worked to build the foundations of education, infrastructure, and cooperative spirit that in time would enable the Korean people to once again engage in "self governance, self support, and self propagation"

27. Underwood, *The Call of Korea*, 109–10. The influence of Nevius' Three Self Policy—i.e., self-supporting, self-governing, and self-evangelizing—is clearly evident, together with emphasis on the evangelism of women and working classes and the education of children, the effects of which can still be easily seen in Korean Christian demographics today. James Kim, "A Copernican Re-evaluation," 211–34. See also Vinton, "Presbyterian Mission Work in Korea," 665–71; Charles Allen Clark, *The Korean Church and the Nevius Methods*, 33–34; both excerpted and included in Min, *A History of Christian Churches in Korea*, 156–59. For Nevius' mission methods, see Nevius, *The Planting and Development of Missionary Churches* (1899).

of their land, with the spirit of the gospel to direct, unify, and ultimately renew the culture and the people as a whole. Later, he would write of how the
Koreans more than any other peoples are "ripe and ready harvest" for the
gospel.[28] The Neo-Confucian ethos deeply saturated in the culture had in
many ways laid the groundwork for Underwood long before his arrival, and
in time would also give him a newly enlarged understanding of his God as
"Ha-na-nim," the Korean indigenous monotheistic term.

It may be said that in many respects Underwood's missional works
themselves were modeled on those of his better-known predecessors such
as William Carey (1761–1834), Adoniram Judson (1788–1850), and Hudson Taylor (1832–1905), all of whom he greatly admired. Like them he
worked tirelessly to translate the Bible into the native language, to produce
a dictionary, to found orphanages and schools, to plant fledgling churches
when and as he could,[29] to train natives in evangelism and church leadership, to establish women's study and support groups, all the while working to get to know everyone from the highly educated elites including the
King and Queen themselves down to the common people, etc. He was
particularly proud of the newspaper and tracts he published on a regular
basis to share medical and other kinds of scientific knowledge with the
general public. After he married Lillias Horton (1851–1921), a medical
missionary eight years his senior, in 1889, their joint ministry came to
include frequent medical mission trips to outermost regions of Korea as
well, including on their honeymoon.[30] He also published two books, *The
Call of Korea: Political, Social, Religious* (1908), and *The Religions of Eastern Asia* which had originally been a series of six lectures he gave at New

28. Horace G. Underwood's letter to Thomas, November 14th, 1896 (see p. 172 in
the present volume); see also Underwood, *The Call of Korea*, 98–99.

29. Underwood planted a total of twenty-three congregations in Korea during his
thirty years of work there, among which twenty-one congregations are still active today.
One of the events for which they come together is the Annual Underwood International Symposia (since 2008) at Sae-mun-an, the first church he started, in Seoul.

30. Despite Lillias' relatively advanced age they had a son, Horace Horton Underwood (1890–1951), who would follow in his father's footsteps by remaining in Korea
and serving the cause of education. He served as the third principal of Yonsei College
until he died of a heart attack in 1951 during the Korean War while his wife was killed
in a communist terror attack in 1949. Books by Horace Horton Underwood include
Modern Education in Korea (1926); *Korean Boats and Ships* (1934); and *Tragedy and
Faith in Korea* (1951). The grandson, Horace G. Underwood Jr. (1917–2004), served
as a first lieutenant during both World War II and the Korean War, for the latter taking
part in the Inchon Landing. He also served as the chief interpreter for the Panmunjom
Armistice negotiations. For his writings see H. G. Underwood Jr., *Korea in War, Revolution and Peace: The Recollections of Horace G. Underwood* (2001).

York University in 1910 as part of the Charles F. Deems Lectureship of Philosophy and published the same year.[31]

But to prevent Korea in its vulnerable state from becoming carved up into so many denominationally dominated regions, Underwood also insisted against all odds on the principle of inter-denominational cooperation among all the Protestant missions in Korea, himself personally recruiting as many missionaries for Korea as were willing regardless of denomination. For example, on his first sabbatical leave from Korea Underwood traveled to recruit prospective fellow missionaries from throughout North America and Canada irrespective of denominational affiliation, and on his return was accompanied by four Southern Presbyterian and one Canadian Methodist missionaries.[32] This led to the founding of the first Korean Southern Presbyterian mission in Korea in November, 1892, which continued to work closely with Underwood and his Northern Presbyterian Church to the end. Oliver R. Avison (1860–1956), the Canadian Methodist medical missionary recruited by Underwood, not only allowed himself to be underwritten by the Northern Presbyterian mission but carried on the founding of Yonsei University after Underwood's untimely death to bring it to fruition. Such union between denominations was work that often tested the strength of his patience, leadership, and personal sacrifice, but remained, according to Lillias, his "ideal" toward which he persevered to the end.[33]

Underwood set great store by sharing with the people an impartial, accurate understanding of the world and its affairs—a theme, as we shall see, that he would return to repeatedly in his letters. As early as 1886 he expressed hopes of establishing a college as well as a seminary in Korea, showing his prioritization of education for the long-term development and well-being of the country as well as taking full advantage of the Koreans' native zeal for schooling and education. Although that dream would be realized only posthumously, the idea translated into his offering classes on such modern subjects as chemistry and other sciences, printing and distributing tracts on diverse subjects, publishing gazettes that included reliable and up to date news about Korea's national affairs, establishing schools and the YMCA, and of course laying the groundwork for what would eventually become Yonsei University—not a seminary but a secular university, which from his initial planning included a business school to help prepare young Koreans to participate in the new world of industry and international business. At

31. Later the lectures were published as *The Religions of Eastern Asia* (1910).

32. See Rhodes and Campbell, *History of the Korea Mission Presbyterian Church*, 1:558; available in Korean as *Miguk Puk-janglo-gyo Han'guk Sŏn'gyohoesa*, translated by Jai-Keun Choi (2008).

33. Lillias Underwood, *Underwood of Korea*, 16. Underwood himself wrote of this often, including in *The Call of Korea*, 125–26.

that time being Confucian Korea regarded merchants/businessman as the lowest profession for its association with profit-mindedness. In founding Yonsei University, however, Underwood foresaw that when Korea became independent, it would face the challenges of urbanization and industrialization posed by the Western world. Himself both son and brother to highly successful yet deeply devout entrepreneurs who stood fully behind his calling as a missionary, he sought to prepare young Koreans for these challenges as capable and ethical leaders of the business world.

Underwood died six months before the University first opened on April 7, 1917, but his foresight has since made Yonsei the *alma mater* to many of Korean leaders, and a major center of social consciousness and political activism. Because Underwood saw education as a partner in the Christian renaissance of Korea he believed in maintaining the highest standards of academic and moral excellence for Christian educators, pastors and workers, as well as for education in general. He pushed for the admission of non-Christians into mission schools and colleges while upholding the Christian values of the institutions at the same time. He even promoted native folk culture and supported its artistic expression. He published the first Korean hymnal in 1894 and included seven hymns written by Korean composers and writers. In all, his vision was to establish a Christian *Korea* in the true sense of inculturation rather than to establish churches *in* Korea. He did not limit himself to the creation of isolated Korean Christian enclaves. Instead, he sought to transform Korean culture as a whole on Christian terms.

Horace G. Underwood passed away at age fifty-seven in Atlantic City, New Jersey, on October 12, 1916 where he had gone to recuperate. His last words, spoken to his wife, were "I think, I think, I could travel that far." Guessing where his thoughts were, his wife said, "Where, dear, Korea?" "His face brightened and he nodded in reply."[34] It took, however, much longer to realize Underwood's wish of traveling back to Korea. In 1999, nearly a century after his death, Underwood was finally moved from his family plot in Grove Reformed Church, New Jersey, to Yang'hwajin, the now well-known cemetery for foreign missionaries in Seoul Korea, where his wife, son, daughter-in-law, and granddaughter-in-law all had preceded him.[35] It is on this note, then, that we now turn to examine more closely the nature and effect of his own education on his person, his mission, and Korean Christianity.

---

34. Lillias Underwood, *Underwood of Korea*, 332.

35. His wife, Lillias Horton Underwood (1851–1921) in 1921; son, Horace Horton Underwood (1890–1951) in 1951; daughter-in-law, Ethel von Wagoner (1888–1949), who was killed by a group of young Communists in 1949; and granddaughter-in-law, Joan Vida Davidson (1915–76) in 1976, were buried at Yang'hwajin. In 2004 his grandson, Horace Grant Underwood III (1917–2004), and in 2000 great-granddaughter-in-law, Gale Clarke (1955–2000) were also buried there.

Dr. John R. Mott (rear, fourth from left), with Underwood (rear, second from right) and others during his visit to Korea, shortly before he and Underwood attended the 1910 World Missionary Conference in Edinburgh.

Scene of the 1910 World Missionary Conference.

Chapter 2

Three Formative Strains in the Education
of Horace G. Underwood

THIS CHAPTER IS DIVIDED into three distinct yet inter-related sections pertaining more specifically to different aspects of the education of Horace G. Underwood. By coincidence each period covers roughly thirteen years of his life: (1) the Thirteen Years in London and France; (2) the Thirteen Years in America; (3) and the Thirteen Years in Korea covered by the letters presented in this book.

The organization of the three sections is by more than chronological happenstance, however. The focus of first section is to establish the national and cultural contexts in which Underwood's basic Christian consciousness would have been formed. This included the many educational reforms taking place, especially in England, as it sought to on the one hand maintain its position as the leading imperial power around the world, and on the other to produce a workforce capable of manning the industrial revolution at home. Born to a successful scientific entrepreneur and his educated wife, schooling would have been an important element of Underwood's boyhood years. Equally if not even more important to his formation, however, would have been what he absorbed growing up in his family: the legacy and legend of his great-grandfather and Scottish Presbyterian minister Rev. Alexander Waugh who had been a charter member and longtime President of the London Missionary Society; his father's studies under Michael Faraday who was not only commonly known as the "greatest experimental scientist" of his time but a devout Christian deeply invested in popular education; and the family's long friendship with George Müller, the eminent evangelist and director of Ashley Down orphanages in Bristol. All of these and more would have had a role in helping to form Underwood's fundamental evangelical and at the same time ecumenical and inter-denominational orientation as well as lively entrepreneurial social consciousness.

Likewise in America, it was not his formal liberal education alone—albeit at some of the best schools available—that shaped Underwood. There was also all that he observed and absorbed as an impressionable newcomer to the social experiment that was the United States, especially in wake of the Civil War (1861–65)—ideas about race and ethnicity, class, equality, difference, tolerance, the importance of institutionalizing associations, etc. Far from learning about these as mere abstract intellectual ideas, under the influence of his pastor at the New Grove Church, i.e., Rev. William Mabon (1822–92), the young Underwood got practical experience of them through unmediated personal encounters with wide swaths of immigrant population by way of passionate if youthful evangelism. These, together with his participation in the Inter-Seminary Missionary Alliance and meeting Arthur T. Pierson (1837–1911), gave him the visceral exposures[1] that would find expression in his advocacy for unity in diversity and difference, as embodied in his envisioning of a Christian Korea rather than Christian churches in Korea.

Nor did Underwood's education stop there. He encountered in Chosŏn Korea the five-hundred-year Neo-Confucian culture and ethos that deeply saturated its people and that in many ways not only both echoed and complemented Underwood's Christian spirituality and fundamentally Enlightenment sensibilities, but ultimately also transformed Underwood's own understanding of the Christian gospel and mission.

Thirteen Years in London and France: Underwood's Early and Family Education

Early Schooling

John Underwood took the education of all his children very seriously—about which more will be said later in this section—but that of his son Horace seems to have been one of special priority. His earliest formal education took place at a school called Cox's Collegiate Institute, near his boyhood home in central London. Given that the family had suffered bankruptcy in 1866 when Horace would have been just the age to enter school, this meant he was either sent to school despite the family's financial straits or only just as it was beginning to get back on its feet. Little is known about Cox's Collegiate today, though its categorization as a "collegiate" would identify it as a fee-paying preparatory ("prep school") for university, with a curriculum in keeping with the expectations—if not of the English aristocracy headed

1. See chapter 1, p. 11; also this chapter, pp. 48–51 and n94.

for such exclusive public schools as Eton, Harrow, and Winchester—of the English gentry and upper middle class. Despite great variances between such schools, education in Great Britain was in high swing by the latter half of the nineteenth century. The greatest empire in the world had tremendous need to produce an educated, well trained workforce at all levels of society to keep it running, and with concerted public as well as private efforts beginning in the 1840s education was made a requirement for even the most destitute children. Indeed according to some accounts, by the last quarter of the century more than 95 percent of all children in England of elementary school age had at least a year or two of schooling with the establishment of hundreds of so-called Ragged Schools.[2] For better schools, the Grammar School Act of 1840 made science and literature required subjects alongside the classics as part of regular curriculum, while in 1861 centralized examinations in reading, writing, and arithmetic were instituted to determine which schools would continue to receive public funding.[3] Underwood's early education, in short, took place in the context of a society that, as the world's leading power, was investing in education as a means of not only improving individuals' chances at upward social mobility but also of raising general social welfare.

Underwood's attendance at Cox Collegiate was cut short, however, by his being sent with his brother Frederick rather abruptly to the Catholic boarding school of *Ecole Dié*, in Boulogne-sur-Mer, France, in 1869.[4] Although Boulogne-sur-Mer was only a Channel crossing away from London, it remains a question why John Underwood would suddenly decide to send two of his sons to a boarding school in France. One possibility put forward has been that it might have been by the influence of his new wife, Caroline Nunn, who may have been Catholic.[5] But if Caroline did indeed push to send two of her stepsons—just at the sensitive ages of ten and eleven—away during what might have been the key period of settling into her new marriage,

2. Walvin, *A Child's World*, 114–19.

3. Gillard, *Education in England*.

4. Lillias Underwood, *Underwood of Korea*, 19.

5. This is somewhat speculative, as there is no hard evidence regarding her religious affiliation. But it has been argued that the noticeable absence of Caroline Underwood's name later from the registry of the New Grove Reformed Church where the rest of her second husband's family would eventually belong, as well as her absence also from the family plot at New Grove, make it possible she was not of the Protestant faith. If that had been the case it might also explain Lillias Underwood's wall of silence regarding Caroline in her *Underwood of Korea*. In memorializing her Protestant missionary husband Lillias may have felt it unnecessary, indeed awkward, to explain the role of a Catholic stepmother. See Hyoung-Woo Park, "A Study on the Coming to Korea," 75. See also chapter 1, n11.

it was likely agreed to only because of the sweeping changes taking place across the school system throughout England in precisely the years 1868 and 1869. Underwood had declared his decision to enter into ministry and especially the life of a missionary at the precocious age of four; whether his father took the declaration itself seriously or simply saw his character as particularly suited for study, John Underwood lavished particular care over his youngest son's education above even those of his elder brothers. It could therefore hardly have been a casual decision for him to send that son to a foreign Catholic boarding school, especially at a time when his oldest son John Thomas—only two years older than Horace—would soon be working at an iron foundry for five dollars a week.[6] But by the late 1860s English schools—public, proprietary, and elementary—were undergoing massive restructuring. Following several royal and parliamentary commissions to investigate the school system throughout England and Wales, the Public Schools Act (1868), the Endowed Schools Act (1869), and the Elementary Education Act (1870) were passed to reform and regulate the three classes of schools respectively throughout the country according to the accepted class divisions of England at the time—the upper, middle (itself divided into upper, middle, and lower), and the laboring classes. Most relevant for our purposes, the Endowed Schools Act gave the Endowed Schools Commission extensive powers over endowments of individual schools to reorganize them into a national system of three "grades" of secondary education with curricular changes fit "for modern purposes":

- *First-grade schools* with a leaving age of eighteen or nineteen would provide a "liberal education"—including Latin and Greek—to prepare upper and upper-middle class boys for the universities and the older professions;

- *Second-grade schools* with a leaving age of sixteen or seventeen would teach two modern languages besides Latin to prepare middle class boys for the army, the newer professions and departments of the Civil Service; and

- *Third-grade schools* with a leaving age of fourteen or fifteen would teach elements of French and Latin to lower middle class boys, who would be expected to become "small tenant farmers, small tradesmen, and superior artisans."[7]

6. Lillias Underwood, *Underwood of Korea*, 23.
7. Gillard, *Education in England*, ch. 6.

It was a common saying at the time that the Commission could "turn a boys' school in Northumberland into a girls' school in Cornwall" in the name of meeting the needs of the current population, and across England and Wales schools formerly endowed to offer free classical instruction to boys were remodeled as fee-paying schools (with a few competitive scholarships) teaching broad curricula to boys or girls. In response, headmasters of thirty-four of the top-tier public and proprietary schools joined together to resist the Endowed Schools Commission, led by Thomas Arnold, Headmaster of the famous Rugby School and a notable advocate for inclusion of more natural sciences in the curriculum.[8] It is unclear where in the new order Underwood's Cox Collegiate Institute fell, but if John Underwood was not in a position to be able to afford a school of choice under the new regulations in 1869, the Catholic Ecole Dié just across the Channel may have offered an affordable alternative. It apparently also proved a generally happy experience for Underwood, once he and his brother stood their ground to maintain their Protestant faith and practice of daily prayers amidst the school's own French Catholic orientation.[9] The experience may have given them also at an impressionable age an intimate, open, sympathetic understanding of faiths different from their own.

The Legacy of Alexander Waugh

But as indicated by the Underwood boys' strength of standing their ground at Ecole Dié, a basic foundation or orientation to the schooling had already been sown by the education they received within the family itself. In her biography of her husband, Lillias Underwood makes mention of a number of figures she herself did not know and could not have known about except through significant remembrance of them by her husband or by members of his family during her infrequent visits with them in America. In other words, these were figures who loomed large in the minds of Underwood and his family and in their conversations as significant to their upbringing and experience, thus coloring Lillias' own understanding of them in the character of her husband and in-laws. Of these figures it was clearly Underwood's great-grandfather Alexander Waugh and his father John Underwood who had place of the greatest influence, not only on Horace but his siblings who were to play such a large part in his mission as well. Of Rev. Waugh Lillias Underwood writes,

8. Gillard, *Education in England*, ch. 2.
9. Lillias Underwood, *Underwood of Korea*, 20–21.

If there is anything in the theory of heredity, we have here in this
great resemblance in the character and deeds of this man and those
of his great-grandson a marked example. The broad-mindedness,
the wide-reaching philanthropy, the love of unity, the charity, the
qualities of leadership and organization, the intellectual gifts, all
so similar, make one feel a bit creepy and we wonder whether
Alexander wasn't pretty close to Horace, or at least whether the
mantle of the one had not fallen upon the other.[10]

Given that none of the immediate Underwood family, including John Underwood, ever had chance to know Alexander Waugh personally (he passed
away in December 1827, probably after giving baptism to John Underwood
born that year) the confidence with which Lillias Underwood claims simi-
larities to her husband may seem extraordinary. But then Rev. Waugh had
been much more than just the spiritual head of the Underwood family
known through the stuff of private family lore. Widely respected as minister
of decades to the important Scottish Presbyterian Secession Church at Wells
Street, London, he was also a founding member and for twenty-eight years
repeatedly elected President of the London Missionary Society.[11] His work
for the London Missionary Society went well beyond the scope of merely
personal interest in missions:

It was by a minister of the Secession church (the late excellent
Dr. Waugh, of Wells Street, London) the fundamental principle
of the London Missionary Society was originally framed; and
the high place which that Society has long occupied in public
estimation, has been in a great measure owing to the catholic spirit by which that principle is characterized. The pledge
which the Associate synod gave to the Society, when it was first
formed, has been faithfully redeemed. The pulpits of the Secession have, generally speaking, been cheerfully thrown open to
the successive deputations that have periodically visited Scotland, to plead the cause of that Society; and, by the members
of the Secession congregations, comparatively poor though they
be, many thousands of pounds have been cast into its treasury.
When Dr. Waugh visited Scotland in 1815, on behalf of the Society, he carried with him to London the very liberal sum of
£1,420, which was collected almost exclusively in the churches

10. Lillias Underwood, *Underwood of Korea*, 17.

11. Some accounts imply that he was the central force behind the founding of the
Society. For more on his career, see Hay and Belfrage, *Memoir of the Rev. Alexander
Waugh*. The work was reprinted in 1839, then again in 1851 in New York. See also
Black, *The Scots Churches in England*, 208–10, 327.

of the Secession. . . . These instances are a few of the many that might have been here recorded, for the purpose of showing the liberal support which the London Missionary Society has received from the ministers and people belonging to the Secession church. A similar spirit of liberality has been manifested by them to the Baptist and other missionary institutions.[12]

Alexander Waugh's attitude regarding the mission, moreover, founded as it was on strong principles concerning ecumenical unity as well denominational freedom, was far advanced for its time. True, the Church of Scotland, while adhering to the Westminster Confession of Faith (1647), had long tended to uphold "liberty of opinions on points which do not enter into the substance of the Faith."[13] Without an official line differentiating what constituted substantial versus insubstantial matters, it had become a Church relatively tolerant of a variety of theological positions, including those who would term themselves conservative and liberal in their doctrine, ethics and interpretation of Scripture. But as early as 1794 Rev. Waugh took this stance a step further by proactively working for the united cooperation of the Anglican, Presbyterian, Methodist, Baptist and other denominational churches for purposes of mission and the publication of a shared religious periodical. Considering that many of these were still relatively young, often controversial denominations in conflict with one another in the late eighteenth century, it says much about Waugh's open-minded, "one gospel above and beyond all" understanding of Christianity, which his great-grandson would take up in turn with passionate commitment. The likes Arthur Tappan Pierson (1837–1911) would later be associated with similar ideals of inter-denominational unity for world mission in America,[14] and have—as will be discussed later in

12. M'Kerrow, *History of the Secession Church*, 575.

13. Article V in the Constitution of the Church of Scotland reads, "This Church has the inherent right, free from interference by civil authority, but under the safeguards for deliberate action and legislation provided by the Church itself, to frame or adopt its subordinate standards, to declare the sense in which it understands its Confession of Faith, to modify the forms of expression therein, or to formulate other doctrinal statements, and to define the relation thereto of its office-bearers and members, but always in agreement with the Word of God and the fundamental doctrines of the Christian Faith contained in the said Confession, of which agreement the Church shall be sole judge, and with due regard to liberty of opinion in points which do not enter into the substance of the Faith." Church of Scotland, *Articles Declaratory of the Constitution of the Church of Scotland.*

14. See Robert, *Occupy until I Come: A. T. Pierson and the Evangelization of the World.* One can argue that the idea had been present in earlier American mission movements as well—for example in the orientation of the American Board of Commissioners for Foreign Missions (ABCFM, founded in 1810) where participants consisted of members from various denominations, albeit mostly from the Reformed traditions of Presbyterians, Congregationalists, and German Reformed churches.

this chapter—no small impact on the young Underwood, but clearly for Underwood the roots of the principle went back further than the world mission movements such as the Inter-Seminary Missionary Alliance and the Student Volunteer Movement (for Foreign Missions) he encountered and became a part of in America. Indeed, it is as the essence of her husband's work also that Lillias Underwood quotes almost as her opening gambit—with admiration bordering on incredulity that such foresight should have been possible in 1795—a passage from the principles of the London Missionary Society as preserved in Rev. Waugh's own handwriting:

> As the union of God's people of various denominations in carrying on this great work is a most desirable object, so to prevent, if possible, any cause of future dissension it is declared to be a fundamental principle of this missionary society that our design is not to send Presbyterian, Independent, Episcopalian or any other form of church order and government, about which there may be a difference of opinion among serious persons, but the Glorious Gospel of the Blessed God to the heathen, and it shall be left to the minds of the persons whom God shall call into the fellowship of His Son from among them to assume for themselves such form of church government as to them shall appear most agreeable to the Word of God.[15]

Implicit in the above statement is Rev. Waugh's non-judgmental cognizance of the complex historical conditions that had led to the proliferation of denominations in Europe and England, together with an almost prescient awareness of how a necessary solution arrived at in one context can yet sow seeds of far-reaching problems in another, unless checked with utmost self-awareness and self-restraint. We can also read in his stated principle the profound respect and trust with which he, in anticipation of the fellowship God will call the heathen unto Godself, regarded the nature of such fellowships as founded on self-determination, guided by the Word of God but otherwise free from the imposition and interference of denominational interests. Needless to say, his argument presages the continuing impact on our own times of the issues of mission and contextualization.

---

15. Lillias Underwood, *Underwood of Korea*, 16. I have elsewhere stressed the global significance of Underwood's successfully spreading a united, cooperative, interdenominational model of mission and evangelism in Korea. See James Kim, "A Copernican Re-evaluation," 212.

The Scientific Legacy of Michael Faraday

Aside from his commitment to mission, Rev. Waugh devoted his considerable energies also to issues of social welfare. He took an "active interest" throughout his career in supporting the Scottish Hospital, the Hibernian Society (a Catholic society formed to provide mutual aid and support to members), the Irish Evangelical, the Religious Tract Society, and Anti-Slavery Society. Their variety across Protestant/Catholic, Scottish/Irish/English as well as racial divides show the catholicity of his interests, giving weight to the claim made throughout his biography of his having been in all things and above all a "peace-maker."[16]

To this rich evangelical, supra-denominational-minded family legacy, Underwood's paternal grandfather Thomas Underwood (1795–18??) and father John Underwood (1827–81) added yet another layer of influence through their interest in the sciences as well as philanthropy. What little scholarship there has been about the family's connection to the great English scientist Michael Faraday (1791–1867) has generally focused on Horace's father's relationship to him; having been an ardent admirer of Faraday even as a boy, John eventually became his student.[17] But the connection may have gone back further to Thomas Underwood, whose name appears on numerous occasions among Faraday's correspondences in the 1820s in the capacity of a trusted associate to both himself and of his mentor the chemist Sir Humphry Davy (1778–1829), often entrusted to convey various papers and messages between them and to various colleagues.[18] Widely

16. As quoted in Lillias Underwood, *Underwood of Korea*, 16. James Hay describes Waugh as one "who was so peculiarly characterized as a *peace-maker*." Hay and Belfrage, *Memoir of the Rev. Alexander Waugh*, 414.

17. John Underwood is described as "a graduate of the laboratory of the celebrated Michael Faraday" in *Chicago and Its Resources Twenty Years After*, 145. It may have been at the Laboratory of the Royal Institution where Faraday had assumed Directorship in 1825 that John Underwood studied with Faraday as a young man before going on to study at the University of Colchester. In fact it would seem John Underwood had considerable scientific mind of his own even as a young man. According to Lillias, her husband used to "love to tell" how while still a mere student at Colchester his father had engaged in—and was declared the winner—of an anonymous newspaper debate on the potato disease; to his own great surprise it was later revealed that his opponent in the debate had been the illustrious German chemist Justus Freiherr von Liebig (1803–73), considered by many even today to be the founder of organic chemistry. See Lillias Underwood, *Underwood of Korea*, 17–18.

18. References to "Mr. Underwood" appears numerous times (at leas nineteen) in the correspondence of Michael Faraday, both by Faraday himself and by those with whom he was in communication, among whom was the great French physicist and mathematician André-Marie Ampère (1775–1836) who referred to Underwood as "*mon excellent ami* Mr. Underwood" and "*mon savant et respectable ami* Mr. Underwood."

considered "the greatest experimental scientist" of his day, Faraday was in many ways a highly unusual figure for his time. Son of a blacksmith who as a boy was apprenticed to a bookbinder, it was against incredible odds that he rose through the ranks of class-conscious England to become the first Fullerian Professor of Chemistry—a lifetime appointment with no obligation to deliver lectures—at the Royal Institution of Great Britain.[19] Largely self-taught through books he encountered during his years as a bookbinder's apprentice, it was only at age twenty-two and through the unexpected attentions of the Sir Davy that Faraday was able to begin working as a scientist in earnest as Davy's assistant.[20] Over time Faraday's numerous pioneering discoveries, including of electromagnetism and electrochemistry, among others, laid the foundations of modern physics and chemistry, popularizing along the way such terminology as "anode," "cathode," "electrode," and "ion." But possibly sharing in a certain "strong tendency" within Scottish Enlightenment thought generally to maintain "a central place for the divine" in the rational, practical, and empirical investigations of things,[21] Faraday

---

Since the letters date from the 1820s the references cannot be to John Underwood, born in 1827. See James, *Correspondence of Michael Faraday*, 268–70, 275–76, 287, 321, 350–51, 365, 376–77, 414, 531–39. It is interesting to speculate whether Faraday and Thomas Underwood might have been brought together by their mutual connections to the publishing industry, since Faraday had apprenticed as a bookbinder while Thomas Underwood became a publisher of medical books. Such relative proximity to one of the greatest scientific minds of time would certainly help explain young John Underwood's wanting to embark on a scientific career of his own. There is, however, also the possibility that the "Mr. Underwood" mentioned in the Faraday correspondence refers to another Thomas Underwood altogether—i.e., Thomas Richard Underwood (1775–1832), thought to be a minor naturalist and painter.

19. According to Gillard, in many ways education for the poor in early nineteenth century England was "even worse" than it had been in previous centuries. This was because "although England's poor had never been educated en masse, there had been parishes where exceptional provision had been made, and a few able boys from poor homes had even been offered university places. But by the start of the nineteenth century—after fifty years of industrial revolution—education was becoming organised, like English society as a whole, on a more rigid class basis. The result was 'a new kind of class-determined education. Higher education became a virtual monopoly, excluding the new working class, and the idea of universal education, except within the narrow limits of "moral rescue," was widely opposed as a matter of principle.'" Gillard, *Education in England*, ch. 5, quoting Williams, *The Long Revolution*, 136.

20. Sir Humphry Davy was an important chemist in his own right, known primarily for isolating a number of elements including potassium, sodium, barium, and magnesium, as well as discovering the elemental natures of chlorine and iodine. Davy served as President of the Royal Society between 1820 and 1827. Faraday, in the early days of his assistantship with Davy in class-conscious Europe, sometimes had to travel as Davy's valet as well as assistant.

21. Merikoski, "A Different Kind of Enlightenment," esp. 11–12.

was equally and widely known for the total faith and devotion with which he held to beliefs as a Christian of the Sandemanian denomination, a small offshoot of the Church of Scotland to which his parents had belonged and he himself joined with a public profession of faith at age thirty, as for his scientific discoveries. In a lecture delivered in 1854 at the Royal Institution with the Prince Albert in attendance and later included at his request at the end of his *Researches in Chemistry and Physics*, Faraday wrote,

> Before entering upon the subject [of mental education], I must make one distinction which, however it may appear to others, is to me of the utmost importance. High as man is placed above the creatures around him, there is a higher and far more exalted position within his view; and the ways are infinite in which he occupies his thoughts about the fears, or hopes, or expectations of a future life. I believe that the truth of that future cannot be brought to his knowledge by any exertion of his mental powers, however exalted they may be; that it is made known to him by other teaching than his own, and is received through simple belief of the testimony given. Let no one suppose for an instant that the self-education I am about to commend, in respect of the things of this life, extends to any considerations of the hope set before us, as if man by reasoning could find out God. It would be improper here to enter upon this subject further than to claim an absolute distinction between religious and ordinary belief. I shall be reproached with the weakness of refusing to apply those mental operations which I think good in respect of high things to the very highest. I am content to bear the reproach. Yet even in earthly matters I believe that "the invisible things of Him from the creation of the world are clearly seen, being understood by the things that are made, even His eternal power and Godhead"; and I have never seen anything incompatible between those things of man which can be known by the spirit of man which is within him and those higher things concerning his future, which he cannot know by that spirit.[22]

22. Faraday, *Experimental Researches in Chemistry and Physics*, 464. Concerning the inclusion of the paragraph in his book Faraday wrote, "These observations were delivered as a lecture before His Royal Highness the Prince Consort and the members of the Royal Institution on the 6th of May 1854. They are so immediately connected in their nature and origin with my own experimental life, considered either as cause or consequence, that I have thought the close of this volume not an unfit place for their reproduction." The phrase "through simple belief in the testimony given" is probably a reference to his Sandemanian faith (founded by Robert Sandeman [1718–81]) which held that "justifying faith is a simple assent to the divine testimony concerning Jesus Christ, differing in no way in its character from belief in any ordinary testimony." See Wikisource, "Glasites."

Faraday's profession of faith was not limited to words only but imbued all his actions and interests. Even as he got involved in social and environmental causes too numerous to mention here, he remained steadfast in his refusal to participate in the creation of chemical weapons for the Crimean War on religious and ethical grounds. Likewise, "offered the presidency of the Royal Society, Faraday flatly refused, as he also refused the offer of a knighthood. He did not believe Christ of the apostles would accept these worldly honors."[23] He assumed instead in 1825 the directorship of the Laboratories at the Royal Institution (RI) based in London.[24] Distinct from the Royal Society, RI had been founded in 1799 for the purposes of scientific education and research, especially for "diffusing the knowledge, and facilitating introduction, of useful mechanical inventions and improvements; and for teaching, by courses of philosophical lectures and experiments, the application of science to the common purposes of life."[25] Ever the egalitarian, in 1827 Faraday founded there the Christmas Lectures series in an effort to make the sciences more accessible to young people and the general public, which garnered popularity even among London's gentry, and between 1827 and 1860 personally gave nineteen lectures for the series.[26] His successor at the RI, the physicist and agnostic John Tyndall (1820–93), is to have said of Faraday, "[In his case] you cannot separate the moral and the emotional from the intellectual."[27] For the Underwoods, not only John but his sons Thomas, Frederick and Horace, the example of such a great scientific mind making public declaration of his faith through the minutest of his everyday actions as well as professional papers, could not have been small, especially given the pride they took in their personal— however small and, in the case of the boys, indirect—acquaintance and discipleship with him. Indeed Lillias Underwood makes a great point of emphasizing the rare seamless integration of faith and rare scientific gifts in multiple generations of the Underwood family:

> The energy, the versatility, the sunny, kindly, jovial nature, the wonderful indomitability and the scientific bias which, chanced they to be making inks, dictionaries or typewriters, founding missionary societies or schools and colleges, marked the character of Dr. Waugh and his grandsons and great-grandsons are extremely interesting to note. Not only was Horace's father a

23. Graves, *Scientists of Faith*, 110.

24. For a biography of Faraday see Hirshfeld, *The Electric Life of Michael Faraday*.

25. James, *Guides to the Royal Institution of Great Britain*, 2.

26. James, "Faraday, Michael."

27. See Seeger, "Faraday, Sandemanian," 101.

remarkable instance of this but his brother John [Thomas] and his cousin Dr. Arthur Underwood were cast in much the same mold, though each had a different calling.[28]

A Spiritual Legacy: George Müller

Another major figure Lillias Underwood mentions in connection with the Underwood family is the evangelist George Müller (1805–98) whom she goes so far as to describe—presumably based on Underwood's own remembrances of his father—as one of her father-in-law's "closest and most intimate friends." This intimate friend, however, also happened to be "the founder of the great orphanage in Bristol, carried on only by faith and prayer."[29] Müller was in fact said to have cared for over ten thousand orphans over the course of his life at the orphanage he founded in Ashley Downs, all without ever asking a single person for donation. Once imprisoned at the age of sixteen for dissolute living, he had an epiphanic conversion in 1826, and from 1830 "adopted the principles that trust in God and sincere prayer were sufficient for all purposes in material as well as in spiritual things. He accordingly abolished pew rents, refused to take a fixed salary or to appeal for contributions towards his support—simply placing a box at the door of the church for freewill offerings—and resolved never to incur debt either for personal expenses or in religious work, and never to save money for the future"— a resolution he apparently kept for the remainder of his long life without much ado (he lived to be ninety-two).[30] Anecdotal accounts of "miraculous" provision peppered his life, not just in terms of getting the Ashley Downs orphanage built using only unsolicited donations, but of occasions such as the time he sat down to give prayer of thanks with the three hundred hungry orphans under his care literally before an empty table. Just as he was finishing

28. See Lillias Underwood, *Underwood of Korea*, 17–18, 23, 25.

29. Lillias Underwood, *Underwood of Korea*, 25. He was born Johann Georg Ferdinand Müller, in Kroppenstedt, Prussia (present-day Saxony-Anhalt, Germany). If it seems unusual that Müller befriended a scientist twenty-two years younger, i.e., Underwood's father, John (born in 1827), Dana Robert describes how he and Arthur T. Pierson [born in 1837] "felt strong kinship for each other, despite Müller being thirty-two years older." Robert, *Occupy until I Come*, 104. Later, Pierson would go on to befriend Horace Underwood, twenty-two years younger than himself.

30. Johnstone, "George Friedrich Müller." "The substantial funds associated with building and maintaining the enterprise were voluntarily contributed without even direct appeal, often as a result of the wide circulation of Müller's autobiography." This was the very famous *A Narrative of Some of the Lord's Dealings with George Müller* (1837; 2nd ed., 1841; 3rd ed., 1845).

THREE FORMATIVE STRAINS IN THE EDUCATION OF HORACE G. UNDERWOOD   33

the prayer he heard knocking on the door by a baker and a milkman, each separately, who provided just enough bread and milk for the children. There was even an instance where, faced with a broken boiler on a cold winter night, Müller prayed both that the workmen would find it in their hearts to work through the night to fix it and that the weather would stay warm until it was in working order—with God answering both prayers![31] If it seems Underwood's modus operandi—accepting the very modest annual salary from the Mission Board for his work in Korea, frequently appealing to the Board as well as his brother Thomas for more support for mission work, and engaging in exhausting fundraising tours during trips to America—differed significantly from Müller trusting in prayer and unsolicited funds, the difference may yet be understood as one of context rather than of faiths. That is to say, Underwood's solicitations and acceptance of funds may be more properly understood as necessitated by the context of carrying out mission work in a foreign land where one could not expect—at least in the beginning—native sympathy for, or in some cases real comprehension of, the work required. Lillias Underwood wrote of her husband:

> His open-handed freedom in the use of money left him too often with an empty pocket, not knowing at all from whence his next meal was to come. However, his absolute faith in God was such that he never felt a moment's anxiety; he never knew the meaning of worry. Often have I marveled, when remittances were delayed, or when we seemed face to face with some critical emergency and could see no way out, he was perfectly cheerful and calm; not in appearance only but in reality. 'It will be all right,' he averred, and so it always was. For example, on two different occasions several years apart, our supply of hard coal, very rare in the East, failed during a bitter winter, and none could be had either from dealers in Seoul or from the mine or from the ports. More and more ghastly the vacancy in the coal bin yawned, while lower sank the thermometer, until at last there was only one scuttleful of the precious commodity left, but still he was as confident that the Lord would provide as though the coal were there; and before the last scuttle was empty the coal came on both occasions from utterly unexpected sources.[32]

31. Steer, *George Müller*, 124–26. Müller was also known for providing an education to the orphans under his care, much more than usual, to the point where some accused him of raising the poor above their natural station in life. His work apparently pleased Charles Dickens, however, "whose concerns about the standards of the operation were apparently removed" after making a personal visit to the Ashley Downs. Johnstone, "Müller, George Friedrich."

32. Lillias Underwood, *Underwood of Korea*, 31.

The descriptive account, even to such phrases as "never knew a moment's anxiety" and "as though the coal were there" is very much in accord with Müller's own writings in his *Autobiography*.[33] It should be taken into consideration, too, that Underwood's mission was in a sense largely "self-supporting" if we accept that it was very much a *family* endeavor in which each of the brothers understood their individual callings as complementing the work of the other.[34]

Besides being above worries for material support Müller was source of yet another important point of influence for John Underwood—and through him for Horace as well—and this was his strong premillennialist belief. Lillias Underwood makes it a point to mention how "especially was Horace filled with his father's eager hope and longing for the return of the Lord. It was his constant thought and he never ceased to look and pray for that Glorious Appearing in his own time. This hope he passed on to the Koreans from the first days when he could teach them at all, and now probably the whole Korean church is one in looking and waiting for that day."[35] This avowed impact makes the subject of the relationship between Underwood's theology and mission a potentially important one warranting further future study, especially in light of the momentous conversion in 1879 by Arthur T. Pierson also to premillennialism through his meeting with Müller while the latter was traveling through America. By that time Pierson, then in his early forties, was already well established as a towering figure in American urban ministries, and known, too, for his strongly postmillennialist views which—despite the many social problems that inspired evangelical activism or perhaps because of them—was the popular belief in late nineteenth century America. His public conversion to premillennialist position—one Dana Robert describes as "a lonely position to hold" at a time of growing economic and political confidence in America—resulted in his suffering "public misunderstandings and broken relationships," but also became "the inspirational focus of [his] mature years,"[36] one that may have led to the

---

33. Müller, *The Autobiography of George Müller.*

34. See Underwood's letter to Thomas, August 23, 1897 (p. 175 in this volume). Note also Underwood's letters to Thomas of early December, 1887 (pp. 138–39); August 2, 1895 (pp. 152–53); May 29, 1896 (pp. 161–62, 164), and December 28, 1898 (p. 199).

35. Lillias Underwood, *Underwood of Korea*, 19.

36. See Robert, *Occupy until I Come*, 107–8. As a postmillennialist Pierson would formerly have believed that Jesus would return after the millennium, i.e., after a thousand years of peace and prosperity brought about by human effort and benevolent Christian civilization. For those who experienced the nineteenth century as one of prosperity and even more importantly of "progress," the involvement in social justice issues would have "grown out of their postmillennial convictions that working hand-in-hand with God's purposes on earth, humanity would effectively solve the problems of modern society." To

shift in his focus from ministry to world mission, and to the keen sense of kinship and mutual respect that would develop between Pierson and Underwood despite their age gap of twenty-two years.

These few accounts of figures who had place in Underwood and his family's consciousness show something of the richly woven tapestry in his early education—the commitments Underwood would have imbibed almost as matter of course, not only toward the gospel and the idea of the mission in general, but to principles of supra-denominational cooperation, the practice of unity and peacemaking, to socially-minded evangelism across national, class and racial divides, to egalitarian ideals of which standards of scientific excellence and truth without compromise of Christian faith was itself an expression, and to a way of life made both more urgent and more free of all worry for focusing so intently on the imminent coming of Christ. These would have been the very air Underwood breathed, not as some high ideals of heroes set apart, but as familiar mundanities of living lives of faith that was the stuff of his natural home environment as a young boy, together with the British outlook that saw venturing into the unknown—whether it be to America, India, Amoy, Africa, Australia, South America, or even the "last hermit kingdom" of Korea—as par course for citizens of the empire in which the sun never set.[37]

The Thirteen Years in America: Professionalization

The family's singular attention to Underwood's education continued even after they took up residence in New Jersey. Underwood, now age thirteen, was encouraged to continue his studies at the Hasbrouck Institute in Jersey City even as each of his other siblings worked variously as gardener, at the family ink factory, or at home to help the family.[38] Founded in 1856, Hasbrouck was a small but elite private "preparatory school" run by headmaster

---

this Müller argued that society—far from progressing gradually toward any kingdom of God on earth—was held in the control of Satan, and that events on earth would worsen until Jesus returned in person. Rather than trying to improve naturally through human effort, the world would only be cleansed and purified through "a supernatural act of God—the return of Jesus Christ." Robert, *Occupy until I Come*, 107–8.

37. It may have been that there were numerous other members of Underwood's extended family who were also called to be witnesses for the gospel. Lillias Underwood mentions several cousins as serving variously in India, Africa, Australia, and Brazil, and the general "*sang froid*" with which everyone seemed to consider the prospect of dying abroad unknown to anyone. Lillias Underwood, *Underwood of Korea*, 36.

38. Lillias Underwood, *Underwood of Korea*, 23.

Washington Hasbrouck (c. 1824–15) for area students aspiring to enter the nation's foremost universities and proceed thereafter to lives of public service. Hasbrouck himself remained head of the Institute until 1876, before becoming principal of the State Normal School at Trenton (now the College of New Jersey), so it seems likely Underwood studied with him.[39] The school is said to have been progressive in its philosophy, curriculum, and facilities for its time, but unfortunately little is known now about its program. Given, however, that admissions to the School of Arts & Sciences at New York University (then known as the University of the City of New York) required sufficient knowledge of mathematics (algebra through quadratic equations, Euclidean geometry), English grammar, geography, American history, Latin (Caesar's *Commentaries*, Virgil's *Aeneid* and/or the *Eclogues*, Cicero's orations, Sallust's *Conspiracy of Catiline* and *Jugurthine War*, and Arnold's *Latin Prose Composition*), and Greek (Xenophon's *Anabasis*, Homer's *Iliad* as well as the prosodies), it seems likely his preparation at Hasbrouck would have been along those lines, together with enough background in the natural sciences for Underwood to get excellent grades in the sciences at New York University.[40] In short, it offered the kind of education associated with the progressive, liberal American gentleman who, while not necessarily competing with the older and assertively aristocratic "public schools" back in England such as Eton and Charterhouse, nonetheless boasted a liberal, "more modern" and "well-rounded" education for its time and place. Notably, too, Underwood did not immediately matriculate at New York University upon graduating from Hasbrouck, instead studying Greek along with several other students under the tutelage of the family pastor, Rev. William Mabon (1822–92), while continuing to take active part in local mission activities.[41] He received admission to New York University on June 12, 1877, five weeks before his eighteenth birthday.[42]

39. See "Professor Washington Hasbrouck," *New York Times*, February 26, 1895.

40. See Karnoutsos, "Jersey City Past and Present." According to a 1902 history of Jersey City, many of its graduates rose to "positions of prominence and responsibility in the city. It has since then greatly developed, and is recognized in educational circles as an institution second to none in its facilities for and methods of instruction." Van Winkle, *Old Bergen*, chapter XLIV, "Early Other School Accommodations."

41. Lillias Underwood, *Underwood of Korea*, 23.

42. University of the City of New York, *Class Merit Book, July 1835–June 1888*, Vol. 4.

Formal Education: New York University and
New Brunswick Theological Seminary

New York University of the late 1870s was a non-denominational, private university comprised of programs in the Arts & Sciences, Law, and Medicine. Admission to its four-year Arts & Sciences curriculum was especially competitive due to privileges of its free tuition. Underwood maintained a rigorous academic schedule while there; he is listed in New York University's *Matriculation Book*, 1853–93, as having taken the following courses:

> Freshman Year: Mathematics, Greek, French, Rhetoric, Oration, and Latin;
>
> Sophomore Year: Classics, Economics, Oration, Chemistry, Trigonometry, Greek, Latin, Analytical Geometry, and English Literature;
>
> Junior Year: German, Epistemology, Natural Philosophy, Oration, Modern History, Latin, Greek, Astronomy, and Logic;
>
> Senior Year: Ethics, Latin, Greek, Oration, Geology, Constitutional Law, Botany, International Law, and Analytical Chemistry.[43]

His status as a commuting student may have helped him develop a strong physical constitution during this time. According to Lillias, Underwood commuted daily from his home in New Durham to New York University, which involved walking the seven miles each way to take either the Weehawken or Hoboken ferry between New Jersey and New York. To make that trip in time to attend the daily chapel at New York University, followed by classes from 10:00 am until 1:30 or 2:00 pm, extracurricular activities, and studying, before making the return commute home each evening helped build a certain stamina and discipline that would serve him well throughout the rigors of hard work in Korea.[44]

Interestingly, the courses for which he received his highest grades were mostly in the sciences and mathematics, such as trigonometry, chemistry, analytical geometry, natural philosophy, and astronomy.[45] But the subject he most excelled in was oration. Alongside the required Latin and Greek it was the one subject he took each of his four years. As a junior he received the Webster Award for Oration, and was one of ten speakers chosen to give a

43. University of the City of New York, *Catalogue of the University of the City of New York, 1876–1877*, 62–64.

44. Lillias Underwood, *Underwood of Korea*, 24.

45. University of the City of New York, *Matriculation Book*. See also Hyoung-Woo Park, "A Study on the Coming to Korea," 64.

speech at the graduation ceremony in June, 1881.[46] The title of his piece was "The Valley of Glencoe—As It Is and As It Was." Though no copies are extant, the Valley of Glencoe was known as the birthplace of Ossian, the legendary bard of Irish mythology and literary symbol of Romanticism. Lillias gives an interesting indication of Underwood's early talent for oration when she notes that it was he rather than his older brothers who, even as a young child, led the Sunday services by preaching to his siblings on the rare Sundays when the family could not attend church.[47] Underwood graduated with a very respectable GPA average of 87.7, and was tenth in a graduating class of twenty-two. This might not seem a remarkable achievement, but at the time of his matriculation the class size had been fifty-two students. By sophomore year that number had dwindled radically to thirty-two, then further down to twenty-eight and twenty-two in subsequent years. Grades were given on basis of written and oral exams on an absolute scale. Of the 879 graduates of NYU Arts & Sciences between 1831 and 1882, 141 became clergy, 144 served in fields of law, and eighty-three became doctors.[48]

Graduation would have been a bittersweet time for Underwood. His father who had done so much to support his dreams of becoming a missionary passed away on June 6 that year, after two years of fighting cancer. In light of his father's extended illness it is rather remarkable that Underwood was able to maintain such strong extracurricular activities in literary publishing as he did throughout his university days, as the editor and later vice president of the University's literary Philomathean Society, as well as the editor of the student newspaper, *The University Quarterly*. Perhaps it had been a way to honor his paternal family heritage (i.e., of Thomas Underwood, his publisher grandfather). In any case both experiences would contribute to the effectiveness and efficiency with which he later made use of printing and publications in Korea.

Before we go on to examine Underwood's more vocation-specific training three observations are in order about his general education up to this point. In the first place, the Underwood family took enormous pains to ensure that the son who was committed to a life of mission and ministry received the best, broadest, and most advanced education available to him, at considerable cost and apparent sacrifice to other members of the family destined to carry on the family business in commerce. While it was true that university education was traditionally often required for careers

46. Lillias Underwood, *Underwood of Korea*, 24–25.

47. Lillias Underwood, *Underwood of Korea*, 24–25.

48. See University of the City of New York, *A General Catalogue of the University of the City of New York*, 55, also 40. Cited also in Hyoung-Woo Park, "A Study on the Coming to Korea," 64.

in ministry, other, less rigorous means of entering the career were also available, especially in America. Despite the family's tremendous regard for life devoted to religion, the decision could hardly have been a foregone conclusion for a family starting out fresh from a recent bankruptcy as immigrants in a new country. This is not to say the education he received in his time was without problems from our present point of view. The point here is not necessarily an evaluation of the quality of the education per se so much as the consistent and shared understanding and attitude within the Underwood family of the broadest and best possible education being the proper preparation deserved for a life of ministry.

Secondly, Underwood demonstrated keen interest in, commitment to, and talent for the sciences in his studies alongside the "arts and humanities." This love of sciences was of course something he shared with his father and brothers, whose entrepreneurial success was very much in the applied sciences (even his paternal grandfather had been a publisher of medical sciences). But in his work as a missionary we may also say it helped him grasp with great clarity not only the usefulness of sciences for improving people's everyday lives but the necessity of its creative mastery for a people to be able to compete in the global market as such. When Underwood left for Korea in December 1884, his brothers were still operating a relatively small business producing typewriter ribbons for companies like Remington. It was only after they began producing their own, more advanced typewriters in 1896 and especially after the development of the famed Underwood No. 5 in 1900—widely regarded "the first truly modern typewriter"—that they became an "international" company selling more typewriters around the world than all other typewriter companies combined.[49] Through his family background and training Horace Underwood—however much confessing himself lacking in business sense—developed a keen appreciation of the centrality of sciences and entrepreneurship for participation in the world community of his time.

A third point of note is that his curriculum through college was founded on classical liberal education—that is, an intellectual engagement with Greek and Roman classics in the original languages that, though considered "pagan" at one time, since the Renaissance was routinely accepted by even those training to become ministers and missionaries as an integral part of the so-called "Western" intellectual tradition together with biblical studies. From today's global perspective one can point to this as another case par excellence of interculturation through which the substantively different Judeo-Christian and Greek/Roman intellectual traditions had come

49. Engler, "The Typewriter Industry," 30.

to effectively enlarge and in fact redefine each in terms of the other. It is suggestive of the possibility that Underwood would have been open in turn to a similar process of meaningful, fundamental interculturation or mutual enlargement of East and West.

Underwood's formal education continued with his matriculation at the Dutch Reformed Theological Seminary in New Brunswick, New Jersey (today's New Brunswick Theological Seminary) in September 1881.[50] During his three years of study Underwood took the following courses:

> First year: Hebrew and Greek Languages, External Study of Messianic Predictions in the Original Language, and of the Greek Harmony, Biblical Geography, Biblical Antiquities, Sacred Chronology, Ancient Sacred History, Sacred Rhetoric, Composition, and Delivery of Sermons.
>
> Second year: Didactic and Polemic Theology, Ecclesiastical History, Church Government, Biblical Criticism, Chaldee and Syriac Languages, Exegetical Study of Messianic Predictions continued, Exegetical Study of one of the Pauline Epistles, Liturgics, Catechetics, Composition and Delivery of Sermons.
>
> Third year: Didactic and Polemic Theology continued, Ecclesiastical History continued, Pastoral Theology, Exegetical Study of Prophecies continued, Exegetical Study of the Pauline Epistles continued, Theses, Composition and Delivery of Sermons, Constitution of the Reformed Church, Full paraphrases of the Epistles which they study.[51]

Some important members of Seminary faculty to influence Underwood at New Brunswick included Samuel M. Woodbridge (1819–1905), Professor of Church History; David D. Demarest (1819–98), Professor of Pastoral Theology and Rhetoric, and not least, Rev. Dr. William Mabon, Underwood's former pastor at the New Grove Church and pre-college tutor

---

50. New Brunswick Theological Seminary dates its founding to 1784, when the Reformed Protestant Dutch Church in North America (renamed the Reformed Church in America in 1867) elected its first professor of theology, John Henry Livingston (1746–1825). Livingstone at first taught his students in New York City, but removed to New Brunswick, NJ, in 1810 as president of the Reformed Church's undergraduate college, called Queen's College (to be renamed Rutgers in 1825), where he continued to exercise his role as the Church's professor of theology, thus establishing the foundation of what at first was called the "Theological Institution of Queen's College" but soon afterward came to be known as the Reformed Church's Theological Seminary. The seminary continued to share quarters with the college until 1856, and the two institutions had official ties until 1867. See Coakley, *New Brunswick Theological Seminary*, 1–16.

51. University of the City of New York, *Catalogue of the Officers and Students*, 6–11. On the Seminary in the time of Underwood's presence there, see Coakley, "The Seminary Years," and also his *New Brunswick Theological Seminary*, 27–53.

who, shortly after Underwood's enrollment at New Brunswick, was himself appointed there as Professor of Didactic and Polemic Theology.[52] The chief impression his classmates had of Underwood seems to have been of his energy and passion for evangelism, always running from place to place "with his coattails flying."[53] Upon finishing his first year Underwood was already traveling around the country, ostensibly to sell books but earning converts and friends among the all sorts of people he met along the way, as well as money. The enthusiasm and orientation toward evangelizing present in him since early childhood had been given practical action and experience under the constant encouragement and guidance of Rev. Mabon during the years at the New Grove Church, to which we now turn.

The Experience of America and the Example of William Mabon

To the values and commitments Underwood received through family and early education, life in America gave him visceral understanding and experience of the practical challenges to creating unity from many different peoples, cultures, and classes. Late nineteenth-century America was a society undergoing tremendous change. Newly connected by railways, steamships, and the telegraph, millions of Americans were spreading out to the growing number of cities that were mushrooming throughout the continent. The cities themselves also grew at exponential rates. New York had numbered a half million people in 1850 but was 3.5 million by 1900; Philadelphia went from one hundred thousand to 1.2 million people in the same period; Chicago's rise was even more dramatic, going from 4,470 in the 1840 census to well over a million by 1890.[54] All in all, American population around the time of the Underwoods' arrival in the early 1870s had been about 38.5 million; by the time Horace Underwood set out for Korea a little more than ten years later the number was closer to sixty million, or increased by about 33 percent, both through large-scale immigration as well as domestic births.[55] A major draw was the prospect of new jobs created by the booming Second Industrial Revolution throughout the country, with its emphasis on large-scale steel and iron production, the building of railroads and factories, and all that they required and represented. Legendary fortunes were built during

52. University of the City of New York, *Catalogue of the Officers and Students*, 3; Coakley, *New Brunswick Theological Seminary*, 46–48. Mabon taught at the Seminary until his death in 1892.

53. Lillias Underwood, *Underwood of Korea*, 27.

54. Rees, *Industrialization and the Transformation of American Life*, 44.

55. Wright and Porter, *Compendium of the Eleventh Census*, 46.

these times, from the Vanderbilts (shipping and railroads) to the Morgans (banking), the Rockefellers (oil) and the Carnegies (steel), but it was also a time of enormous suffering for the working poor who toiled long hours in terrible conditions with few labor laws to protect them. There were many movements toward unionization, but they were often thwarted by the many more desperate strikebreakers eager to gain a foothold in the cut throat economy by accepting jobs on any terms. The fast-rising middle class was not without its anxieties either. It was a volatile time, with one's fortunes liable to turn for better or worse on the wisdom of a decision or a connection, and pressures coming from both above and below.[56]

For the Underwoods this dynamic itself was not necessarily new; they were after all an educated upper middle-class family from the epi-center of the British Empire, experienced in the ways of the new economy driven by industrialization and familiar with the evangelical response to its problems.[57] Pastoral training in America at the time, too, was dominated by Scottish "common sense philosophy" after its effective promotion by the Scottish-born and University of Edinburgh trained John Knox Witherspoon (1723–94) who had wielded enormous influence first as the sixth president of Princeton College in 1768, and later as a member of the Congress.[58] What *was* new in America instead was its concentration of demographic diversity and the experimental spirit of democracy—not only as a political system or ideology but equally much as a social dynamic—harnessed to forge order out of the potential chaos. The Civil War that had ended in 1865 sent nearly four million newly freed slaves on the move, seeking to either leave or find new ways of surviving the devastated South. Many moved to cities in the North, but were rarely welcomed since they meant another source of competition for jobs alongside the urban poor already resident there, together with the continual stream of newly arriving immigrants. Between 1840 and 1870 American population had more than doubled from a little over 17 million to nearly 38.6 million, not only through native births but an average of 2.2 million newly arriving immigrants per decade. Between 1870 and 1900

56. May, *Protestant Churches and Industrial America.*

57. To provide a sense of context from something like Underwoods' point of view, the population of London grew from about one million in 1800 to 6.7 million in 1900. See Emsley et al., "London History."

58. Robert, *Occupy until I Come*, 31. Witherspoon was president of Princeton until 1775, at which time his second son-in-law Rev. Samuel Smith succeeded him to the position. He had in the meantime become much more involved in the cause of the American Revolution, joining the Committee of Correspondence and Safety in 1774, then becoming both elected to the Continental Congress in 1776 and appointed Congressional Chaplain in 1776. He continued to serve in Congress as one of its most active and influential members until 1782.

the population would double again to over 76 million, and the number of immigrants rises from 2.8 million in the 1870s to an unprecedented 5.2 million in the 80s. This time, moreover, many were from southern and eastern Europe—Italy, Greece, Poland, and Russia—as well as a small but regular contingent from Asia, rather than from Ireland and Germany as in the earlier decades. When tensions inevitably flared under volatile economic conditions, they tended to lash out with ethnic, cultural, and religious overtones, and vice versa.[59] It was in this context of late nineteenth century America that Underwood would gain a deeply felt appreciation for both the ideals and limitations of the "melting pot," witness the powerful need for ecumenical cooperation to combat social problems, and absorb also the effectiveness of equal and open participation in the infrastructure of associations for the building up of a *culture* of Christian democracy.

Initially, Underwood and his family settled in a small town seemingly at considerable remove from the cosmopolitan New York City, which was then as now the largest city in the country with about 924,000 residents, of whom nearly 45 percent were foreign born.[60] New Durham was situated in North Bergen County of New Jersey, on the Hackensack turnpike about four miles north of Hoboken. Known as the Marshland until 1803, as late as 1844 it was a backward town described as having "1 Reformed Dutch and 1 Baptist church, and about 50 dwellings."[61] Being conveniently situated right next to the railway, however, by 1870 it had grown into a "thriving manufacturing center" in its own right, with residents made up mostly of Dutch, English, and German descent, and the town's upper section described with some pride as "one of the finest residential sections in the county."[62] Lillias Underwood gives few details about Underwood's early days in America, merely mentioning in general terms his family's "brave struggle under difficult circumstances" toward slow but sure success "earned by vigilance, energy, determination, brains, and courage."[63] The major nexus of their social life seems to have been around the little community at the Dutch Reformed Church where they "took part in all the church work," including in evangelistic work:

> During these early years in America, the boys were engaged in
> much evangelistic work. Besides three or four regular services

59. "Decennial Census Historical Facts." See also Handy, *A Christian America*, 73–77; May, *Protestant Churches and Industrial America*, 36.

60. Rosenwaike, *Population History of New York City*.

61. Barber and Howe, "North Bergen, NJ," 234.

62. Feldra, *History of Hudson County*, 1917, 27–28.

63. Lillias Underwood, *Underwood of Korea*, 22–23.

of church and Sunday school, they attended a mission school and engaged in tract distribution in some of the worst localities of Union Hill. They met active opposition in one of the saloons and were roughly ordered to keep away. They bowed politely and calmly, went again the following week quite undisturbed by bluster and profanity . . . the saloon men eventually capitulated with what grace they might and even grew to be friendly with the indomitable and polite young evangelists.[64]

The new influence in these early evangelistic activities in America was Rev. Mabon, whom Underwood frequently referred to as his "beloved pastor." A graduate of Union College (class of 1840) as well as of New Brunswick Theological Seminary (Class of 1844), Mabon was already a man in his early fifties by the time he met the Underwoods, and described as a "genial man, a lover of nature, a lover of humanity, and a lover of God," with his life very much that of a local pastor.[65] Having begun serving the New Grove Church in 1846 as a young man of twenty-four, he would remain its pastor for thirty-five years until 1881 when he was appointed faculty at the New Brunswick Theological Seminary the same year his pupil Underwood became a student there. But as John Coakley notes, in many other ways Rev. Mabon and his ministry likely "served as a model" for Underwood.[66] Given to practical ministry and evangelism more than scholarship, Mabon was nevertheless deeply interested in education and not only personally tutored many young men, including Underwood as he prepared for college, but also served seven years as the County Superintendent of Public Schools and seventeen years as Examiner of Teachers during his time as pastor, so that his writings included papers on the proper task of public education and the raising of children in home and church.[67] He was also extraordinarily dedicated to evangelism, with "[his] wise counsels" helping to found "no less than seventeen sanctuaries, in connection with thirteen regularly organized churches" described as daughter-churches.[68] Unlike the so-called "parachute method" of church planting where a minister simply moves into a new location to start a church from scratch, or the case where small cell churches network and periodically meet together as a larger group, "daughter-churches" are those where an

---

64. Lillias Underwood, *Underwood of Korea*, 22–23.

65. E. T. Corwin, *A Manual of the Reformed Church in America*, 407.

66. Coakley, "The Seminary Years," 67.

67. University of the City of New York, *Union College 1795–1895*, 385. He also served for five years as commissioner for equalization of taxes.

68. E. T. Corwin, *Manual of the Reformed Church in America*, 590.

existing "mother-church" provides the initial leadership and resources—
i.e., money, people, and/or training—to get the new church started. Their
success depends on the agreement of the whole of the mother-church's
congregation to engage in such mature, "selfless" enterprise, to sustain as
well as adjust the assistance over time enough to give the daughter-church
a fair start, and then to let go and let it become an independent, self-governing entity free of the oversight of the mother-church that had given it
life. To carry out such an enterprise, enough members of the congregation
would have to be sufficiently persuaded not only of the endeavor's Christian rightness but of sound financial and administrative planning, as well
as the subtler issues of church "politics." To have successfully orchestrated
such sustained cooperation for so many daughter-churches over a lifetime,
it is no wonder that upon Rev. Mabon's death an editorial in the Reformed
Church's newspaper wrote of his "rare business tact."[69]

While there is no way to know how much of Underwood's similar success in daughter-church planting later in Korea was due to what he observed
and learned from his "beloved pastor," his mission reports from throughout his ministry in Korea demonstrate a similar sense of business tact (as
distinct from business sense, his lack of which he frequently lamented to
his brother!), notable absence of personal ambition, as well as keen judgment when it came to the spirit and training needed to nurture a daughter
church to self-sufficient maturity.[70] Not surprisingly an early and strong
advocate of the so-called Nevius Plan, Underwood strove to plant churches
according to principles of self-sufficiency long before he invited John Nevius
(1829–93), to visit Korea in the summer of 1890 to explain his version of
these principles as a basis for missionary work.[71] This was in keeping with
Underwood's belief in the importance of building up a *culture* of free and
open participation in the infrastructure and decision-making process of the
church as in every other form of association, even though it might mean
taking a longer, more difficult path to the establishment of each church. For
example, though there might be sufficient number of believers in a region

69. Quoted in Coakley, "The Seminary Years," 68.

70. Underwood planted a total of twenty-three congregations in Korea during his
thirty years of work there, among which twenty-one congregations are still active today.
See Choi, *Story of Underwood*, 22–23. See also chapter 1, n36. The list and detailed
information concerning the twenty-one congregations still extant are available in
several sources, including *the Proceedings of the 10th Annual Underwood International
Symposium*, 121.

71. For Underwood's own account of results from Nevius' visit to Korea, see Underwood, *Call of Korea*, 109–10. For an account of the visit itself, see Lillias Underwood,
Underwood of Korea, 99–101. For further description and sources see also chapter 1,
p. 15 and n27.

who wished to build a church of their own, he did not help them appeal to the Presbyterian mission or to other, more established congregations in Korea to help. Instead, he focused on making the *process* of sustained effort, coordination, and cooperation among the would-be congregants to build a church on their own become itself an essential part of the training needed for them to learn to manage the church and to have the joy and confidence of independent achievement. He also made sure there were trained native leaders in Christian doctrine among them, often graduates of his bible study program which later became the foundation for the first Presbyterian Seminary in Korea. For all the good of self-sufficiency as a goal, of course, he like an experienced parent, understood when a congregation was ready to make its wobbly road to independence and when it didn't understand the nature or the responsibility of independence, and could demonstrate a different kind of "business tact" on such occasions. In one instance, in 1898, he was asked by the congregation of the Central City Church to give the sermon celebrating their decision to become an independent church free of missionary oversight. Underwood shared the concern of other missionaries that the congregation's abrupt decision to declare its independence had been motivated more by the general stirring for national independence sweeping across the country in the wake of Japanese and Russian presence and interference in Korean affairs, than any reasoned understanding of the life of a church. Nevertheless, very much against the advice of his colleagues, he at once agreed to give the sermon, then used the podium to gently persuade them of the difference between "independence and inter-dependence," thus bringing them back into the fold without damaging their pride, stirring resentment, or stunting their striving toward independence.[72]

Such "business tact" and peace-keeping went hand in hand with skills he developed also in association building. In his *Democracy in America* (1835, 1840) Alexis de Tocqueville astutely noted the much greater necessity and proliferation of associations in America than elsewhere, ironically because Americans more than anyone "learn from birth that he must rely upon himself to combat the ills and obstacles of life."[73] To better assert or actualize one's interests in a society of equals one therefore needs to form an association with those of similar interests, since in a democracy of equals lone can only claim a legal right or a legal majority, and only very rarely if at all approach issues by presuming a position of moral majority.[74] Moreover, Tocqueville observed, instead of looking to authority

---

72. Lillias Underwood, *Underwood of Korea*, 186–88.

73. Tocqueville, *Democracy in America*, 220.

74. Tocqueville contrasts this with the context in Europe where associations claim/

of governments to solve problems, Americans prefer to come together as assenting individuals to consider and resolve matters themselves whether it be to organize public festivities, resist ideologies and/or social excesses, or lobby for change on a larger scale. In that sense learning to understand the organization and running of associations—its legal, administrative, and moral aspects, and their practical implications in ensuring one's self interests—become something of a basic survival skill and *modus operandi* in America, so deeply saturated into the culture that the young more or less imbibe it unconsciously "as mother's milk," and not just for those serving in government. Tocqueville noted furthermore the close relationship between such power of assembly and freedom itself.[75]

Underwood clearly understood the importance of this dynamic even as a young college student, and would continue to rely on it throughout his ministry in Korea. While at New York University he became a passionate member of the Delta Upsilon, a distinctly non-secret "social fraternity." Delta Upsilon originally had been a fraternity founded in 1834 to oppose the secret, Freemason-style fraternities then popular. The preamble to its constitution read in part,

> Believing that secret societies in college are calculated to destroy the harmony of college life, to create distinctions not founded on merit, to produce strife and animosity, we feel called upon to exert ourselves to counteract the evil tendencies of such associations. We would have no class of our fellow students invested with factitious advantages but would have all upon equal footing in the race of honorable distinction. We unite to maintain and diffuse liberal principles and to promote the great object of social and literary improvement. In doing this, we are confident that we have at heart the best interests of the institution to which we belong and that we are directed by the light of experience, the suggestion of reason, and the dictates of conscience.[76]

believe they represent the wishes of the *majority* who are the oppressed *moral* right. Tocqueville, *Democracy in America*, 225–27. For a more expansive description of the significance of associations in America, see Tocqueville, *Democracy in America*, 595–609.

75. Tocqueville, *Democracy in America*, 220–21.

76. Gurney, "History of the Colby Chapter," 201. Delta Upsilon was originally founded in 1834 at Williams College in response to the presence of secret or professional fraternities on campus suspect for their "successful placement of members into high campus offices, regardless of their qualifications." It was in "opposing the unjust and, at that time, alleged barbarous practices of the secret fraternities" that Delta Upsilon took as its motto, "*Ouden Adelon*" or "Nothing Secret." See "History of Delta Upsilon."

In short, the Delta Upsilon original purpose had been to uphold ideals of open and egalitarian meritocracy—a value very much at the heart also of Neo-Confucianism of which Chosŏn Korea took and practiced as its founding ideology. By 1879 it had formally disavowed its mission of anti-secrecy in favor of a mere general policy of "non-secrecy," on the view that the battle against secrecy had been so successful as to change the very character of secret societies such that they no longer merited the earlier hostility.[77] If the blunting of a well-defined, finite objective brought on a crisis of identity both internally and externally at Delta Upsilon, especially at relatively young chapters such as at New York University, which had been founded only fourteen years before, nevertheless its continued general purpose of promoting equality, openness, and liberal principles clearly meant much to Underwood. He joined it despite the chapter being in a "very weak and in rather a critical condition," then in a demonstration of association-building par excellence, with "ardent enthusiasm, foresight, energy, diplomacy and skill" managed, against "a determined fight" from other societies, to "claim and initiate, apparently at the risk of life and limb, enough first-rate men of an incoming class to insure the future life of their fraternity."[78] Later he would bring the same spirit of egalitarian meritocracy to Korea and pour similar effort and skill to uniting missionaries toward an ecumenical Christian movement regardless of denominational affiliation.

Ecumenical Evangelicalism and the Inter-Seminary Missionary Alliance

Underwood may well have been a most sincere and successful practitioner of inter-denominational or ecumenical cooperation in context of nineteenth century Anglo-American foreign missions, coming as he did from his family background, but he was far from alone in holding to the principle.[79] It

77. Gurney, "History of the Colby Chapter," 202–3.

78. Lillias Underwood, *Underwood of Korea*, 24.

79. Such close colleagues of Underwood as Homer Bezaleel Hulbert (1863–1949), James Gale (1863–1937), and Oliver R. Avison (1860–1956), as well as Henry G. Appenzeller (1858–1902) and Robert A. Hardy (1865–1949), shared the same spirit of interdenominational cooperation. Starting with joint prayer meetings begun on January 1, 1888, under the leadership of Underwood and Appenzeller and their two respective Jŏng-dong churches (i.e., Jŏng-dong First Methodist Church and Jŏng-dong Presbyterian Church later known as Sae-mun-an Church), missionaries engaged actively in inter-denominational meetings and projects. The Korean Tract Society was created as an inter-denominational entity in 1890; in 1893 the four Presbyterian missions, i.e., American Northern and Southern, Australian, and Canadian, united to create the Presbyterian United Council; in 1905, 150 Presbyterian and Methodist missionaries

had in a sense been developing naturally since the mid-nineteenth century as yet another form of association building among many of America's urban evangelicals. Faced with the situation of extraordinary high ethnic, religious, and linguistic diversity concentrated in the newly forming cities throughout the country and especially among the urban poor, many evangelicals, as Dana Robert has written, "sought fellowship with like-minded brethren across the denominational spectrum for the purposes of Bible study and addressing social problems."[80] The Civil War also had the effect of dividing existing denominations along their northern and southern loyalties while at the same time also strengthening cooperation *across* denominational lines to meet overwhelming needs of wartime suffering. As Robert notes,

> The 1880s were the height of an ecumenical and evangelical consensus about the role of the church in the world. People who would eventually be remembered as either "liberals" or "conservatives" were still working together in the 1880s. Shared practical activism and inter-denominational cooperation from the ground up dominated the thinking of progressive clergy of varied theological views and different denominational traditions. The public split between "social" and "individual" methods of Christian work lay in the future. Pierson's generation, forged in the crucible of Civil War, still clung to hopes that American Protestantism could embody a broad consensus.[81]

More formally, some 800 Protestant delegates from England, Europe, and America had gotten together in 1846 in London for the first ever meeting of the international Evangelical Alliance where they agreed on certain basic elements of the Christian evangelical faith, leaving room for more nuanced differences of belief and right to private judgment in biblical interpretation; by 1873 the Alliance meeting held in New York City had more than fifteen thousand delegates in attendance. If actual membership in the American branch of the Evangelical Alliance never numbered more than a few hundred, their prominence as urban pastors, editors of religious journals, academics, denominational leaders, and even businessmen who shared common concerns for finding evangelical solutions to burgeoning social problems brought them into contact with a "vast inter-locking

---

gathered together to found the General Council of Evangelical Mission in Korea. In June, 1910, Underwood together with Yun Chi-ho (1865–1945) and Samuel A. Moffett (1864–1939) participated in the Edinburgh World Missionary Conference where A. T. Pierson presented a paper on the theme of "Cooperation and Unity." For an extensive description see Choi, *The Founding of Chosŏn Christian College*, 357–63, 372–74.

80. Robert, *Occupy until I Come*, 70.

81. Robert, *Occupy until I Come*, 125.

directorate of evangelical voluntary societies, publications, church boards, and assemblies which enabled the Alliance to reflect the general evangelical opinions of the time"[82]—yet another instance of association building for a good cause. At one end of the spectrum there were people like Arthur T. Pierson, a prominent and passionate leader of the Alliance, working on a grand and international scale, writing articles and giving sermons on issues pertaining to "The Unity of the Church";[83] at the other end were dedicated local pastors such as Rev. Mabon writing in a similar paper but on more locally relevant topic such as strategy for uniting the Dutch and German Reformed Churches.[84] Their shared reasoning was that social problems such as intemperance, atheism, corruption, materialism, rape and violence, and racism did not stop at denominational lines; certainly one of Underwood's earliest evangelical forays under Rev. Mabon's tutelage had been to the local taverns to discourage drinking, which at the time was widely considered the root of many social and personal problems.

Underwood understandably shared in the ecumenism of the Alliance completely. The Inter-Seminary Missionary Alliance which he first attended in 1883 along with Henry Appenzeller (1858–1902) was also ecumenical, and would in time become an important seed for both the Student Division of the American YMCA and the Student Volunteer Movement associated with Arthur T. Pierson, Dwight L. Moody (1839–99), Robert Wilder (1863–1938) and John R. Mott (1865–1955).[85] Overall, as Lillias Underwood notes at some length,

> The truth was that whenever he saw people working for Christ he saw brothers who had a claim upon his great sympathy and service. He never had any strong sectarian, class, or race bias. More than anyone else I have ever seen he seemed to feel a real brotherhood with people of all races, nationalities, classes, ages, and sects. The whole current of his being set toward unity. He involuntarily tended to draw into close, helpful, loving fellowship with all living souls. No one was too low or too high, too broad or too narrow; too white or too black for his sympathy, interest and love. . . . This marked trait of character was

---

82. Robert, *Occupy until I Come*, 72.

83. Unity in these instances referred to a "practical union," such as inviting pastors from other denominations to speak at one's pulpit and sharing the Lord's table of fellowship, rather than absorption of one church by the other. In 1877, the Presbyterian Alliance became the first international body to bring the Presbyterian and Reformed churches together. See Robert, *Occupy until I Come*, 72.

84. See Coakley, "The Seminary Years," 67n15.

85. Coakley, "The Seminary Years," 72–76.

often illustrated in his life in the East, in a foreign community
made up of Europeans and Americans of all classes of society,
all shades of religious beliefs, from the titled diplomat to the
flotsam and jetsam of wandering ne'er do wells; from the high
Anglican church missionary to the atheist; and all in the midst
of the great non-Christian Oriental races of China, Japan and
of Korea. He was the friend and brother of everybody, from the
king to the coolie . . . realizing the often over-looked truth that
everybody in this sad world needs a friend. But especially did
he make light of or set aside altogether all sectarian barriers
in his relations with other Christian workers, longing to bring
them all into the closest unity. This was one of the great desires
of his life, "that they all should be one."[86]

It is significant that this ecumenical tendency was in equal parts evangelical, evangelistic, and socially minded. There was tremendous belief among
those in the Evangelical Alliance that social problems were best solved by
each person's deeply personal religious or conversion *experience* irrespective of denomination (as long as it was of Protestant origin); policy changes
from the top down, while important, merely helped create an environment
conducive to sustaining the narrow path. Underwood's unstoppable zeal for
evangelism from an early age and throughout his Seminary years has already
been much noted by others—whether converting the residents of a "very
rough and lawless people" in the remote hills of New Jersey (possibly the Ra-
mapo Mountain people), exhorting support for foreign missions while having charge of the congregation in Pompton, New Jersey, for several months,
or simply going on a "book-selling tour" of the country to earn money.[87]
His equally enthusiastic support for the Salvation Army during his days at
the Seminary[88] is evident not only of his interest in alleviating the suffering
of the poor, destitute, and uneducated as part of Christian evangelical and
evangelistic responsibility, but a basic stance of trying to resolve problems
through practical, systematic approaches on the level of culture.

The Example of Arthur Tappan Pierson

In this regard the personal example and leadership of Arthur T. Pierson was
likely to have been both a significant reinforcement and a lasting source of

86. Lillias Underwood, *Underwood of Korea*, 28–29.

87. Lillias Underwood, *Underwood of Korea*, 31–32; Coakley, "The Seminary Years,"
69–70.

88. See Coakley, "The Seminary Years," 68–69.

encouragement and support for Underwood. Considered by many to be the father of inter-denominational mission as well as the world mission movement of the nineteenth century, Underwood looked up to Pierson while the elder minister found in Underwood someone who faithfully and intelligently applied his evangelical vision in the frontlines. Indeed their mutual respect inspired Pierson, in December, 1910, at the advanced age of seventy-three, to include the politically unstable Korea among the destinations of his first and last tour of various mission sites in East Asia. Then, having witnessed for himself the dynamic intensity with which Koreans were converting to Christianity, he made it his will that a Normal Bible School be erected after his death—not in any of the mission sites already prepared in India or Japan by his own children who were established missionaries there, or in China—but in Chosŏn Korea.[89]

As a Presbyterian, Pierson along with many of the American clergy of his time worked under something like a general cast of Scottish Enlightenment thought in which, unlike its Continental counterpart, the criterion of moral behavior included the promotion of the general welfare of mankind, to be achieved through rational and practical social change as motivated by the centrality divine presence in human moral development. But Pierson, born of abolitionist parents and even named after the famous New York abolitionist Arthur Tappan (1786–1865), had been also trained to develop methods in his ministry incorporating political activism, especially support for anti-slavery and the Civil War. Beginning in the late 1860s his sense of the urgency and enormity of social problems in America expanded, and with it was also his study of the historical and theological issues of foreign missions. His ecumenical vision increasingly included parachurch ministry as well, for a brand of evangelism that promoted building schools, modern medicine, and other markers of social and scientific progress associated with the Enlightenment. He popularized holding bible study as open, informal discussions on the text, much in the style of the liberal arts education he had received, and personally took to training lay people to teach Sunday school, while at the same time leading prayer meetings for the outpouring of the Holy Spirit.[90]

---

89. His son Delavan Leonard Pierson (1867–1952) consequently worked closely with Underwood to found the Arthur T. Pierson Memorial Bible School (today's Pyeongtaek University) to be managed jointly by the Northern Presbyterian, Southern Methodist, and Northern Methodist Churches. For more detailed information regarding Underwood and Pierson, see Cho, *Arthur T. Pierson Memorial Bible School*, 33–59. There is also a brief but helpful account of Pierson's stay in Korea in Robert, *Occupy until I Come*, 296–97.

90. Robert, *Occupy until I Come*, 42.

We might note that in many ways these "mission programs" within America were quite similar in purpose and orientation to what Underwood later would undertake in "heathen" Korea. Pierson would shape the Bethany Church in Philadelphia, which he had been invited to pastor in 1883, into a model "institutional church" where doors were kept open at all times to provide for the educational, recreational as well as spiritual needs of the working poor who could not always attend regular church meetings. Some of the programs he instituted there early on included sewing classes, a savings program, a mutual aid society, a children's temperance organization, the Sunday school teacher training, and general education of the congregation toward democratization of the church infrastructure—literally offering every man, woman, and child the opportunity to become involved in some way that ultimately would help improve themselves and their standing in the world at large.[91] We can see here as well the American penchant for working through associations, and of Pierson taking a proactive approach to essentially "training" people—many of them new immigrants—in how to participate in the actual running of organizations and infrastructures, the better to prevent autocracy of any sort and to help spread and integrate with a democratic Christian *culture* in its stead beyond simply democratic *politics*. According to Dana Robert, Pierson helped launch "the greatest wave of missionary enthusiasm in American history,"[92] in large part because he

> absolutely refused to separate the spiritual from the intellectual. The mission movement thrived on its emotional appeal to personal spiritual instincts toward holiness, combined with logical analysis of the world's needs and of the church's responsibilities to meet those needs. Missions drew upon both the latent emotion of American popular religion and a system of rationality

91. The night school at Bethany Church included classes in German, Bookkeeping, Mechanical Drawing, Dressmaking, and Elocution as well as religious studies, with tuition for members of Bethany Church kept at only 25 cents per term. The program was Pierson's brainchild, supported by businessman and founder of the Bethany Church, John Wanamaker. See Robert, *Occupy until I Come*, 119–25.

92. Robert, *Occupy until I Come*, 156. The United States had begun sending forth foreign missionaries in 1812, but the endeavor had been initially slow to grow. The country did not have many churches as yet that could afford to finance missionaries, nor did the U.S. have much clout politically to send or to protect missionaries outside of itself. The Civil War was a further blow to missionaries from the South as many of them lost their home base churches. It was not until the 1880s and 90s that a wave of missionary enthusiasm began sweeping America, by which time Pierson had "become master of missionary facts and senior statesman for the student missionary movement of the century's end" by having begun to study it in the 1860s. Robert, *Occupy until I Come*, 47.

that valued certainty and the classification of historical facts as the "fingers of God."[93]

Underwood's call to a life of mission may have had its start much before—and across the Atlantic from—the wave led by Pierson, but as a young impressionable immigrant who took to America and its social dynamics with such enthusiasm he must nevertheless be counted an exponent of and influenced by the dynamics of his new home country. If Pierson's vision of the church and its programs were developed to both transform and become an integral part of the broader "Christian" democratic and therefore inter-denominationally united America, the greater challenge awaiting Underwood was to carry out similar social reform-minded evangelism toward a unified Christian *culture* in context of an unknown and scientifically backward Korea.[94]

But this gives us an important point to consider: If inter-denominationalism had been a well-known and widely practiced idea in America in the late nineteenth century, one might ask why it was less actively practiced in context of foreign missions? Compared for example to China where many denominational conflicts and rivalries took place between 1860–1900,[95] why was Underwood (and his fellow missionaries in Chosŏn Korea) so much an exception for making it a principle of his work as a missionary to be insisted upon, rather than something to work toward only when easily to be had? Even in Korea it is interesting to note that such inter-denominational cooperation seems *not* to have been the case or the plan from the beginning. According to recently discovered letters of George C. Foulk (1856–93), an officer in the naval diplomatic corps responsible for the safety of missionaries stationed in Korea, petty rivalry between denominations was a common source of his administrative frustration in the early days of the mission.[96] While the question surely deserves a separate, in-depth inquiry, we might conjecture that inasmuch as

93. Robert, *Occupy until I Come*, 300.

94. As mentioned earlier in this chapter, Pierson and Underwood were joined by another, earlier bond. Pierson had for over twenty years been an admirer of George Müller—the same the Christian evangelist and highly respected Director of the Ashley Down orphanage in Bristol that Underwood's father John had supported faithfully while in England, and ultimately converted to Müller's premillennialism. See this chapter, 34. Robert notes, however, that although Muller's cynicism concerning the visible denominational churches may have made more sense in context of Europe's established churches, the American context in which people joined denominations of their own free will made it different. See Robert, *Occupy until I Come*, 106.

95. See Joseph Tse-Hei Lee, *The Bible and the Gun*.

96. Foulk, "Letter [to the Family] of August 18, 1885."

inter-denominational cooperation was considered necessary and appropriate to forge a united Christian culture for a united America, such a motivation did not become a sufficient priority or concern for the Christian leaders and congregations behind the foreign missions. As far as most missionaries and their congregational supporters were concerned heathen conversion to Christianity was the goal, not Christian unity working for a united culture of the people after their conversion. In short, there was a lack of long term planning or vision regarding the mission field despite their own experience and recognition of the need for supra-denominational cooperation in their own contexts. The general practice was for each denomination to form its own mission board, commission its own missionaries with funds raised from within the denomination, and therefore expect mission reports pertaining to the needs and successes of "their" mission as such.

Put more negatively, the commissioning of foreign missions was not impervious to taking on the character—however subconsciously—of an imperial project—i.e., objective material markers of "their" work and generosity and achievement for Christ. Such an implicitly imperial and hence divisive underlying conception of mission could not but affect the workings of individual missionaries as well. Could it be that Underwood, who from his birth in his native England had been steeped in the far-seeing supra-denominational principle of mission drafted by his great-grandfather—i.e., that mission's design is "not to send Presbyterian, Independent, Episcopalian or any other form of church order and government . . . but the Glorious Gospel of the Blessed God to the heathen . . . [for them] to assume for themselves such form of church government as to them shall appear most agreeable to the Word of God"[97]—not only had absorbed the dynamic inter-denominational mission movement under the likes of Mabon and Pierson in America with greater appreciation, understanding, and resolve, but experienced that cooperation in America as itself taking place *at a mission site* no different from Korea? He had, after all, been committed to life as a missionary since a tender age, dreaming of eventually serving in India. Engaging in non-stop evangelism almost from the moment he set foot in America if not earlier, he may well have viewed the country less with the mindset of an immigrant and more as a missionary learning

---

97. Lillias Underwood, *Underwood of Korea*, 16. Interestingly, it has been said that "one of the most striking facts in the earlier history of the Scots Presbyterians in England is their remarkable unanimity of purpose and subordination of the denominational differences that lay between them. Thus . . . 'Established Kirk' ministers and their Secessionist brethren worked harmoniously together on the Scots Presbytery in London. The relations between Scots and their English Presbyterian comrades [also] were remarkably fraternal." Black, *The Scots Churches in England*, 16–17.

from—as well as serving in—one place "en route" to another. If so, it would help explain why he held the "union of all evangelistic sects on the field"[98] to be a principle as natural and necessary in Korea as in America, and why there could be less of a divide in his mind even between senders and "sendees" in mission, as demonstrated in the letters to his family. And so for Underwood, as Lillias described upon his death, "The great aims of his life were: The conversion of the Korean nation to Christ, the organic union of all evangelistic sects on the field, the establishment of self-support in the whole native church and general study of the Bible by all Korean Christians. But 'Union' was his great ideal."[99] Perhaps equally importantly, his time in America may have impressed upon the young Underwood a mindset in which a mission site is quite naturally a place of learning, of growing, of assimilating for oneself. As a boy just entering his teens he might have been a precocious "preacher" at home but hardly likely to think himself in a position to command authority. All of these dispositions factored favorably in his mission in Korea, where the learning would continue.

The First Thirteen Years in Korea:
Beginnings of Interculturation

If one had to capture in a few words the essence of what Underwood would learn from Korea it would probably be the deeply ingrained and pervasive Korean sensibility of "rightness" that transcended both the Confucian concept of rites and Western concept of rights. In Korea Underwood found an extraordinarily fertile ground for the gospel, one that by his own excited and repeated admission far exceeded both his expectations and—to his continued frustration—the imagination of the Mission Board back in America.[100] Indeed, the ideals of the Christian gospel as prepared by much of the nineteenth century Anglo-American missions arguably came to their fullest complete circle in Korea, having there much greater impact than even in China or Japan where Christianity had enjoyed a much longer missionary presence as well as far greater missionary resources and interest, because

98. Lillias Underwood, "Horace Grant Underwood," 909.

99. Lillias Underwood, "Horace Grant Underwood," 909. This article was submitted shortly after Underwood's death in 1916.

100. Not long after his first setting foot in Korea Underwood began to write, especially through the *Missionary Review of the World* edited by Pierson, about the exciting potential of Christian gospel work among the Korean people. During his furloughs as well he traveled not just throughout America but all over Canada, England, and as far as Europe to recruit more missionaries for Korea. See Rhodes and Campbell, *History of the Korea Mission Presbyterian Church*, 1:558.

of the Neo-Confucian values and ethos deeply saturated within the foundations of Korean culture. These values resonated more deeply and more intimately with the way Underwood had been prepared to present Christian ideas and ideals, and I argue, at the same time enlarged his own understanding of the potential power of the gospel.

Neo-Confucianism as a Historical Movement

It is now beginning to be more recognized that certain central tenets of the European Enlightenment had been significantly reinforced—if not necessarily acknowledged as inspired by—Confucian and Neo-Confucian ideas, communicated back home by such Jesuit pioneers as Matteo Ricci (1562–1610) and others since the late sixteenth century. These ideas (and ideals) included that of egalitarian and benevolent governance with particular emphasis not only on providing sufficient livelihood for the people, but also universal education for the formation of a rational and moral society—ideas that moreover had at their base an understanding of human nature and society as purposeful. Such ideas influenced a remarkable body of European intellectuals including Voltaire and Leibniz, and through them succeeding generations of thought throughout the eighteenth and nineteenth centuries.[101]

Long before this, however, Neo-Confucianism had been adopted in its totality as the founding ideology of Chosŏn dynasty (1392–1911) in Korea, making it the only country then or in subsequent history to do so. Neo-Confucian learning had been making its way into Korea since the late thirteenth or early fourteenth century of Koryŏ dynasty (918–1392) as seeds of reform. Initially, Korean scholars who got to study the new learning in Yuan China (1260–1368) brought back Neo-Confucian books and ritual vessels to spread the teaching in Korea, including at the state schools (kwanhak 官學).[102] At nearly four hundred years old Koryŏ was in need of revitalization, and it did not take long before Korean scholars began writing their own commentaries on Neo-Confucian texts, and producing such outstanding and reform-minded Neo-Confucian

101. See Mungello, *Leibniz and Confucianism*; Mungello, "Confucianism in the Enlightenment"; Mungello, *Curious Land*.

102. According to *Koryŏsa*, the Royal Confucian College (Sŏnggyun'kwan) sent two officers (Yu Yŏn and Yu Chŏk) to the Kiangnan area in China in 1314 in order to get Chinese classics and other books numbering 10,800 volumes (*Koryŏsa*, 34:20a–b). According to the *Late Chosŏn Reference Compilation of Documents on Korea* (hereafter, CMP), Emperor Jen-tsung (r. 1312–21) of the Yuan dynasty also sent 4,071 copies of books from the Imperial Library (Pikao t'u-shu) of the Sung dynasty to Koryŏ court that same year (CMP, 202:12b).

scholar-officials as Yi Saek (李穡1328–96), Chŏng Mongju (鄭夢周, 1337–92), and Chŏng Tojŏn (鄭道傳, 1342–98).[103] The Yuan court's adoption of Neo-Confucian texts as part of its Civil Service Examinations (CSE) in 1313 also functioned to provide impetus and support for the newly rising class of scholar-officials in late Koryŏ Korea, especially after the power of its hereditary aristocracy was weakened through military confrontations with the Yuan during this period. As Neo-Confucian thought gathered strength among the rising class of scholar-officials in Korea throughout the fourteenth century, so did calls for more radical reforms. Their targets included rites, education, land and tax policies, and Buddhism, which was widely regarded as depleting the national treasury via its extensive holdings and lavish ceremonies under royal patronage. Ultimately, their concern for restructuring society at political, social, and cultural levels led to a largely bloodless *coup d'etat* and the founding of the new Chosŏn dynasty in 1392 with General Yi Sŏnggye (later King T'aejo, r. 1392–98) as its head. The reforms instituted by the new regime included "constitutionally" limiting the power of kings and the royal family in very significant ways, and discouraging Buddhist and Daoist practices and drastically reducing their institutions while encouraging in their place the establishment of Neo-Confucian family ancestral shrines, which was eventually made a duty for all households including those of commoners.[104]

But possibly even more important than these in terms of long-term change was their two-pronged reform of the educational system. This involved on the one hand overhaul of the CSE system to make it more topically relevant to actual needs of governance and administration, to encourage egalitarian diversity among applicants, to dismantle longstanding master-to-disciple lineages and cliques toward merit-based transparency, to standardize and centralize the military examinations to bring it in balance with the civil examinations, and to systematically connect the institution to study in state-sponsored and public schools. On the other, the school system and its curriculum were overhauled to promote Neo-Confucian learning. Public schooling was greatly expanded throughout the country as a way to nurture worthy applicants to the CSE and ultimately to government posts, with the

103. When Neo-Confucian texts were incorporated into the new Civil Service Examination (CSE) system of the Yuan dynasty, Koreans were "the best prepared and the most adept of students" among those eligible to take part in the ethnically diverse and highly cosmopolitan field of candidates. For example, Yi Saek (1328–96) took the CSE in China while accompanying his father on a trip there, and was appointed to an official position in the Yuan government. See de Bary and Haboush, *The Rise of Neo-Confucianism in Korea*, 3–4.

104. *T'aejong sillok* [*The Annals of King T'aejong*], 2:22a–b. For an English translation, see Byonghon, *Annals of King T'aejong*.

establishment of not only a new Royal Confucian College in the new capital and the four district academies replacing the earlier Koryŏ private schools, but also *hyanggyo* (鄉敎) or provincial schools in every county. The new Chosŏn government often endowed these schools with land, facilities, and servants for their unhampered operation, and in 1406 also decreed the construction and stimulation of local schools to be one of the seven required duties of county magistrates.[105] To promote interest in learning, students registered in local schools were exempt from military and community services, while students of the Royal Confucian College—consisting of those who had already passed both stages of either the classics or literary licentiate examinations—also received "fellowship grants" in the form of their lodging and board. Indeed, Chosŏn Korea was "a singular instance in which Neo-Confucians played a large role in the creation of a new regime and in the formulating of its institutions" from royal lectures at court to learning in local communities.[106] The approach was efficacious not only in the dissemination of Neo-Confucian values top down but to their saturation in culture through gradual changes from the bottom up.

This was not so much the case in China where Neo-Confucianism originated, or in Japan. Historically, Neo-Confucianism had its origins among several generations of scholars in Song China (960–1279), culminating as a comprehensive philosophy with systematic metaphysics, principles of governance, and a graduated "core curriculum" toward that end as put together by its great synthesizer, Zhu Xi (1130–1200).[107] Though widely recognized as a brilliant scholar and made a member of the scholarly elite at court at the age of nineteen, Zhu Xi, due to his criticism of the incompetency and corruption of some influential court officials, was subsequently demoted to minor outlying posts when given office at all, and his teachings were labeled heterodox at time of his death. The importance of his contribution was recognized not long afterward, however, and in 1208 he was posthumously elevated to honor as Wen Gong (文公), meaning "Venerable Gentleman of Culture." Even so, it was not until the Mongol Khubilai Khan (1215–94)

105. *T'aejoing sillok*, 12:8b.

106. de Bary and Haboush, *The Rise of Neo-Confucianism in Korea*, 36–37.

107. The term "Neo-Confucian" generally refers to the ideas, texts, and practices identified with Zhu Xi 朱熹 (1130–1200), as his interpretations gave Confucianism new meaning and vitality, and for centuries dominated not only Chinese but also Korean, Vietnamese, and Japanese thought. For more general purposes the term Neo-Confucian may also be applied to that movement of thought which arose in Song dynasty China and later came to be known as *xin-xue* (新學 new study), in the broad sense of these terms as used by such historians of Neo-Confucianism as Huang Zhongxi, Fung Yu-lan, and Carsun Chang. See Chan, *A Source Book in Chinese Philosophy*, 588–90. See also de Bary and Chaffee, *Neo-Confucian Education*, 1–2.

conquered Song China and established the Yuan dynasty (1271–1368) in its stead that Zhu Xi's ideas were first adopted as the secular ideological basis of the new hybrid state. The Mongols were hardly dedicated to the propagation of Chinese culture, but they saw the political usefulness of Zhu's teachings and curriculum in creating a new class of elite scholarly bureaucracy to check the powerful hereditary landed aristocracy of China, and in 1313 adopted Zhu's interpretation of the classic texts as the standard for CSE, the official channel by which all members of the new bureaucracy were to be recruited. When the Yuan dynasty fell, the succeeding Ming dynasty (1368–1644) continued to endorse both the civil service examinations and Zhu Xi's interpretation of Confucian classics as standard. However, the Ming Taizu, its first emperor, became aware of the many restrictions Neo-Confucianism placed on rulers, and with his considerable power set the dynastic precedent to ensure that the authority of his imperial ruling house would remain largely outside and above the purview of Neo-Confucian principles as well as of its scholar-officialdom. Thus Neo-Confucian learning was relegated to becoming a kind of elite culture among the bureaucratic officialdom in service of imperial power, with little motivation to promote its egalitarian ideals among the enormous and illiterate general populace. Not surprisingly, the Manchus who in 1644 conquered the Ming in turn chose to adopt Ming Taizu's more autocratic interpretation of supposedly Neo-Confucian rule as the model for their Qing dynasty (1644–1912).

In Japan it was not until several centuries later in 1601, after Tokugawa Ieyasu (1543–1616) took the title of Shogun for himself and brought an end to what in practical terms had amounted to hundreds of years of civil war, that Neo-Confucianism first became a topic of conversation in any significant political connection. The brief but well-known conversation between Ieyasu and the Zen monk Hayashi Razan (1583–1657) resulted in the founding of the Hayashi School, which, though traditionally recognized as the seat of Japanese Neo-Confucian studies and patronized by generations of Tokugawa Shoguns, was never granted any official status as the avowed school of the Tokugawa or had any official political function. Japan would go on to produce a number of important independent Neo-Confucian scholars, but always their work would be as essentially "freelance" philosophers and/or political consultants in the patronage of this or that individual daimyo (feudal lord), not as a body recognized as commissioned by the state and accountable to Heaven for a defined function within the social infrastructure to serve the people. In short, no ruling power before or after Chosŏn Korea had justified its political legitimacy on the basis of upholding Neo-Confucian principles, or held to them with such single-minded tenacity for so long.

Neo-Confucianism: Its Four Foundations

Why would the above history of Neo-Confucianism be a significant factor for understanding the effectiveness of Underwood's ministry in Korea and the subsequent explosive spread of Christianity there? To answer that question, we need to understand some of Neo-Confucianism's main ideological tenets—its highly sophisticated metaphysics of nature and human nature, and the programs for popular education and egalitarian social renewal—that over the course of more than five hundred years helped lay the groundwork for the gospel message as brought by Underwood. While a system of thought as broad and all encompassing as Neo-Confucianism can hardly be given comprehensive discussion here, I outline below five main points each of which I argue helped prepare in Korea a culture of deep resonance with the gospel as brought by Underwood. The first three of these form the backbone of Neo-Confucian thought generally as systemized by Zhu Xi himself—that is, the main structural pivots having to do with nature, human nature, and the human obligation toward their harmony through cultivation. The remaining two points pertain more specifically to developments that arose as a consequence within Chosŏn Korea through its long commitment to and practice of Neo-Confucian ideals.

The first foundation for Neo-Confucian thought was its fundamental affirmation of the "substantiveness" of the material world and all things and events in it, including that of human experience. This was an important pushback against certain doctrinal elements of Buddhism that had come to saturate popular culture during the Tang and Song dynasties China wherein all phenomena are characterized by the quality of "Emptiness," i.e., constancy of change and therefore "empty" of any unchanging or constant essence. For Buddhism the recognition of this fundamental transience of all things functioned positively as leading to detachment from desire, but over time it was also seen as promoting widespread social apathy and moral irresponsibility in the world on account of its "meaninglessness." Daoism, while purportedly more grounded in the world of phenomena, had over time also come to be associated with ideas of freedom from worldly cares by "transcending" the cares brought on by change. In important ways Neo-Confucianism agreed with Buddhism and Daoism that material existence of all things is subject to constancy of change, but turned the significance of such transience on its head with the famous—and famously concise—five-character phrase formulated by Zhou Dunyi (1017–73): "Non-Ultimate *yet* Supreme Ultimate."[108] In other words, the great non-differential Unity, here

---

108. 無極而太極. The metaphysical Implications carried by Zhou Dunyi's succinct five-character phrase is arguably comparable in richness to the concept of *Creatio ex*

referenced as "Non-Ultimate" devoid of polarities, *manifests* itself *in and through* the constancy of change and the infinite range of endless differences of things and affairs of the material plane (i.e., "Supreme Ultimate" representing principle of polarities and differences), thus giving both existential purpose and legitimacy *to* change and even to differences themselves *qua* unchanging Unity. In short, differences arising in the phenomenal world are integral to the life generating essence ("*shengsheng* 生生") of the Non-Ultimate by the idea of moral authenticity. Another expression of a similar idea but more directly apropos the plane of phenomena was, "Unity of principle 理, diversity of its applications 用," and its equally important inverse statement—i.e., that "principle 理" as such is perceptible and has (human) meaning only *qua* its calibrated application in the distinct nature of each and every context.

As might be surmised, such affirmation of the purposive nature of the phenomenal world and its endless contextual variations carries within it tremendous potency for adaptation to a wide range of fields, from political and social thought, sciences, education, and the arts, and led to a veritable renaissance in these and other fields in early Chosŏn dynasty. More relevant to our perspective, without becoming a systematic theology Neo-Confucian metaphysics nevertheless acclimated the Korean people to a rational basis for the moral meaningfulness of life and all that happens in it, including what one does and how one relates to others. This was no small point. The gospel message as witnessed by Underwood's person in terms of his social consciousness and engagement, his personal demeanor of caring for rich and poor, young and old, men and women alike, of wanting to improve to the living conditions of people, would have been immediately and broadly recognized and welcomed as partaking of the "unity of principle," however diverse or unusual the particularities of the doctrine he brought. In short, insofar as Underwood's *demeanor and actions*—purportedly inspired by his Jesus Christ—were seen as in line with the fundamentally moral worldview of "Non-Polarity yet Supreme Polarity" Koreans gave him their trust.

Secondly and integral to the above point, Neo-Confucian ideas worked to reaffirm the Mencian view of human nature in which, for all the infinite differences of individual human natures, *human* nature—insofar as it is human and not some other—is given *to develop and to be developed* into qualities of "humaneness, rightness, propriety, and wisdom." According to Mencius (372?–289? BC) all human beings are born with the capacity for feelings of commiseration (which is the seed of humaneness), of shame and aversion (seed of rightness), of modesty and compliance (seed

***

nihilo, but that is beyond the scope of discussion here.

of propriety), and of right and wrong (seed of wisdom). These four capacities together comprise the so-called "Four Sprouts" of "human nature," and insofar as one is human it is their development to maturity that constitutes the sum total purpose of being human.[109] On a superficial understanding Mencius' "positive" view of human nature might seem to run counter to the Christian idea of Original Sin. But Mencius was far from unaware of the powerful presence of less noble human traits and instincts; indeed he acknowledged that compared to such tendencies the part he calls the "Sprouts" of human nature are sometimes so small and subtle as to be barely perceptible.[110] But he called those other tendencies human *destiny* (*ming* 命), as distinct from human "*nature* (*xing* 性)" which for him bespeak the *purpose* of being human—or as he put it, the purpose that differentiates humans from birds and animals. Indeed Mencius went so far as to write, in ideas evocative of St. Augustine's *Confessions*,

> The responses of the mouth to flavors, of the eye to colors, of the ear to sounds, of the nose to fragrances, and of the four limbs to comfort are our nature. But there is destiny in them, and the noble person does not call them "'nature." Humaneness between parent and child, rightness between ruler and minister, propriety between guest and host, wisdom for the worthy, and the Way of Heaven for the sage are destiny. But our nature is in them, and the noble person does not call them "destiny."[111]

In other words, despite the absence of the concept of Original Sin Mencius defined human "nature" in the *aspiratory* moral sense, and aspiratory as existentially assigned to the condition of being human rather than individually or even socially determined. Not all apple seeds grow into fully mature apple trees—many are thrown away and not given a chance to grow, others might not be given the proper care after planting, a few may be less hardy than others or even contain "genetic" flaws, etc. Yet, just as all apple seeds are deemed apple seeds in that their purpose, encoded as their very essence, is to grow into apple trees (as opposed to orange trees or frogs), according to Mencius differences of individual circumstance, capacity, or outcome in no way detract from the latent purposive principle of human nature or, in a sense, its obligations.

109. Of course the best-known description of the Four Sprouts as human nature occurs in *Mencius*, 2A6.

110. "That wherein human beings differ from the birds and beasts is but slight. The majority of people relinquish this, while the noble person retains it." *Mencius*, 4B19. All English translations of *Mencius* have been taken from Irene Bloom's translated volume.

111. *Mencius*, 7B24.

If there is a difference between an apple seed and the sprouts of human nature, it might be that whereas in the former the measure of a mature "treedom" is not in terms of its relationships to other seeds or trees (except possibly in terms of its fruits becoming carriers of more healthy seeds), with respect to Mencian human nature the quality of one's engagement with others is precisely the locus of its measure. As such, the measure of one's development is less dependent on "faith" as such in any particular doctrine as in the practice of how seamlessly one's interactions and/or relations embody the values of humaneness, rightness, propriety, and wisdom. If absolute isolation were possible these values would have no purpose, no meaning, no way even of being understood as such, for—what would "rightness" or "propriety" be in a blank devoid of context?[112] The idea that society or social interaction is necessary for individual human development as much for human survival is of course widely accepted in the West as in the East; but in Neo-Confucian thought even what is commonly termed "*self*-cultivation" is fundamentally, integrally, and indivisibly two-pronged: to nurture the human nature in one's own person is to embody the Four Sprouts in the material *practice* of one's interactions with others, and the standard by which one's interactions can be determined as nurturing the Sprouts or not is essentially by the degree to which those interactions affirm, respect and support the development of the *other* person's Sprouts or human nature. Logically at least, self-cultivation in Confucian/Neo-Confucian terms thus invariably involves what might be called "other-cultivation" as simultaneous and co-terminus to one's own.[113]

112. This clearly resonates with the idea of "Non-Polarity yet Supreme Polarity" in that human nature can only be known and have meaning only *qua* its manifestation in activity.

113. This over time may have given rise to the popular misconception that Confucianism is oriented toward "collectivism" and lacking in individualism. On another front, while Confucian self-cultivation was defined by what I have called "other-cultivation," the measure of one's self-cultivation did not depend on any external "success" in the *outcome* of that other person's own self-cultivation. In other words, though the concept of self-cultivation welcomed, hoped for, and possibly even expected utilitarian benefits, neither its measure nor its ends were understood as utilitarian ("The noble person is not a tool" 君子不器. *Analects*, 2:12). This, of course, is not to deny the inevitable gap between Neo-Confucian idealism and its realities in practice—especially over course of half a millennium. Like any doctrine the important place of classic texts as guiding this process of self/other-cultivation also often veered toward "book knowledge" and material achievement of degrees and licenses of higher learning, and with them expectations of rewards of social class and often lucrative positions in government. While not the intention of Neo-Confucianism it was understandably a common result of human "character" and ignorance.

This aspect of Neo-Confucian thought can be seen as resonating deeply with the ideals of Christian evangelism (and perhaps also carrying the potential to contribute meaningfully to it). Although as a philosophy Neo-Confucianism did not engage in proselytizing, it had as part of its essence components of a socially-minded movement, and as such found Underwood's approach to Christian evangelism both natural and easy to understand. In this a brief introduction to Neo-Confucianism's origins may be instructive. Neo-Confucian thought had its start as a small movement among scholars of the Song dynasty (960–1268) to find alternatives to what they felt were socially debilitating effects of Buddhist and Daoist doctrines. Their vision, however, went beyond wanting to engage in more stringent Confucian self-cultivation for themselves, which would have posed little problem since Confucianism, Daoism, and Buddhism had co-existed more or less peacefully for centuries, including as complementary values and scholarly endeavors within individuals. Rather, in spirit of the Confucian teaching "to first cultivate your-self then to help others," these scholars—especially Zhu Xi—extended their inquiry to the problem of how to transform and elevate society at large.[114] Moreover, having witnessed the earlier failure of Wang Anshi (1021–86)'s autocratic reforms, these scholars recognized that social reforms could not succeed on strength of policies from the top alone but instead depended on more members of the general population having some sense of doing right by the community. Here several points of historical context also played an important role. By Song dynasty society in China had become much more urban and complex. Much of the earlier ritual traditions directed to the governance of large extended clans or conversely the relative self-sufficiency and stability of villages were increasingly becoming set aside as obsolete. "Private" or family values likewise were becoming insufficient if not outright a force in opposition to sustaining the public good. Too, as a politically weak state, the Song dynasty was constantly under attack from "barbarians" at various borders as well. So, at issue for the tiny band of Song Neo-Confucian scholars was how to persuade people to be concerned for the welfare of those beyond "me and mine" in such contexts.[115] It was in working with

114. The idea that "loving the people (*qin min* 親民)" should be understood as "renewing the people (*xin min* 新民)" where "'To renew' means to reform the old . . . that once one has clearly manifested his own clear and bright virtue, he should extend it to others so that they too can do away with the stain of earlier soiling," is one of Zhu Xi's most famous and influential commentaries on the *Great Learning*.

115. Here we might recall that Mencius began his treatise by referring to his meeting with King Hui of Liang in which Mencius tells the King how pursuit of profit at the top results in the corruption of everyone below to self-interest. See *Mencius*, 1Aa.

these essentially "evangelical" or socially "other-cultivating" motivations that Neo-Confucian metaphysics was developed over a century as an argument for why it's something humans are *meant* to do, why it's a *natural* and a *good* thing to do—albeit without recourse to concepts of hell, a God who rewards and punishes, or an eschatology.

This Mencian understanding of human "nature" and its moral obligations as emphasized by Neo-Confucianism came to so saturate Chosŏn culture that "*Kwŏnsŏn-jing'ak* 勸善懲惡" or "Advocate good and reprimand evil" continues to be widely accepted as the moral norm even today irrespective of religious affiliation and however much its practice might be wanting in reality. The idea that no human being is exempt from social moral obligation, and that the cultivation of one's own "personhood" and one's respect for the nurture of the "nature" of others go together—these would have found immediate resonance with the evangelistic purpose and passion as demonstrated by Underwood, especially as he appealed to moral piety for the benefit of others. It may also help explain the high zeal among Korean Christians today to undertake evangelism in their turn, and potentially suggest a new way of articulating the Self-Other dynamic often experienced in the witnessing of Christ. Underwood's carrying out of the mission—energized by his social consciousness, free of interest for himself or the American "benevolent" empire,[116] and dedicated instead entirely in the service of realizing the Kingdom of Heaven among a people different from himself to lead toward a Christian Korea—would have found ready recognition and appreciation among the Korean people as the essence of Mencian cultivation of human nature, as well as of the spirit of "Benefit humankind (*Hong'ik-in'gan* 弘益人間)" attributed to Tan'gun the legendary founder of the Korean people, and formed a meaningful common ground with especially the Neo-Confucian scholars known as "*sŏnbi*."[117]

116. William Hutchison attributes the neglect in both religious and general histories of the considerable influence missionaries as a group have had on East-West relations well into the late twentieth century to "more than a little embarrassment. . . . The problem has been that the missionaries' stated purposes, while expressive of service and sacrifice, bespoke a supercilious and often demeaning attitude toward religions that the recipient peoples considered integral to their own cultures. The missionaries who embodied such complexities have seemed too admirable to be treated as villains, yet too obtrusive and self-righteous to be embraced as heroes. The most common reaction, therefore, has been simple avoidance." Hutchison, *Errand to the World*, 2.

117. Of course, evangelism—whether Christian, Neo-Confucian, or anything else—carries potential for many problems, especially when undertaken for the wrong motivations, without sufficient training and/or understanding of context. I have alluded to some of these problems, especially as pertaining to contemporary Korean mission practices, in James Kim, "Copernican Re-evaluation," 229–31. See also Moll, "Missions Incredible," 28–34.

The third important aspect of Neo-Confucian thought as laid down by Zhu Xi, to continue the organic metaphor coined by Mencius, was the provision of certain necessary pre-conditions for the systematic nurture of the human "Four Sprouts." The responsibility of providing for these conditions through several specific practical supporting institutions formed the central function of governance, while the responsibility of effort at self-cultivation or "learning" lay with individual persons—hence the constancy of Neo-Confucian concern with both principles of governance and the development of proper personhood as forming the two wings of civil society.[118] In Neo-Confucianism proper, then, a government—*qua* government independent of any individual ruler's will—is charged or "mandated" by Heaven, as it were, to model humaneness and rightness. In practical terms this included obligations of reasonable economic wellbeing and security as requisite measures for not reducing people to such states of want and desperation that they lose their human compassion and dignity.[119] Another equally important responsibility of governments, however, was to provide such universal education as would enable the populace to actually learn what it is to live in human moral dignity, i.e., in nurture of their human nature.[120] Whereas in China such Neo-Confucian idealism—especially regarding education—was soon met with challenges of the enormity of the size, poverty, and illiteracy of its population, as well as the dynastic imperial ambitions fundamentally at odds with the ideology, in Chosŏn Korea where the ideals of actualizing man's moral existence on social as well as individual levels had both inspired its founding and was professed to be the source of its legitimacy, the social program was adopted and applied with greater sincerity of will and under arguably more favorable conditions. To be sure,

118. On the concept of "learning for one's self" and Confucian "personhood" as distinct from "individualism" see de Bary, *The Liberal Tradition in China*, 21–66.

119. See *Mencius*, 1A3-7.

120. "At present, the regulation of the people's livelihood is such that, above, they do not have enough to serve their parents and, below, they do not have enough to support wives and children. Even in years of prosperity their lives are bitter, while in years of dearth they are unable to escape starvation. Under these circumstances they only try to save themselves from death, fearful that they will not succeed. How could they spare the time for the practice of rites and rightness? If the king wishes to put this into practice, he should return to the root of the matter. Let mulberry trees be planted around households of five mu, and people of fifty will be able to be clothed in silk. In the raising of chickens, pigs, dogs, and swine, do not neglect the appropriate breeding times, and people of seventy will be able to eat meat. With fields of a hundred mu, do not interfere with the appropriate seasons of cultivation, and families with eight mouths to feed will be able to avoid hunger. Attend carefully to the education provided in the schools, which should include instruction in the duty of filial and fraternal devotion, and gray-haired people will not be seen carrying burdens on the roads." *Mencius*, 1A7.

corrosions to that ideal over the course of half a millennium—especially toward the last third of the dynasty's long reign—meant its actual practice often fell grossly, even critically short, on the part of both government and the citizenry. Even so, the principle was reflected in multiple aspects of Chosŏn society and practice, both in terms of the proliferation of schools and the social institution known as "community compacts 鄉約."

The presence of schools in civic life is well illustrated by something Underwood encountered early during his mission in Korea. One of the first things he sought to do upon arriving in Korea was to found a school for orphans. By late nineteenth century there was nothing new about mission schools. Since the time William Carey (1761–1834) had used the school as a means to approach native peoples of India as early as 1800 it had become an accepted—even expected—practice of Protestant missions. But whereas for Carey and most missionaries schools often also served as the principal means of financial support for the mission endeavor, Underwood faced a very different situation in Korea. On January 20, 1886, Underwood wrote:

> The Korean government in their schools have no charges at all but virtually pay the scholars for attending in providing them with their food, clothing, and a certain amount of money and it will therefore not be the easiest matter to find those that are willing to pay for what costs nothing elsewhere. If a free school were opened it would be filled at once if in addition we would pay the pupils enough to live on and in fact I have been told that we could have all that we could teach if the latter clause were left out but we feel that there is a danger of giving the Koreans the idea that we are backed by a rich board at home and that it would be a pretty good idea to become a Christian. There is one way in which we could begin work at once and be at the same time building up for Korea a Christian youth. My attention has been called to the fact that there are in Seoul a great many homeless and destitute children as orphans and those of illegitimate birth and they could be taken and clothed and fed and trained up in a right way and taught to love the Savior.[121]

The Chosŏn dynasty from its inception had demonstrated unprecedented commitment to popular education, even inventing a writing system not long afterward that continues to this day to be widely lauded for its simplicity, logic, and accuracy.[122] The emphasis on popular education reflected

121. Letter dated January 20, 1886, in In Soo Kim, *Rev. Underwood's Missionary Letters*, 622–23.

122. Han'gŭl, the Korean reading and writing system invented and/or commissioned by King Sejong (r. 1417–50) was completed in 1444 (promulgated in 1446),

not only the Neo-Confucian desire to raise the general welfare of people but also the ideals of social mobility and rule by meritocracy—i.e., the recruitment of scholar-officials to serve in positions of governance through civil service examinations based on learning and merit. As a result, academies sprouted up in every village, and teaching became a highly respected profession. In an effort to ensure meritocratic social mobility there were even laws put in place returning upper-class families or *yangban* to commoner status if they failed to produce a successful civil service candidate over the course of three generations. Over time, however, the national enthusiasm for learning itself began to lead to problems. Education could be an expensive, time-consuming gamble. A farmer's son, instead of helping his family prosper and preparing himself to take over the farm, might devote years to master the difficult literature in classical Chinese, depleting the family's financial resources and possibly getting into debt, only to find himself unable to pass the examinations even after repeated attempts.[123] If he did pass it he would bring great honor to his family and raise their social status to that of *yangban*,[124] but in the limited and increasingly competitive job market it was still uncertain whether he would be given a civil post for his efforts.

More than a couple of centuries into the dynasty the government simply could not create enough government bureaucratic posts to absorb the

---

and gave Koreans two different writing systems—the Chinese ideographic and Korean Ural-Altaic syllabaric. Many scholars attribute the success of Christian Protestant propagation in Korea in part to the availability of Han'gŭl which is so easy to master and made literacy so accessible to all that by year 1900—i.e., less than two decades since the first translation of the Gospel of Luke into Korean—Christian missionaries had printed and distributed more than an astonishing over two million copies of bible books in Han'gŭl (including separate gospel books) in a country with total population of just twelve million. Han'gŭl allowed Korea to achieve the highest literacy rate in the world early on. John Ross (1842–1915), the Scottish Presbyterian missionary to China who in 1881 initiated translating the bible into Korean with the help of Koreans in Manchuria, wrote in his landmark book on Korea that Han'gŭl is the most efficient linguistic system in the world: "Their alphabet is so beautifully simple, that half-an-hour's study is sufficient to master it; and as, like Pitman's Phonography, it is employed phonetically, it is universally known and used by men, women, and children. So much so, that a Corean, who 'did not know a single character [of Chinese]' sat down to a MS copy of John's Gospel, and left it off only when he had read it all, not a single word having escaped him. This proves the great superiority of Corean over Chinese for the purposes of translation." Ross, *History of Korea*, 374–75.

123. In principle the examinations were held every four years, but in practice they were held more often. It was not uncommon to honor the birth of a prince or other such celebratory occasions with the dispensation of a "special examination."

124. Yangban 兩班 literally stands for "pair of classes," consisting of the civil (文科 mun'gwa) and the military (武科 mu'gwa) officers. However, in late Chosŏn Korea it became a way of characterizing the de facto prevailing "aristocracy."

large number of successful candidates vying for them. This meant that the more desirable posts and promotions increasingly began to go to those with the wealth and connections to "buy" into them, and many with the means also took to ensuring the success of their children by hiring private tutors or sending them to exclusive private schools created for the purpose of preparing them for the examinations. The obstacles gradually led to locking out certain parts of the population from competing altogether. By law, as also indicated in Underwood's letter above, these included those of illegitimate birth (often sons of legal concubines to *yangban*), descendants of national traitors, and those born to lowest ranks of society such as shamans, butchers, executioners, etc.; by practice it often also included the very poor. The way was still open for a "poor boy" without family background or the "scholarship student" sponsored by his village to succeed, but it could be an uphill battle even after he attained a post of some distinction when the bureaucracy itself often operated more like an "old boys club."[125]

It should also be remembered that even the highest ranking posts paid surprisingly low salaries, on principle that one entered government service out of one's humane desire to serve the people rather than for one's own gain. Ideal in theory, it often left those who had incurred debts along the way—and those who hadn't—vulnerable to requests for payback in favors within their newfound authority, as well as to a culture of bribery and corruption. But even so, despite the general poverty and floundering politics amidst growing international pressures, despite the corrupted meritocratic system and fractured society, despite the increasing spiritual vacuum left unfilled by Neo-Confucian idealism depleted of its practice, the nationwide cultural commitment to education in late nineteenth-century Korea remained surprisingly high. Underwood himself noted that "all over the land in every village of any size there have been established schools that give a mental drill in the Chinese classics," and characterized Koreans as a "people of good minds" and a "nation of scholars" as compared to commercially-minded Chinese and the warrior-like Japanese:[126]

> [Koreans] are not as phlegmatic as the Chinese nor as volatile as the Japanese. Without the stolid conservatism, often amounting to impregnable obstinacy, of the one or the easy adaptability,

125. One might compare this to the challenges someone like Michael Faraday faced in early nineteenth-century England, who—even upon wide recognition as a great scientist—was nevertheless not considered a "gentleman." See this chapter, 29nn19–20. Women of all classes were also excluded. Female members of gentry were expected to study within the confines of their homes, but there were no public schools for women regardless of class.

126. See Underwood, *The Call of Korea*, 46, 49, 72–73.

amounting to fickleness, of the other, calmly weighing pros and cons, they are willing to accept change if it is really good and receive what is new without too rashly discarding long-established beliefs and customs. They are not as slavishly bound by superstition, not as devoted to their old religions, not as faithful, perhaps, to the traditions of the past, as the Chinese, nor so imitative and ambitious as the Japanese.[127]

The proliferation of schools and popular zeal for education long encouraged by Chosŏn Neo-Confucianism had tremendous impact in preparing the ground for Underwood's message of the gospel. In a most important way it established a general predilection among Chosŏn Koreans, including its poor, for learning about the gospel *for themselves*. In other words, their faith did not depend merely on the hearsay of missionaries. Far from it, once the gospel message interested them, many read the bible for themselves (or learned to read Han'gŭl so that they could!), studied and debated it among themselves, and thus made it their own to be applied in the intimate contexts of their own lives. Underwood gives the example of a Mr. No (Ch'unkyŏng) who came to his English classes merely as pretext for an opportunity to read the bible for himself, only afterward to engage in further study of the gospel with him; and of the many trips on which the books he carried for sale sold out so fast that although he limited the number of copies for sale at each place and had many more sent to him en route they continued to be sold out long before he reached his destination. Underwood made the further point that "it must be remembered that these people did not buy the books because they were Christian, but the fact that they purchased them in spite of this proved that a wide door was open to the Gospel."[128]

The importance of this early Korean ability and desire to study and make the gospel their own on individual and community levels cannot be stressed enough, minimizing the gospel's ties to Western imperialism and enabling them to take a role in propagating the gospel on their own.[129] Underwood wrote,

> The individual Christians who first learned the truth, generally became the teachers of others in their district, or village, and naturally the leaders of the groups that they had started . . . It

127. Underwood, *The Call of Korea*, 45–46.

128. Underwood, *The Call of Korea*, 105–8.

129. I have elsewhere written about the significance of this unique phenomenon in the history of Korean Christianity, extending to the propagation of both Catholic and Protestant Christianity, especially concerning the practice of "ersatz clergy" in Chosŏn Korea. See James Kim, "Bible versus Guns," 35.

soon became necessary to hold leaders' classes, which were . . . put through a graded course of instruction and have gradually grown in numbers varying from 200 in the south, in a class, to 1300 in the north. The attendants return to their own sections, and, under the guidance and direction of the missionaries and district leaders, hold local classes, so that in the past year [1907] in the one station of Peyng Yang [Pyongyang] in the north, 191 such local classes were reported in the Presbyterian Mission alone, with an attendance of over 10,000. These methods have developed in Korea an intensely active native Church, with an ardent desire for the study of the Word.[130]

Korean Christians also often took the initiative in the education of their own children. One clear though hardly exceptional example was the Christian school built by the church in Sorai. The Sorai church had been started not by missionaries but by Mr. Soh Sang-Ryun (1848–1926) who had converted to Protestantism even before the arrival of Underwood in Korea, through his encounter with the missionaries John Ross (1842–1915) and John McIntyre (1837–1905) during a trip to China. Not only did the Korean Christians of Sorai—converted to Christianity through the work of Mr. Soh and not any foreign missionaries—build in 1895 the first church ever for that exclusive purpose in Korea, but even before that established its own "Church primary school with its Christian teacher."[131] By 1908 Underwood could write that there were 337 such primary schools in one Mission alone, of which 334 were entirely self-supporting.[132]

Together with schools, another important Neo-Confucian institution for the renewal of self and society was the community compacts or associations called *hyang-yak* (鄉約). As the most important voluntary self-governing institution within individual villages, members came together in basic commitment to upholding moral values such as not gambling, drinking, or fighting, and contributed to longstanding practical programs such as the community granaries and pledges of mutual aid. Moreover, the leadership within these compacts was usually given to the oldest (male) member of the village itself rather than the local official. Like the many associations in America, then, in important ways participation in these compacts served to empower the people, to interest and to train them in self-governance and what that entails in terms of following due process, organizational planning, and cooperation. The purpose, infrastructure,

130. Underwood, *The Call of Korea*, 110–11.
131. Underwood, *The Call of Korea*, 107–12.
132. Underwood, *The Call of Korea*, 112–13.

and dynamics of these compacts would have made the idea of a church as a communal institution meant to aid one another in both spiritual/moral and practical welfare easy to understand and accept for many Koreans, as well as cooperation across larger district lines. Underwood noted, for example, that it was usually the Korean Christians themselves who would recommend those among them who showed "most proficiency in the Bible and in the work" to be made a superintendent of a district, and work among the various groups to raise his salary.[133] Needless to say, this would have been very much in keeping with Underwood's strong advocacy for cooperation across denominational lines as essential to the enterprise.

Fourthly, grounded as it was on "Unity of principle, diversity of its applications," Neo-Confucianism was adaptive and practical within its fundamental moral direction, as evidenced by the rise of Silhak or "Practical Learning" movement beginning in the mid-Chosŏn period. If over time there was increasing distance between Neo-Confucian ideals and its practice—even its abuse—in society, there was also in Neo-Confucianism the capacity to generate new resources from within. In one sense the very fact that Chosŏn dynasty had sustained a society stable and balanced enough to hold its own for half a millennium despite its powerful neighbors is testament to both the strengths of the system and of Chosŏn Korea's commitment to its principles. Silhak was an important example of movements generated internally from within Neo-Confucian thought and practice by reform-minded scholars.[134] To the basic Neo-Confucian emphasis on the moral purpose of life as lived in this material plane, beginning in mid-Chosŏn period Silhak scholars brought general awareness of the urgent need for—and legitimacy of—more practical, "scientific" learning and its application for the material well-being of the people at large. They sought to improve practical living standards by engaging directly with the many urgent problems people faced especially in the wake of the Imjin (1592–98) and Pyŏngja (1636–37) Invasions,[135] advocating for policy changes ranging from land, bureaucratic, social, and economic reforms; the leveling and professionalization of the four classes of scholars, farmers, artisans, and merchants; and improvements to national transportation, currency, infrastructure and communications. Investing in scientific research had been among the core values from the very

133. Underwood, *The Call of Korea*, 110.

134. Silhak 實學 literally means "practice" (sil) and "learning" (hak).

135. The Japanese invasion in the year of Imjin (1592) 壬辰倭亂 lasted for seven years and so decimated the population across the country Korea did not recover its former numbers for another two hundred years. The Manchurian (later Qing Dynasty) attack in the year of Pyŏngja (1636) 丙子胡亂 only three decades later also severely devastated the entire country.

earliest days of Chosŏn dynasty as part of the general Neo-Confucian affirmation of the fundamental substantiveness of the material plane. But under a social structure that rewarded humanistic scholarship as the highest learning and moreover actively discouraged mercantilism as leading to the disease of profit-mindedness among peoples, sciences had become secondary in importance. Silhak scholars revived the legitimacy of the sciences so that their work led to important advances in such fields as astronomy, medical and biological sciences, agricultural sciences, map-making, historiography, linguistics, mathematics, the social sciences, and increasing interest in and publication of encyclopedia-like works. The renewed interest in history and its contextual realities also led to a renaissance in national arts and literature. Not surprisingly, Silhak scholars were also among the earliest in Korea to seek out and study "Western Learning" (called sŏhak 西學), brought earlier by Jesuits into China. The great scholar and innovator ChŏngYag'yong (丁若鏞 1762–1836) was such a one. Perhaps best known among Koreans as the author of the important *Mokmin simsŏ* (牧民心書; 1818),[136] the magisterial yet practical guide for provincial officials covering the broad array of their responsibilities and powers for serving the people, Chŏng was also a scientist, inventor, and an early convert to Catholicism (before Protestantism was known in Korea). Silhak's contributions to practical reforms and to the development of science as well as of "national culture" had significant impact throughout every aspect of life in Korea.

There is no denying that despite these efforts Chosŏn society in the late nineteenth century was not only poor but poorly prepared to meet the challenges brought on by global developments of the time. Still, Korean Neo-Confucian culture in general and Silhak scholarship in particular had laid down a foundation particularly suited to appreciate and welcome with open arms the harmonious synthesis of faith and science brought by Underwood.[137] Indeed Underwood noted,

> It has been said that the Koreans are an uneducated people, but this has been said by those who fail to make a proper distinction between education and instruction. The Koreans have not been instructed in all the technical details of Western science. While they lack in knowledge, all over the land in every village of any size there have been established schools that give a mental drill in the Chinese classics, and while we must acknowledge that if it

136. English translation available as Chŏng, *Admonitions on Governing the People*, translated by Byonghyon Choi.

137. This is not to say there were not those who were inclined to Christian faith as to a stronger god or a more likely giver of material gifts. No society is one-dimensional.

stops here the system is at fault, at the same time it has placed to our hand a raw material of fine quality ready to be developed.[138]

It is also worth remembering that although one might take for granted that every Christian missionary of the nineteenth century believed in the central-ity of faith in life, given the intellectual rift in especially continental Europe since the Enlightenment it was by no means to be assumed that every mis-sionary was so at ease when it came to relations between faith and reason/sciences. Too much reason—whether in the form of too many questions, questioning of authority, love of disputation, or even love of learning out-side the direct influence of church authority—was sometimes regarded as a potential threat to faith, and especially dangerous among "undeveloped" natives. Others were known to take the Noah's ark approach whereby the Church is to function as a haven from any social reality less than pious on its own terms. It is not difficult to imagine the gospel message taking on a very different tone under such approaches. But as son of a deeply pietistic scientist who had studied under Michael Faraday's example, as well as inspired by the example of evangelically motivated social reforms led by the likes of Pierson, Underwood saw no contradiction whatever in being a carrier of the gospel and applying his final efforts toward the founding of Korea's first business school for the nurture of industrial and commercial leadership capable of serving the common good. However much he might regret laws that pre-vented him from teaching Christian doctrine in schools, he had no qualms about founding schools for children that taught English, chemistry, or other secular subjects. His thoughts on the subject may be surmised from what he wrote about the weekly *Christian News* he had begun publishing:

> The paper is already doing no small amount of good. It is unit-ing our church members, is a good medium of communicating between churches & church members as well as between the missionary & his friends & adherents. In addition to this it is steadily working its way into the homes of those who are not Christians. It's [sic] general news, its firm stand for truth & justice regardless of position & party, its [firm?] & practical scientific notes all are tending to make it a necessity to all par-ties Christian &non Christian& thus a weekly tract goes into hundreds of heathen homes & already in several cases direct conversion has been the result while not a few have been led to say that they did not know there was so much good in Christi-anity. All this is an advance.[139]

138. Underwood, *The Call of Korea*, 72–73.
139. Horace Underwood letter to his brother Thomas, August 21–23, 1897. Each

Here again we can see Underwood envisioning a Christian *Korea*, as opposed to enclaves of Christians *in* Korea sufficient and privileged unto themselves. As with Silhak scholars, for Underwood the scientific spirit and benefits of scientific learning was something to be shared with the widest possible number of people without thought to exclusivity of privileges. He continued the trajectory initiated by Silhak scholars, but advanced and revitalized it with new ideas, new scientific and world knowledge, new motivation for action, and new vision.

"Rightness"

If each of the four elements of Neo-Confucianism in Korea described above helped prepare an extraordinarily fertile ground for the gospel brought by Underwood, there was yet another element unique to Korean Neo-Confucianism that I believe was particularly critical in enlarging Underwood's own appreciation of the power of the gospel in a fundamental way. This was what I call the Korean ethos and egalitarian spirit of "rightness," as distinct from mere adherence to established Confucian rites or the more modern and arguably Western concept of rights. Whether and to what degree rites serve to approximate the function of rights has been subject of much discussion among scholars and politicians alike in the last twenty years of East-West studies.[140] "*Rightness*," on the other hand, while related to concepts of both rites and rights as their root, speaks to a more subtle, fluid, intimate, holistic, and often a more intangible aspect of balance in interpersonal relations. It was, as mentioned earlier, a concept central to Confucian notions of human nature and social relations from the start, but being subtle and fluid, sensitive to the least nuance of the infinite and constantly changing dynamics of human relations, it was also a principle that defied codification. It could not and did not function as did laws or rituals, on basis of externally verifiable standards, instead depending on there being a widely shared, cultural foundation of *feeling* or ethos for the totality of what more or less satisfies a given relation or situation toward a point of mutual fulfillment. As such, rightness may encompass actions of ritual propriety but essentially goes beyond them to such proffering of sincerity that it satisfy the other's soul (and/or Heaven)

---

issue of the newspaper ran four to five pages. Underwood wrote that at the time of the letter had about six hundred annual subscribers in addition to non-subscription buyers; the King and his household read it every week, as well as sent to every magistracy in the country.

140. A pioneering publication in this regard was de Bary and Tu Weiming, *Confucianism and Human Rights*. There have since been many more written on the subject.

in ways mere propriety and established rites cannot, and sometimes even where ritual propriety has been violated. The intangible and unique nature of sincerity "right" for the nuanced particularities of each individual relational dynamic makes it difficult to document as part of a broad culture; indeed one may argue that the very power of rightness to move lies in part in their being beyond what is codified or codifiable.

We have one instance of what egalitarian rightness meant for Korean people in the late nineteenth century in an account of an incident given by Underwood himself. In a letter to his brother Thomas dated November 8, 1898, which will be discussed in more detail in chapter 3, Underwood wrote:

> The last few days we have been on the very verge of a popular uprising. The people are waking up to the fact that they have some rights and in a dignified way they are insisting upon them. The King has yielded to them, but some of his advisors thought best to try and stop what was going on absolutely, and got the order for the arrest of 19 of the peoples [sic] leaders. They were arrested one night, [and] when it was learned the next morning some 30 thousand people gathered on the street and big square and in a dignified way sent in a request that as the leaders of the people had been arrested and the leaders had only done what the people had asked, they too might all be arrested. For some four or five days this crowd with bonfires etc. have continued night and day waiting to be arrested. They in a quiet way simply say that if they have done wrong they are ready to die and there they stay. The leading stores and merchants have all stopped business and closed their doors on the plea that if they have no rights they might as well die of starvation as oppression. They have in the main been quiet and orderly. The only thing that they have done that might be said to be wrong was that when a company of soldiers was sent to disperse them and the order was given to prepare to fire they rushed up and disarmed the soldiers but nothing more, and then gave them back their arms and let them go. There they still are camped, and there they say they will wait and die if they do not get justice. I tell you the fact that we see these people are getting a little backbone is most encouraging and as we see this we feel that there is some hope for this country after all if only the outside countries will keep hands off and let them work it out for themselves. They have waked up to the fact that they have some rights and that if they can only stick together they have no little power.[141]

141. Underwood, letter dated November 8, 1898. This and other similar accounts of the political unrest in Korea is absent from his letters to the Presbyterian Board.

For thirty thousand people to come together in a city with a population of three hundred thousand at the time was no small incident, similar in scope to the 2.3 million Koreans peacefully coming together between December 2016 and June 2017 to engage in candlelight vigils demanding political change. Notably, not only did the gathering of thirty thousand mostly commoners refrain from becoming an unruly violent mob in spite of feeling they had been wronged, not only did they merely disarm the soldiers without harming them in any way then actually return their weapons to them shortly afterward, these people were protesting the arrest of their leaders by patiently and "in a dignified way" asking to be themselves arrested together with their leaders. Underwood, being a product of Enlightenment thought and educated to the concepts of commonwealth and of political rights of individual citizens especially when it came to rightful defense of life, liberty, and property, was prepared to understand the incident as one of the Korean people "waking up to the fact that they have some rights" and "getting a little back bone." But in fact it was not a new waking up to rights but a longstanding tradition of action based on widespread understanding of *rightness* brought to its limits. Rights refer to moral or legal claims justly due to someone; rightness carries implications of mutuality between parties with equal or greater emphasis on one's *responsibility* alongside one's claim. Both concepts appeal to ideas of basic human dignity, but whereas rights stress dignity as something inherently given to oneself from birth and therefore requiring its recognition by others, rightness puts greater weight on the dignity of one's moral cultivation as both a privilege and a responsibility before Heaven (which Koreans traditionally called Ha-na-nim, which will be discussed further below).

Those gathered on the morning of November 8, 1898, had clearly felt their rights had been violated to such an extent that they needed to protest the abuse for redress, but even under real threat of imprisonment and/or death it was the responsibility of maintaining peaceful civil disobedience that they considered the appropriate expression of rightness called for. On some level, too—notwithstanding the recognition that the sacrifice of their lives might not lead to any change—they were holding to the hope and trust that perseverance in such acts of moral sincerity to the death would inspire a responsive rightness on the part of the King and government, or to move Heaven itself on their behalf. Without belaboring the point we may describe it as an ethos very like "Turn the other cheek" of the New Testament[142]—and

---

142. Confucius put it another way. When someone asked, "What do you think of the saying, 'Respond to injury with virtue (*de* 德)?'" Confucius said, "How then will you respond to virtue? Respond to injury with uprightness and to virtue with virtue." *Analects*, 14:36.

significantly, this quiet civil protest by thirty thousand had not needed any extraordinary exhortation by a figure of leadership to guide it. It had instead been the spontaneous response of thirty thousand protesters who had been deprived of their leaders over night despite having been promised otherwise, and themselves threatened by soldiers carrying guns.[143]

The "dark" side of such culture—that it is not based on the realities of human society but rather on what is hoped for and should be, in the matter of human character—may be that it is quite possibly detrimental to the development of a sense of political rights as such. The social and political implications of the complex Korean Neo-Confucian ethos of rightness certainly warrant separate in-depth study in the future. Even so, it may be to such saturation of Neo-Confucian values that we can attribute the deeply ingrained belief widely shared among Korean people even today that governments are morally—rather than merely legally—accountable to the people, and that the people's voice—when it rises to the point of representing Heaven—must nevertheless be one of peaceful, *civil* disobedience. For better or worse, both embody Neo-Confucian civility founded on the notion that sincerity to human "nature" as defined by Mencius is more of the essence than even the materiality of life itself.[144] But if as a result Korean Neo-Confucianism over time did not always succeed in inspiring those in power—however much or little—to share more of that power in an egalitarian manner, it nevertheless sensitized the desire in people for rightness in human relations and heightened their appreciation toward those individuals who demonstrated its qualities. However far the principle of self-sacrifice was from being practiced universally, especially by those in power, it was widely understood to be how people should be, and in effect laid the path for the Korean people to receive the gospel message

143. A good example of how deeply the long-suffering denial of one's rights in favor of Neo-Confucian "rightness" had saturated the Korean cultural psyche is that such ideals formed the central themes in each of the five most popular folk "operas" collectively known as the "P'ansori Five" performed everywhere by itinerant professional singers since at least the eighteenth century if not before. Regarding the centrality of p'ansori in expressing such Korean ethos Rachel E. Chung observes, "[The five primary works of p'ansori] present . . . the whole web of Neo-Confucian values, tensions, and conflicts that had acculturated Chosŏn popular consciousness for several centuries." Chung, "The Song of the Faithful Wife Ch'unhyang," 367.

144. "I desire fish, and I also desire bear's paws. If I cannot have both of them, I will give up fish and take bear's paws. I desire life, and I also desire rightness. If I cannot have both of them, I will give up life and take rightness. It is true that I desire life, but there is something I desire more than life, and therefore I will not do something dishonorable in order to hold on to it. I detest death, but there is something I detest more than death, and therefore there are some dangers I may not avoid." *Mencius*, 6A10.

with particular appreciation for its message of social ethics and personal practice of spiritual reverence.

For Underwood at least, the witnessing of the November 1898 incident marked a kind of dividing line for his understanding of Korean culture, especially in relation to *its independent relation to the gospel of Christ*, and thus his long-term vision for a Christian Korea. Although we unfortunately do not have many letters dating from after the incident, there is a notable change of tone in his next letter to his brother Thomas dated December 28 of the same year. He reported,

> Politically things in Korea look strange, everyday and almost every hour sees changes in the Cabinet. . . . History is rapidly being made out here in Korea and no matter what happens there is always a steady progress forward. There are a good many setbacks as it were but in it all we can see that there is a steady advance . . . the present British Representative in his official report . . . said that progress here is marvelous and that no country had ever advanced as rapidly as had Korea. The king is weak and vacillating; were it not for this I am sure that the progress would be even faster. As it is with such a weak sovereign the great fear is that one of the powers that would be no benefit to the country will step in and practically take over the land. What the end will be we do not know but as long as God gives us an open door to carry on His work it is our place to do so . . . on all sides we see great strides.[145]

Like most missionaries, Underwood in the early years of his mission in Korea had often considered the possibility that having foreigners to run the country would not only have great beneficial effects in terms of opening up the country for Christianity, but actually help bring more order to society in general. What the above letter begins to show, however, is a new found faith in an independent Korea and its future, and of his commitment to working toward the building of *that* Korea to be a Christian Korea. If he had come to Korea with some general dream of a Christian Korea—even much as he might have assumed for a Christian America[146]—we see here the beginnings of its clarification as a concrete idea. Certainly the "strides" he mentions refer to much more than the propagation of Christianity in the narrow sense. As will be shown in greater detail in chapter 2 this was in clear contrast to his earlier view in which he had distinctly divided his work into "proper mission work" and those outside it about which necessity he

---

145. Horace Underwood letter to Thomas, December 28, 1898.

146. See Handy, *A Christian America*, 27–94.

complained as arising from Korean government's prohibition against direct Christian evangelism. But in important ways this change in Underwood did not merely bespeak his coming to have greater hopes for an independent Korea or a clearer crystallization of what Christianization might mean in the context of Korea. Rather, I argue, his own understanding of the gospel had begun to be itself broadened by what he witnessed in Korea and especially that November, becoming aware of the possibility of freedom to be had in the gospel not only in terms of the Church as a community brought together by faith in mutual respect of rights, but also as one expressing or manifesting its faith in the ethos of rightness.

In his landmark book, *The Making of Korean Christianity*, Sung-Deuk Oak points to the extraordinary perspicacity of missionaries for the explosive growth of Christianity in Korea:

> North American missionaries displayed both openness toward Korean religions and culture and a remarkable ability to Christianize certain elements, while rejecting others. Their evangelical mission theology maintained the finality of Christ in relation to Korean religions. Yet they searched for points of contact with Korean religions and welcomed the preparation for the gospel in them. The integration of Christian adaptability, was one of the major factors for the growth of evangelical Christianity in Korea from 1884–1915. In other words, the American missionaries' cross-cultural sensitivity and moderate fulfillment theory helped Korean Christians to stimulate the rapid growth of indigenous Korean Christianity. Therefore North American missionaries' evangelism in Korea moved beyond the level of mere proselytism, proclamation, and cultural imperialism. They were pioneers of a distinctive indigenous Korean Christianity in the specific and particular Korean religious context.[147]

Oak makes the important point that there had been an underlying Korean spirituality, one that was moreover deeply monotheistic at heart despite the seeming proliferation of gods and spirits, and that this baseline monotheism was captured in the Korean word "Ha-na-nim," in etymology a synthesis of the words "One" and "Heaven." Most Western missionaries to Korea, including Underwood's close colleagues James S. Gale (1863–1937) and Homer B. Hulbert (1863–1949), had been quick to understand the opportunity for inculturation offered by Korean spirituality founded on Hananim and argued strongly for the use of the word in proselytizing as well as in Underwood's translation of the bible. Only Underwood, whose stubbornness earned him

---

147. Oak, *The Making of Korean Christianity*, 315.

the nickname "English bulldog," was unconvinced and held to his opposition against all persuasion until he felt confident that the term Hananim's origins were "rooted in a monotheistic religious tradition of Korea."[148] From his initial stubborn refusal to call God by a word so saturated within existing Korean belief system we can read how much Underwood in fact feared for Christianity's syncretization into Korean culture rather than its renewal. In time, he himself would come to point out how "in the Korean concept of Hananim there is even less anthropomorphism than is seen in the Jewish ideas of Jehovah,"[149] but until then, for all his insistence on harmony and inter-denominational cooperation he was not one to compromise on issues he felt endangered proper understanding of the gospel.

By pointing to how the missionaries recognized and sought out those elements within indigenous Korean spirituality as points of integration with Christianity Oak in fact argues for the successful *in*culturation of Christianity in Korea.[150] That is, the many points in common between Korean indigenous—especially shamanistic and Hananim-based—spirituality and the Christian gospel message led to the "incarnation of Christian life and of the Christian message in a particular cultural context, in such a way that this experience not only finds expression through elements proper to the culture in question, but becomes a principle that animates, directs and unifies the culture, transforming and remaking it so as to bring about 'a new creation.'"[151] While that had certainly been the case, what I have suggested is the powerful role of culture and ethos created by half a millennium of Chosŏn dynasty's commitment to Neo-Confucian ideals of self and social cultivation in preparing the people to receive the gospel and for the gospel mission of Underwood. Whereas some might see this as merely differences in the *locus* of inculturation, however, I have also suggested that Underwood's mission in Korea was more than an example of successful inculturation—that in fact it exemplified a case of *inter*culturation whereby his own understanding of his mission in Korea was itself transformed and enlarged—similar to when St. Paul and St. John did not so much acquiesce to "translating"

---

148. Underwood addresses the issue of his position on Ha-na-nim—and the criticism he was facing because of it—in his letter to Thomas, August 1, 1898. For a succinct yet thorough summary account how the word "Hananim" eventually came to be adopted by missionaries, which has been a matter of longstanding study among Korean church historians, see Oak, *The Making of Korean Christianity*, 55–63.

149. Underwood, *The Religions of Eastern Asia*, 132. The book was based on the series of talks he gave as part of the Charles F. Deems Lectureship of Philosophy at New York University the same year. See also Oak, *The Making of Korean Christianity*, 74.

150. Oak, *The Making of Korean Christianity*.

151. Arrupe, "Letter to the Whole Society on Inculturation," 2.

their understanding of Christ into *"logos"* to accommodate and win over the Greeks, but rather the ideas within the Greek cultural concept of *logos* as they encountered it helped *expand* their own understanding of Christ, and thereby led to the mutuality of interculturation—thus changing the dynamic of his mission to reflect in a sense a more Korean character, even to affect the understanding of his family back in the America regarding the nature of that mission. Witnessing the Korean ethos of rightness at work in the incident of November 1898 and others like it, over time Underwood would come to see and appreciate something of the nature of the relationship God was preparing for Godself with the Korean people as founded on the latter's Neo-Confucian culture and especially ethos of rightness. This was to be independent of what he in his own relationship to God had been prepared to convey and share. Being able to "see" it is in some sense also to be himself "remade" as a Korean in the ethos of rightness—that is awakened to or imprinted with its spirit—thus empowering him to envision a *long-term* dream of a Christian Korea, even as the thirty thousand powerless protesters had done in their powerful trust of rightness innately connected to Hananim. If Underwood's own long dedication and preparations for life as a missionary had nurtured in him a strong disposition for discerning and doing "the right thing," so apparent in his letters as we shall in see in chapter 2, it also prepared him to recognize and appreciate the ethos of rightness so widespread among the people of Korea. And it was this that allowed him to say, at a time when Korea had all but fallen into Japanese hands with the silent assent of the international community,

> I see this nation, reaching out strong, glad arms of influence—to China on the one hand and to Japan on the other, softening the prejudices and conservatism of the one, and steadying the faith of the other; the three joining the great circle of Christian nations who praise the Lamb for ever and ever, and hail Jesus King of Kings and Lord of Lords.[152]

Conclusion

Underwood was a product of nineteenth century England and America, viscerally aware of the British Empire on which the sun never set and the growing ambitions of the young United States. But he also came from a family that had long been dedicated to the ideals of Christian mission, among them a great-grandfather, i.e., Rev. Alexander Waugh, whose decades of

152. Underwood, *The Call of Korea*, 125–26.

leadership at the London Missionary Society had rested on the principle of there being no denominational politics in mission work but only the glories of the gospel itself, that native peoples called unto Christian fellowship might similarly form different church governments "as to them shall appear most agreeable to the Word of God" while nevertheless united in love with all.[153] But whereas a distinction between "us" and "heathen" may be seen as still present in the statement drafted by his great-grandfather, Underwood's experiences in America—especially the early practical exposure to evangelizing with "business tact" among people older and "different" from himself under the guidance of Rev. Mabon, and the urgent call by the likes of Arthur T. Pierson to realize a world united under Christ—in effect empowered him to go even further with the idea. He wrote, "guiding and influencing it all, I see an organized Church, with a competent, well-trained, thoroughly consecrated native ministry—a united, non-sectarian Church of Christ, where there are neither Methodists, Presbyterians, Episcopalians, Jew nor Greek, Barbarian, Scythian, bond nor free, circumcised nor uncircumcised, but Christ is all in all."[154]

Furthermore, informed by the life examples of his father, John Underwood, as well as his father's teacher the great Michael Faraday, Underwood had not only been infused through and through with their scientific and enterprising spirit but also given discernment enough to distinguish between lack of education and mere lack of instruction. Knowing the difference allowed him to share updated instruction with the Korean people while earnestly respecting the tradition that had so made zeal for learning and education a part of the national culture. The seamless partnership between faith and science that had been planted in his mind from the earliest youth, where each was seen to spur the greatness of the other rather than otherwise, was met with ready response among Koreans and their fundamentally moral cosmology laced with eagerness for new knowledge.

By the late nineteenth century there is no denying that Korea's deeply saturated Neo-Confucian values, at nearly five hundred years old, were much in need of revitalization. Ideas that had once galvanized the nation and renewed it had degenerated to obsolete and yet rigidly maintained rituals, dry book learning, and a calcified social class system, not lacking for criticism from among its own scholars and dissatisfied citizenry.[155] Though

153. Waugh, *Principles of London Missionary Society, 1795*, quoted in Lillias Underwood, *Underwood of Korea*, 16.

154. Underwood, *The Call of Korea*, 125.

155. Yun, Ch'iho (1865–1945), whose harsh critique of the effects of calcified Neo-Confucianism on society Underwood included in the Appendix of his Deems Lecture at New York University in 1910, was one such scholar. See Underwood, *Religions of*

the Christian gospel and Western Learning accompanying it as brought by Underwood may have been regarded as very foreign at first, yet many of its aspects were soon and not infrequently recognized in many respects as striking a deeply resonant chord, as if coming face to face with an updated, revitalized and transfigured version of ideas long cherished as Korea's own in times past. These included faith in a universe that is fundamentally moral and meaningful in fiber, the need to investigate the "things and affairs" of this substantive material universe,[156] commitment to ideals of an egalitarian and meritocratic society, schools and community compacts as places of cooperation across lines for the practical realization of such ideals, and most of all the idea of self-realization as tied to the utmost expressions humaneness and rightness in one's dealings with others. These ideas moreover had so saturated the culture as to transcend mere institutional infrastructures, to find expression as the very ethos of the Korean people at all levels of society, especially in terms of a deeply shared sensibility of "rightness" beyond mere rites or legal rights.

Seeing the passionate hunger with which the Korean people received the gospel Underwood repeatedly called attention to how the Korean people were not only "fertile" ground but "ripe" for harvesting, and deserving of much more interest and support by Mission Boards everywhere. But witnessing, and gradually coming to understand, the nature of the sensibility of rightness he found widespread among the Korean people, he came to dare envision not a Church of consecrated Christians in Korea but a Christian Korea itself as consecrated to Christ and becoming a model for the rest of Asia if not the rest of the world—"reaching out strong, glad arms of influence—to China on the one hand and to Japan on the other, softening the prejudices and conservatism of the one, and steadying the faith of the other."[157] It was not to Western missionaries or to Western models of evangelism—of which there were already plenty in both China and Japan at the time—that he entrusted this task. On the contrary, he increasingly turned his energies to the education of Koreans that would empower them in this task for the long term through both "secular" and "Christian" leadership, not least by working to ennoble leadership in commerce through the

---

Eastern Asia, 180–82. Elsewhere Underwood gives a lively account of how Yun, as "a scion of nobility, this Korean of princely birth, this ex-Vice-Minister of State" from one of the noblest families and of the highest rank himself, did not hesitate to work as a sweeper and duster at a furniture shop in San Francisco while getting an American education there. See Underwood, *The Call of Korea,* 50–51.

156. Zhu Xi, *Daxue zhangjiu* (大學章句), 1:4–5, in de Bary and Bloom, *Sources of Chinese Tradition,* 1:727.

157. Underwood, *The Call of Korea,* 125–26.

founding of Korea's first business school. Nor did he keep this vision to himself. Instead, through him his most ardent partners in mission—his brothers and sisters back home who had supported his education and dreams when young, and later followed the intimate details of the mission in Korea with such interest as to support its needs not only materially but with personal care for the many Koreans Horace sent their way (as we shall see in chapter 4 from his letters)—came forward upon his death to take it upon themselves to bring to fruition the vision he had shared with them of a secular university in Korea.[158] Having been brought up in the same devotion to Christian values and evangelism as their brother, their understanding of the mission continued to grow with him across the Pacific. Put another way, Underwood's importance as a missionary was as much for what he conveyed back from and about the Koreans to his partners and supporters in mission in the U.S., thereby broadening and enlarging their understanding of the mission also, as in taking the gospel to Korea.

This mutual growth and transformation exemplified by Underwood, his "Senders" back home, and Chosŏn Korea suggests a number of ways to rethink the models of global missiology today. The very idea of "Global Christianity" has been threaded from inception with questions concerning the theological as well as political implications of separating the gospel from its historical encasings in Western cultural and political imperialism, and continues to be central to current debates about dynamics of missions. While the very real history of imperialism and its impact on the propagation of Christianity around the world cannot and should not in any way be downplayed, the example of Underwood and Korea also suggests revisiting histories of evangelism from vantage points of how witnessing missionaries themselves were changed and how such changes affected and enlarged the understanding of the gospel "back home." St. Paul and St. John arguably represent the Ur-examples of such interculturation. By rejecting the circumcision many early Christians themselves considered a condition of the faith and arguing for the equal legitimacy of non-circumcision St. Paul recast what had been simply a new development within the Jewish faith into a universal religion; St. John likewise broadened the conception of Jesus to include the Greek concept of "logos" and vice versa. Now, nearly two thousand years later, could Western Christianity—by assuming *its* history to be the essential and standard history of Christianity as such, and insisting on certain "internal factors" as being inherent to Christianity itself to which all Christianities must adapt as to a kind of doctrinal "circumcision"—be

---

158. It was John Thomas Underwood who in 1915 provided both the two hundred acres of land at Yŏnhui Village and the funds for the founding of Yonsei University in Korea.

committing the same mistake of which St. Paul had accused the early Christians in Jerusalem and Rome?[159]

Underwood's example of mission in Korea not only raises the issue of missiology but provides a significant modern case study for its re-evaluation. Stephen B. Bevans' *Models of Contextual Theology* has made a key contribution to our understanding of missiology by detangling the range of historical/theological approaches to their dynamic yet independently articulate components.[160] One might only wish that interculturation in which the possibility of mutuality of transformation is central, were also recognized as a model. Such a model would clearly allow us also to re-think the way we understand the meaning and possibility of unity across denominations in "Global Christianity." If the Church's relation to the structural imbalances in the world's socio-economic and political policies poses a fundamental challenge to the very ontology as well as function of religion in the world, then Underwood's example offers a relevant and thought-provoking case study for the building of a new, viably global missiology to be applied for the future.

159. Stephan B. Bevans uses the term "internal factors" to point to five dynamics "within" Christianity itself. They are the incarnational nature of Christianity, the sacramental nature of reality, the nature of divine revelation, catholicity of the church, and the doctrine of Trinity. See Bevans, *Models of Contextual Theology*, esp. 3–15.

160. Bevans, *Models of Contextual Theology*, esp. 3–15.

Koreans gathered in peaceful demonstration, c. 1898.

Underwood giving a sermon before a crowd of Koreans, c. 1913.

Chapter 3

Analysis of Underwood's Early
Letters from Korea

Findings from Newly Discovered
Letters to His Family

Introduction: The Missionary & Missiological
Vision of Underwood

THE LETTERS PUBLISHED FOR the first time through this collection in-
clude one written during his train trip from New York to California, dated
December 22, 1884, to board the ship for Asia, but the bulk extend from
February 6, 1887 until December 28, 1898, or up to about thirteen and
half years from the time of his arrival in Korea on April 5, 1885, and provide materials of historical interest on an enormous variety of subjects.
Unlike the mission reports and letters he sent to Dr. Ellinwood of the
Presbyterian Mission Board,[1] these personal letters—mostly to his brothers Fred and later John also known as Thomas, as well as one from Lillias
to her sister—provide his inmost assessment of both the difficulties and
accomplishments of his mission work, lively descriptions about his fellow
missionaries and the many Koreans he met along the way—from the king
and queen with whom he and his wife enjoyed rare close friendship, to the
high ranking officials, poor farmers and even the bandits he encountered
during his frequent travels throughout Korea—as well as intimate details
concerning his personal and family life, including a picture of his finances.
These on their own are enough to provide new depth and personality to
our picture of Underwood's life and work as the first Protestant missionary
to set foot on Korea. Equally importantly, the letters here give us for the

1. Frank Field Ellinwood (1826–1908) was the corresponding secretary for the
Presbyterian Board of Foreign Missions from 1871 to 1906.

first time in his own words a detailed account of his increasing involvement in Korean politics and his observations about what was happening in Korea at the time, as well as evidence demonstrating his absolute and whole-hearted faith in the rightness and necessity of inter-denominational cooperation and coordination. Together, these two aspects of the letters show Underwood developing a consistent missiology that envisioned a future best described not in terms of "Christians in Korea" or "Christianity in Korea" but rather of "a Christian Korea."

Underwood's attitudes vis-à-vis Korea's destiny and identity as a nation in the complex international imperial politics in the region have been a longstanding question for scholars and lay Christians alike with an interest in Underwood and the roots of Protestantism in Korea. It was the question that loomed large, for example, in Prof. Mahnyol Yi's recent introduction (2015) to the Korean translation of Lillias Underwood's account of her husband's life and work,[2] because despite the numerous indirect indications of Underwood's support for an independent Korea, in the years following the Japanese annexation of Korea he also went on to court the favor of Japanese authorities in order to obtain permits for the YMCA and a college that later would become Yonsei University. Unfortunately, being under strict orders from the beginning by the Mission Board not to involve himself in Korean politics and to practice utmost care and restraint even in conducting all "proper" missionary work on account of Korean government's official ban on Christian proselytizing, Underwood was careful to refrain from mentioning his thoughts on such matters in his communications to Dr. Ellinwood. Lillias Underwood's record of his life and work, published in 1918 not long after the Japanese annexation of Korea in 1910, likewise largely avoided the issue. In the absence of incontrovertible evidence one way or the other scholars have found it difficult to fathom the true nature of his sentiments on the issue of Korea's national independence in so fraught a period. While the letters introduced here do not extend beyond 1898, their importance is immeasurable for shedding light on the development of his thoughts as well as the extent of his active political involvement in the years prior.

But the letters' witness to Underwood's early views and actions has, in my view, ramifications far beyond the nationalist sensitivities of Korean scholars of Christianity and of modern Korean history. They help us begin to piece together for the first time a coherent—if still developing—missiology for Underwood that arguably allowed him to surpass in achievements those of missionaries far better known than him both then and now, such as

2. See Mahnyol Yi, Preface, 10–11.

William Carey (1761–1834), Adoniram Judson (1788–1850), Robert Morrison (1782–1834), and Hudson Taylor (1832–1905). These missionaries also carried on medical and education missions, established churches under difficult circumstances, published dictionaries and translations of the Bible, hymns and religious tracts, etc. much like Underwood—so what would account for the difference? Part of the answer to that question lies in the global context of nineteenth-century missions, which has been called the age of modern imperialism as well as of the Protestant world mission. Missionaries inevitably worked in highly charged political contexts, and rightly or wrongly were often regarded as the "soft" promoters of Western superiority and imperial agenda—or as I described elsewhere, as messengers of both "bible and guns."[3] It was typical of missionaries, whether consciously or unconsciously, to consider the Western imperial agenda to be only right and natural, as necessary and benevolent as the gospel message itself. Against such a backdrop Underwood dared envision the self-determined transformation of an entire people and a nation by the synergy of the gospel together with their own strongly embedded ethos of Neo-Confucian rightness in Hananim, combining the implications of both of these for the transformation of individuals as well as of society. The two together formed the axis of his vision for a "Christian Korea." This vision alone makes Underwood a highly significant figure in the history of missions, potentially bringing into it a new narrative leading beyond Western imperialism, into a new way of thinking about relations between politics and religion, between sacred and secular, and the building of a "city of God."

In this Underwood had been prepared, even since young boyhood, by the inter-denominational spirit of his great-grandfather Rev. Alexander Waugh; the scientific, entrepreneurial yet devout mindedness of his father John Underwood; by the family awareness of Michael Faraday who had risen from a humble background to become the acknowledged leading scientist of his time without betraying either his devout pietism or his roots; by friendship with George Müller and his famous reliance on prayer in all things[4]; the early experience in practical evangelism in the backwaters of America under the guidance of Rev. William Mabon; the broad liberal education in preparatory schools and college and the professional training he received at New Brunswick Theological Seminary; and the urgent, expectant spirit of the world mission as led by Arthur T. Pierson. Indeed we may even say Underwood's early years in London at the epicenter of

---

3. James Kim, "Bible versus Guns," 33–37. See also Lee, *The Bible and the Gun*, esp. 60.

4. Underwood refers specifically to his having read Müller's *Life of Faith* in his letter to Thomas, August 2, 1895.

the British Empire in its heyday, and his subsequent experiences as a new-comer to America, helped anchor his individual experiences in a more multi-vantaged awareness of arguably the most significant historical context of nineteenth-century missions. Each of these elements together and more not only shaped his understanding of the gospel and of evangelism, but in important ways also gave him the wherewithal to appreciate what he would find in Chosŏn Korea.

Equally important, however, was the nature of what he would dis-cover—unexpectedly—soon upon his arrival in Korea: not only a fertile, prepared ground, but in fact the seed already "sown & already begun to germinate, in many places ready for the gathering" even without having been "watered by man."[5] In chapter 2, I have tried to give something of an introduction to his encounter with the Neo-Confucian culture that saturat-ed Chosŏn Korea, as background to this important synergy between that specific culture and the gospel as he understood it, transforming not only Korea and Koreans but also Underwood himself and—through him—his Senders back in America, in this case primarily his family who were fully invested and engaged in his mission with him. As the main purpose of this book is to introduce his newly discovered early personal letters, the more detailed account of that synergy will necessarily have to be for a next book, to include not only a close analysis of his activities in Korea but consider-ations also of the nearly thirty years between his death in 1916 and Korean independence of 1945 during which time his *legacy* (if not his name) for Korean Christianity and for the world Christian mission was in many ways both deliberately and not so deliberately erased from international aware-ness, and appreciation of Neo-Confucian ideals itself underwent broad erosion in subsequent decades. Sufficient for the contexts of this book will be to merely suggest how Underwood's dynamic of mutuality of transfor-mation—or what I have called "interculturation"—functions as helpful historical ground for rethinking our approaches to globalization of Chris-tianity in the future. In this chapter, therefore, I focus on some of the main points of interest from the letters that elucidate especially Underwood's political thoughts and activities while in Korea, his efforts toward an inter-denominational or ecumenical Christian Korea, and his own transforma-tion through the understanding of Korean people's ethos.

5. Letter to his brother Fred, undated but likely written in late November or early December 1887.

Political Involvement and
Evolving Attitude toward Korea

Evident over the fourteen-year span of these early letters is the significant change in Underwood's attitude toward Korea. In the beginning, like most Westerners of the period, Underwood was more at home and more impressed by Japan's well-ordered strides toward modernization, and persuaded of the its superiority over Korea. By 1885 Japan was already in the seventeenth year of the Meiji Restoration and—despite the continuing rivalry among opposing factions in government—largely united as well as relatively well organized in its efforts to catch up with Western industrialization and im-perially funded economics. It was also home to many more missionaries and an established mission infrastructure, so that missionaries from Korea and China regularly traveled to Japan whenever in need of respite, recupera-tion, and specialized resources. Japan was both better informed and more systematic about its interest in the West, much more directed in its efforts to imitate it, and its citizenry obedient and orderly within the militantly hierarchical social structure. Compared to the political and social disarray he found in Korea it is not surprising that in his letter to Fred dated Febru-ary 6, 1887, Underwood wrote how he had been feeling "a little worn out of late" but that "the very thought" of taking a run to Japan for a few weeks soon was enough to "straighten him out." He continued in the same letter,

> We seem to be degenerating and we need the prayers of those
> who are at home that in the interval of studying the language we
> may be kept from turning into all head and no heart. This is the
> danger that we feel. . . . I am in great hopes that my trip to Japan
> will be a benefit to me in this respect and that my intercourse
> with those who are in Yokohama will do me good.[6]

His thinking of Japan as the "mission base" of Asia would continue for some time; it was after all the place he relied on to get his major publication efforts typeset and printed, as well as for much needed supplies such as quinine, albeit at highly padded prices he tried to avoid. As late as May 20, 1890, Underwood would report to Thomas with satisfaction,

> Our trip to Japan has, we think, done us both much good in
> many ways and in none more than in giving us an insight into
> the work as it is done in other fields and by other missions. We
> have indeed seen much to learn in such a ripe field as Japan, but
> this has not been to us the only experience, for while we were in

6. Letter to Fred, February 6, 1887.

Japan we met missionaries from every field in the world which
you may well imagine would be a great benefit.[7]

In the meantime he seems to have begun to develop friendly relations with
the Palace around early 1887. In a February letter to Fred he describes having been invited to skate on the Palace pond through a Miss Ellers, and
afterward to a supper hosted by Min Pansa—one of the highest men in
the state, according to Underwood[8]—with the King (Kojong, r. 1863–97
as king; 1897–1907 as Emperor) and Queen dining in an adjoining room
separated only by the typical papered sliding doors of Korean interiors.[9]
The scene as described by Underwood—the King and Queen continually speaking through the doors to Min Pansa with messages to give the
company, which Min Pansa then keeps asking Underwood to translate into
English for everyone—anticipates the real affection, curiosity, and intimate
trust that would eventually develop between the monarch and Underwood,
and would almost be charmingly comic were it not also for the tinge of
naiveté and tragedy it presages. Underwood seems to have begun taking
an active interest in Korea's political situation not too long afterward. His
letter to Fred dated October 11, 1887, contains a long section describing
the "muddle" of Korea's status in international politics in which Underwood
takes pains to explain how China had earlier "virtually advised" Korea to
make independent treaties with the other powers in the region, namely
Russia, Japan, and the United States. The King had done so and, having
procured sufficient funds, was about to send a diplomatic embassy to the
U.S. as well when China inexplicably changed its tune and threatened war
if such a diplomatic mission was sent. Describing China's actions as "putting her hand in work that does not belong to her" and "rather up handed,"
Underwood describes the vacillations of the weak King and how "we are
waiting anxiously to see what will be done." As he sees it, Korea's position as
an independent nation hangs in the balance: "If the Embassy does not go or
if they go only after asking China's position Korea is a vassal power, but if

7. Letter to Thomas, May 20, 1890.

8. The reference is probably to Min Yŏng-hwan (1861–1905) or Min Yŏng-ik
(1860–1914), the latter especially a close relative of the Queen [later, Empress] Min.
"Pansa" is a positional title. Min Yŏng-hwan died in 1905 by suicide in protest of the
Japan-Korea Treaty of 1905 (also known as the *Eulsa Unwilling Treaty* or *Japan-Korea
Protectorate Treaty*), which deprived Korea of its diplomatic sovereignty and made
Korea a protectorate of Imperial Japan. Min Yŏng-ik, an emissary to US in 1883 who
met President Chester Arthur at the White House and later founded a court-sponsored
western style school in Korea, eventually fled to Shanghai following the 1905 Treaty,
and continued to work for Korea's independence from there. He died in 1914.

9. Letter to Fred, February 6, 1887.

the king will but say go without awaiting decisions from China, Korea will be independent and China dare not go to war."[10] Despite understanding that the King has long been "in the habit of leaning on China," he closes the section of the letter by saying, "We all hope for [?] independence as this is such a bad [?]—even in all China's work."[11] While the passage still leaves in question whether his support for an independent Korea was motivated more as a response to China's untenable meddling, the anticipated advantages to come from Korea-U.S. relations unencumbered by Chinese interference, or national independence as an abstract/admirable principle in its own right, Underwood's stance for Korean independence is clear.

Two additional pieces of information from this period, in an undated letter from November or early December of 1887, suggest that the Palace also had begun to regard Underwood differently. He mentions having been asked to translate "a tremendously long document for the government," and adds, without describing the nature of the document itself, "They have no one that can do it, and so have come to me. Of course I feel honored that they should ask me and feel I must do it, but I would much rather that they had got it done somewhere else as I am so busy."[12] Later in the paragraph, while expressing incredulity and frustration at the lack of more enthusiasm and support from the Presbyterian Church, Underwood points to the great changes taking place in the country for the spread of gospel: "Who would have thought . . . missionaries would be accorded the position they have today, that they would be on intimate terms of friendship with the officials of the highest rank and this, too, when we were known to be missionaries."[13]

The next several and shorter letters, spread over a few years, make little mention of political matters until one sent to Thomas dated January 11, 1895, some seven years later. In the interval he had made at least three trips through northern Korea, in 1887, 1888, and 1889—the second of which had been cut short due to a sudden and express new decree forbidding Christian work,[14] and the third was a working honeymoon during which Lillias Horton Underwood (m. 1889), as medical missionary, recalled seeing to over six hundred patients. He also oversaw the growth of the Semunan (Sae'mun'an) Church to somewhere between 260 and 400 members, published a Korean grammar as well as a Korean-English dictionary (1890), established the Korea Religious

10. Letter to Fred, October 11, 1887.

11. Letter to Fred, October 11, 1887.

12. Letter to Fred, November or early December, 1887.

13. Letter to Fred, November or early December, 1887.

14. The decree was triggered, according to Lillias Underwood, by the Catholics building the Myŏngdong Cathedral to be taller than the Palace. The impertinence angered the King.

Tract Society (1890), invited the missionary John L. Nevius (1890) from China for an inter-denominational conference, began the Bible Study program (1890) designed to disseminate its close-knit, well-trained native leadership throughout the nascent churches around the country, established a church at Sap'yŏngdong (1893) and at Sŏgyodong (1894), and published a Korean hymnal (1894) containing 117 hymns, the first ever Korean text to contain Western-style musical notation as well as nine hymns newly composed by Koreans themselves.[15] Personally Underwood had suffered the loss of his beloved brother Frederick (d. 1891) as well as the birth of his son Horace Horton Underwood (1890–1951); politically, he had been witness to the First Sino-Japanese War (August 1, 1894 to April 17, 1895) in which Japan shocked the world by its decisive victory against China but was nevertheless forced by the combined cooperation of the European powers and Russia to relinquish its hold on the valuable Port Arthur, in Manchuria, as well as over the Korean peninsula. Given this last, perhaps Underwood's heightened interest and involvement in the increasing political complexities surrounding Korea was inevitable. Indeed, if the letter of January 11, 1895, at the height of the Sino-Japanese War (August 1, 1894 to April 17, 1895), is the first in a while in the present collection to bring up political matters, its contents make clear that his involvement had been ongoing for some time.

In addition to the rather long, conversational update about Lillie's "constant" visits to the Queen as her medical adviser and—in the Queen's own words—"great friend," Underwood includes in this letter his personal assessment of the individual members of the newly appointed cabinet, which he sends to Thomas together with a copy of the *Korean Repository* containing a complete list of the cabinet members and each of their vice ministers and/or first secretaries. The ease with which he saw fit to share both with Thomas points to their having engaged in many earlier and ongoing discussions about what was happening politically, through letters possibly no longer extant. Underwood also points out that "No. 4 [minister on the list] is the man you supported in Washington" and "No. 12 is the man whom Fowler brought down to your office several years ago," alongside other mutual connections and meetings. Clearly, not only Horace but Thomas Underwood also had quietly been giving support to highly placed men within the Korean government on a selective basis, no doubt at Underwood's request and with the Underwood family's implicit trust in his judgment. The exact nature and extent of the Thomas's support for these men must be topic of further research, but it very likely included financial support in at least one case,

---

15. The Methodist hymnal published earlier had only twenty-seven hymns, and no musical notation.

as well as much needed moral support, friendly guidance, and important introductions to society in a foreign land.

It is noteworthy that the cabinet members singled out by Underwood for special mention at this time seem to have been ones familiar with and/ or sympathetic in some way to America and to ideas of change and progress. At least five had been to America either for study or as part of the diplomatic corps; others are described as "progressive" or "enlightened" and "bold enough to assert his independence of custom"; yet another was father to a Korean Methodist missionary already to China. Three are also on apparently intimate terms with Underwood, while another had met with him in Washington. Given his understanding of the ways of governments, as well as by now extensive personal experience with associations of men, Underwood expresses prescient concern that the group appointed to cabinet was badly lacking in someone to be their "balance [wheel]," a person to hold the group's disparate interests and styles together so as to unify their will to work out a coherent policy.[16] Nevertheless he notes the group altogether "makes for a pretty good cabinet," young and spirited but not entirely without experience. He observes, too, that the country is "quieting down" once again, and expresses hope that "When all this is over this whole country will be *open to us & then we must be ready to go in & take the land for Christ*."[17] By "we" here he clearly means missionaries, but his positive assessment of non-Christian members of the cabinet supporting "progress" would also seem indicate a strong bond in Underwood's mind between the Christian mission and more secular progressivism.

In late 1895 an event took place that took the King's reliance on Underwood to a whole new level. A band of pro-Japanese conspirators had taken the King prisoner within the Palace, followed not too long afterward by an attack led by the King's friends to try to free the monarch. Describing the events to her sister Hannah on November 29th—possibly only two days after the attack had taken place—Lillias wrote,

> The attack failed. The king was greatly frightened and called
> out, "Call the foreigners." Mr. Hulbert and Dr. Avison were at
> the palace at Horace's request with Horace, as they expected
> the attack and feared for the king's life, should the conspirators
> become alarmed. As soon as shots were heard they rushed to
> the king's apartments which they found surrounded by a heavy
> guard; bayonets were crossed in front of them but Horace
> pushed them aside and hurried in followed closely by the two

16. Letter to Thomas, January 11, 1895.

17. Letter to Thomas, January 11, 1895; emphasis added.

others, and they remained by the king all night. . . . We seem pretty deeply mixed up in politics, but how can we help it? All these years the king has loaded our Mission and ourselves with kindness—suddenly he is plunged in the deepest distress and calls on us for help—it is pitiful to see how he depends on a few poor missionaries. Our American Minister has asked Horace to act as confidential interpreter and go between, and has asked other missionaries also to stay with the king (or near him) at nights, as witnesses, knowing that the ruffians now controlling the palace would be reluctant to do any open acts of villainy upon the king with foreign witnesses. It is gossiped around here that Dr. A, Mr. H and Horace sat by the king, pistols in hand all night. They did nothing of the kind. Though they had revolvers concealed on their persons for their own possible protection, they were never shown and they simply stayed with the king as witnesses and to give him moral support, that too at the request of the American Minister.[18]

In some Japanese papers the "gossip" apparently turned into "accusations" against Underwood of having taken part in the attack of the night. In a letter dated several months after the incident, Underwood thanks Thomas for sending him a copy of such accusations and makes a point of assuring his brother further that,

I had nothing whatever to do with the attack, and knew nothing about it till a few hours before, as the enclosed account will tell you I have not plotted at all. I have on more than one occasion been sought as interpreter, and perhaps these things have lent color to the statement that I was in the plots. I have felt strong sympathy for the King, when he has asked my advice I have not hesitated to give it. I have cared for no one, been outspoken against wrong, and those who do the wrong of course do not like it at all. They have tried to injure me and to get me out of the way, but I do not mind what they say. I knew when I saw the lies that were cabled to Japan that they would go further.[19]

Underwood states most clearly that the motivations driving his involvement in the politics surrounding Korea were his strong personal, human sympathy for the King, which his many references to the King and Queen in these letters reveal, and his principle of what is right, irrespective of their potential risks to his person or conversely accusations of not doing enough.

18. Lillias Underwood's letter to sister Hannah Horton, November 29, 1895.

19. Letter to Thomas, February 20, 1896.

Indeed in the context fraught with political factionalism both domestic and foreign, the sympathy and affection involved real risks. In her one letter included in this collection, dated November 29, 1895, Lillias confides to her sister that not only had the Queen made her escape from the Palace in the confusion of the night's attack, but that "she is expected to take shelter here in our house for a day or two at least." The Queen never got to do so, but that does not negate the fact that the Underwoods had been willing to embrace the risk of harboring the royal fugitive.[20] With the king "in danger of being murdered ever since" and afraid to partake of the foods prepared for him in the Palace, the Underwoods also took to sending him food under lock and key on a daily basis for a time, delivering them personally with the key on his person. She wrote, "Horace has been almost the only one whom the king could trust to carry secret messages, and it has been with the greatest difficulty he could get even a word in private with his majesty—frequently he has written messages on his cuffs at odd minutes."[21] Not long afterward, Underwood also took up getting one of the King's sons, a young prince more or less held hostage in Japan,[22] safely out of the way to the U.S.—an endeavor in which he once again turned to his brother Thomas for help.[23]

20. Lillias Underwood's claim that the Queen was still alive albeit in hiding at this point in time has been an issue of much confusion and contention among scholars. The Queen's official date of death at the hands of Japanese assassins has been established as October 8, 1895. It is difficult to believe Lillias—so close to the Queen and in discussions with her about opening a new school within the Palace grounds in the preceding months—would not have known about her murder for nearly seven weeks after the event. One possibility is that the news of the Queen's violent death was kept from her for some time for fear of trauma. In a letter dated May 26, 1896, nearly eight months after the death of the Queen, Underwood was still writing from Cheefoo, China, that the "late disturbances in Korea" continued to be a source of "considerable anxiety" for Lillie, and that the death of the Queen especially affected her "as though a relative had been foully dealt with," so as to add to the necessity of taking a respite in Cheefoo.

21. Letter from Lillias Underwood to her sister, November 29, 1895.

22. This was Yi Kang (1877–1955), the fifth son of the King, who the Japanese would later name King Ŭi-ch'in (r. 1910–30). While studying in Keio University in Tokyo, Japan, the prince became interested in learning about and studying in America; he was finally allowed to travel and study in various places in America between 1899 and 1905. It's probably no coincidence that in 1901 the prince became a student of the Roanoke College in Salem, Virginia, where Kim Kyu-sik (1881–1950?) was also student since 1898. Kim was the orphan boy Underwood had more or less adopted not long after his arrival in Korea and whom Lillias nicknamed "little John, Pon Ga-be." See Lillias Underwood, *The Underwood of Korea*, 45.

23. See letter to Thomas, June 17, 1896. The matter became a source of not inconsiderable headache for both Horace and Thomas, though not so much on account of the prince himself. In the process of getting the prince out of Japan Underwood was forced to work with a Colonel Cockerill (John Albert, 1845–96) as well as Mr. Loomis (Henry, 1839–1920)—the latter a missionary in Japan who he did not much

For the King's part, his trust in Underwood must have been indeed great, for he not only told Underwood to come see him freely as he wished, but had him come to visit immediately before and after the latter's every trip outside of Seoul. On these occasions, too, the King frequently cleared the room of all others so that he might speak and ask Underwood's advice confidentially. Indeed Underwood, citing an incident in which the King took immediate action to remove an official from his post upon hearing an account of the man's wrongdoing from him, expressed to Thomas several times the extra care he took to not abuse the situation or the trust placed on him but to use it ultimately only for the good of the gospel:

> We got in on Monday night, & early on Tuesday morning His Majesty sent for me. He was most kind and gracious, cleared the room of all who were there, and asked me to tell him plainly all I thought. I had quite a long talk with him about affairs in this country & made one or two suggestions *all* of which he ordered to be carried out at once. He told me to come whenever I wanted to but I shall be careful not to push myself forward. I shall go when I am called or if urgent demand exists, ask for audience. May God guide me in aught that I may say and in some manner open up the way for me to speak of Christ to His Majesty. It is a very hard thing to do, but may God show me how.[24]

---

like but needed for his connections to Japanese officials. Cockerill went on to spread damaging rumors about Underwood's well-heeled family, while Loomis—whom Underwood described as a "half-cracked individual"—went even further and tried to draw funds from Thomas that Underwood had never authorized (see letters dated February 20, and June 17, 1896).

Another problem stemming from his rescue of the prince was Japanese tampering with Underwood's letters. We can follow his increasing certainty that his communications were being tampered with in the letters dated February 20, 1896 ("I knew when I saw the lies that were cabled to Japan that they would go further"); August 23, 1897 ("We have been wondering whether you ever got my long letters, an oft begun one, that I sent you from Yokohama, Japan. . . . Lillie sent a letter & it was never received. We were so shadowed & watched that we fear our letters were taken out of the mails. Of course we could not prove this, but we know that special messengers were intercepted & their letters opened and read, and that some letters we posted in Yokohama never reached their destination. We also know that during the war letters were opened in transit & their contents copied, published in Japan & criticized before the letters even reached their destination in Japan."); and August 28, 1897 ("I do not know that any of your letters have gone astray as yet, but our letters home we know have been tampered with. I think now that the Prince is in U.S.A. perhaps we will be let alone.").

24. Letter to Thomas, February 20, 1896. For other references to the trust given him by the King, see letters dated May 29, June 12, and June 17, 1896.

Although Underwood understood clearly that "the King needs advice, and if he can get this from a reliable source I believe things will go on well,"[25] he was sincere about not wanting to abuse the trust placed in him by trying to steer the ruler's decisions. Despite having spent months working to get the prince to the U.S., for example, he wrote Thomas, "But when the King was free I thought that he should decide what his son should do. I have talked the matter over with his Majesty, and he desires that he shall first of all come back to Korea. Now when His Majesty says this I have nothing to do but abide by his decision."[26] Underwood had held hopes that the prince, "though not the heir, [as the King's son] will, I feel sure, come to the throne. He desires a good school education and a military one after it. I hope and pray that with his education he may by all means get Christ. What a change it would work in the land if its King were a genuine Christian,"—a hope which he later would come to feel had been dashed by the prince's contact with foreigners while in Japan.[27]

Nor did his personal, human sympathy and willingness to do all he could for the King blind him to the latter's faults and weaknesses which, as one in a ruler's position, could not but be tied to grave political consequences. A little over a year after his earlier, fairly positive assessment of the newly appointed cabinet, for example, we find Underwood reassessing the same cabinet in a different, more sobering tone: "All the present cabinet seem most friendly to me but it is not a strong cabinet . . . most of them [are] afraid for their lives & unless they get over this I do now know what will happen."[28] There is here a new, subtle but significant understanding separating friendliness to his cause and the overall good of the country. He appreciates the importance of the King to the Korean people—"The people love their King & I believe the whole country are glad that he is [safely] at the Russian Legation," he wrote in the letter of May 29, 1896. He also took great pride in the idea to include a large portrait of the King in his weekly newspaper to celebrate the occasion of the King's birthday more than a year later, in August, 1897.[29] But in the meantime Underwood is equally cognizant that "Politically things do not look at all promising. . . . Corruption and abuse of power are on all sides, and there does not seem to be much chance of righting matters. . . . The great difficulty just now is a capable head. There is no capable head in the present government. . . . I wish much that the

25. Letter to Thomas, May 29, 1896.

26. Letter to Thomas, June 16, 1896.

27. Letter to Thomas February 20, 1896.

28. Letter to Thomas February 20, 1896.

29. About the King's photograph in the newspaper, see letter of August 21, 1897.

Queen were alive that she might guide and direct the King."[30] Indeed, his disappointment and concern over the King's "weak and vacillating" character seems to have gradually mounted with time as well as the growing seriousness of Korea's inability to deal with international pressures. By August 1, 1898, Underwood is frustrated enough by the situation to vent,

> There is and always will be a great deal of dissatisfaction with the present government. His Majesty insists that He & He alone is the power in Korea and he does not even give any power to any one of his ministers. He has what he calls a cabinet, but in reality he has no cabinet for He appoints his ministers without any regard to their fitness for the positions to be filled and without any regard to their likelihood of their agreeing among themselves. In like manner the so-called Prime Minister is appointed entirely regardless of his political leadings and as a result what harmony can you possibly have and what can you do with such a cabinet. It has been known to have a cabinet in which no two members out of ten agreed and as a result of the different departments were working in opposition to each other. . . . Everything is so childish and the Koreans from the highest down are just like so many babies. It reminds me of when we as children would be playing and something was done that we did not like we would "I won't play any more if you don't play my way." It will be a long, long while before Korea can govern herself aright and how I wish that she would ask help of old England.[31]

He, however, did not forget to differentiate between the seeming hopelessness of Korea's government and Korea as a whole. He wrote,

> There may be apparent backwards steps but Korea cannot go back now. She has gone too far forward already, and then apparent backward steps are but halts to get breath for another rush forward. *It has been this way in every land, and it must be expected here in Korea.* Things cannot go on all smoothly here and be all rough elsewhere.[32]

---

30. Letter to Thomas, June 17, 1896.

31. Letter to Thomas, August 1, 1898.

32. Letter to Thomas, June 17, 1896; emphasis added. It is notable that even in his most private communications Underwood did not gloss over the social problems, inequities, abuses, as well as the continual efforts at reform both in England and in America despite their far more advanced states of civilization, holding instead for them to be issues common to all humanity irrespective of race, religion, or creed.

Indications of a Missional Vision in Response to the Crisis of Korea

By comparison his criticisms about Japan were much more circumspect and muted. There is no commentary or criticism regarding Japanese leadership by name or group, for example. We might attribute this to at least three causes. First, he did not enjoy access to the kinds of intimate relations with or observation of Japan's governing elite the way he did with the Korean royalty and aristocracy, and therefore was not privy to their motivations, corruptions, and mismanagements in the same way. What he saw of Japan instead was its orderly military organization and a highly competent yet obedient citizenry on the threshold of becoming a major player in the East. The sense of negativity about Japan is present, but as one committed to practicing what is right he did not engage in conjecture but tried to limit himself to reporting only what he observed and knew to be fact, keeping things objective and to the point. Relating Japanese activities on February 20, 1896, several months after the night in which he stayed with the King to protect him, for example, he wrote simply that "[Japan] is trying to stir up sedition among the [Korean] people, is circulating all manner of rumors but whether the people will believe her or not I cannot tell. We still live on a volcano." We sense the negative tone again when he explains to Thomas how he had resigned himself to working with Loomis despite considering him "a *half cracked* individual"[33] because as someone "in with the Japanese officials" he would be best able to get the Prince "*out of their clutches*."[34] Elsewhere, he strongly suggests the debts supposedly run up by the Prince while in Japan were deliberately "manufactured" to embarrass and keep him there.

Secondly, the style of his restraint may have stemmed from his awareness of being under constant surveillance and having his mail intercepted, especially once he became involved in getting the Prince out of Japan. On August 23, 1897, he wrote,

> We were so shadowed and watched that we fear our letters were taken out of the mails. Of course we could not prove this but we know that special messengers were intercepted and their letters opened and read, and that some letters we posted I Yokohama never reached their destination. We also know that during the war letters were opened in transit and their contents copied,

---

33. Letter to Thomas, June 17, 1896; see this volume, p. 168.
34. Letter to Thomas, June 17, 1896; emphasis added.

published in Japan, and criticized before the letters even reached their destination in Japan.[35]

A few days later he stressed again, "I do not know that any of your letters have gone astray as yet but our letters home we know have been tampered with. I think now that the Prince is in U.S.A. perhaps we will be let alone."[36] The passages indicate a level of conscious, deliberate restraint when writing about potentially sensitive matters, above and beyond the pressures and policies of the Mission Board to not get involved in "local" politics. And yet, considering the kinds of political as well as material assistance Thomas Underwood clearly was providing his younger brother's cause throughout this period—including seeing to the affairs of the Prince while in America—it would seem not only highly likely but even necessary that they shared an understanding concerning Korea-Japan relations beyond the sketchy nuances given here.

Thirdly, Underwood avoided confronting the issue directly in the letters—especially given the contexts of above—by referring to rightness as his standard of loyalty, leaving the particulars to be inferred. For example, he made the following observation distancing himself from the "Japs" in his own eyes as in the eyes of the Korean people:

> Everywhere we were recognized as Europeans and not Japs, and everywhere we were greeted as those who were going to change things and save Korea. All whom we saw seemed glad of the change in this city. . . . People that were rising in mobs against the Japanese and the pro-Japan government at once began to disperse. Their work was done and there was nought else for them to do. The people everywhere seemed pleased.[37]

He did not thereby hate without discretion all things Japanese or love unconditionally all things Korean:

> The war, the murder of the Queen, the constant upheavals that we have had here so far in no way hindered our work but [we] rather have shown the people that they have no one on whom to rely, and made them this more ready to receive Christ. . . . The Missionaries' strong trust on the side of right irrespective of [party] has had a good effect upon the natives, & I hope its effects are now being seen. The King and the high officials of the [highest] class all know that we are [always?] to be counted on

35. Letter to Thomas, August 23, 1897.
36. Letter to Thomas, August 27, 1897.
37. Letter to Thomas, February 20, 1896.

on the side of the right that we should of right before anything else, and that the word of the missionaries is to be believed.[38]

He felt that to be perceived as always standing on the side of right "irrespective of party" was the best way to serve the gospel, the ultimate goal from which he never diverged. This speaks in most important ways to the long-term vision with which he began his Korean mission from the start, and it continued to serve as the basic framework from which he navigated the difficult waters of Korea-Japan relations in the years still ahead. But what did "right" mean to Underwood in the complex, changing contexts of the time? Given that he does not offer direct declarations on the issue—and they would likely have been out of place in letters to his older brothers whom he considered his staunchest supporters and fellow missionaries for Christ—we may be forgiven trying to piece together certain fundamental principles implied in the constancy of patterns informing his actions.

In the first place, it would seem Underwood was an advocate for the civil and scientific advancement of humanity, together with rights to independence. Moreover, he recognized and respected the many median steps of the former *as necessary requisites* toward achieving the latter. As a product of the Scottish Enlightenment both through his ancestry in England and Christian education in America, he was a firm believer in faith as a primary moral motivator in bringing empirically sound, practical benefits to society. Whether it was large quantities of quinine brought from Japan to help arrest outbreaks of typhus, the expansion of national infrastructure such as telegraphs and railroads under the direction of Danish and American engineers respectively, or useful new advances in chemistry, mathematics, agricultural sciences, etc. that he tirelessly worked to share through his weekly *Christian News* to be read by Korean Christians and non-Christians alike, for Underwood they meant "progress, and we welcome it gladly but this is not all by any means. We need more."[39] There was no shame to learning from the practical, industrial, and ethical superiority of others, whether they be friends or enemies, when doing so meant alleviating the suffering of humanity and righting its inequities. Indeed, he considered becoming aware of the injustices affecting oneself and others as a first step toward becoming free. He wrote, "We have a fearless paper in the native language that calls itself 'The Independent.' It is edited by Dr. Jaisohn—a naturalized American citizen, a Korean nobleman that has come back to Korea. The paper is very bold in speaking for the right, and takes up everyone's cause that writes a complaint. It has done much good

---

38. Letter to Thomas, June 12, 1896.
39. See letters to Thomas, June 17, 1896, August 23, 1897, and August 1, 1898.

& will do much if the editor is allowed to live. . . . He is courageous and comes out on the side of the right at every step."[40]

Given the lessons already learned through the Opium War and the Boxer Rebellion, as well as the even more immediate Sino-Japanese War, Underwood implicitly understood also that national independence dependent on the steady goodwill and assistance of others could only be an oxymoron of terms. No nation in the newly global world order could hope to secure or maintain true independence without first achieving a united and educated citizenry, a sustainable economy, and sufficient means of self-defense. It was for this reason that he insisted always on including highest available secular education alongside Christian education in the narrow sense; in his mind the two had to work in concert as two wings of a bird.[41] The best example of this principle at work is, of course, his laying the groundwork for the founding of Yonsei University to be a "secular" university that included—against the strong opposition of many of his missionary colleagues—a business school as well as a divinity program. Given his long-term vision for the Christian future of Korea, he foresaw the need to prepare Korea and Koreans to participate effectively as Christian entrepreneurs in the emerging international commercial economy.

As a second principle of "right," Underwood seems to have maintained extreme wariness against dangers of things that came too quickly and/or for "free." He kept the proverbial Trojan horse at arm's length on every level. He was not eager for quick gains in the "head count" of new converts to report back to the Mission Board, and often as not turned down requests for baptism when he felt the person in question had not sufficiently wrestled with the full, life-changing commitment signified by the sacrament. He also advised not offering the customary stipends to students of his mission school for fear people might associate church and faith with becoming beneficiaries of its largesse and power. Although he frequently applied for—and received—liberal financial and other forms of assistance from Thomas for the mission, and freely gave what he could of his own salary as well, he did not allow such funds to go toward the purchase of land, materials and labor needed to build new local churches. Those, he insisted, were to be built only after the community of that church raised the money on their own copper by each precious copper, often

40. Letter to Thomas, June 17, 1896. Dr. Jaisohn was reference to Jaep'il "Jaisohn" Sŏh (1864–1951).

41. It should be noted that this had not always been true even for Underwood. During the early years of his mission he frequently expressed impatience that he cannot find time to engage in "real Christian work." See Letter to Fred, November/ December, 1887.

giving their labor as well. If that meant the faith community in a village had to make do without a church building for years rather than months, Underwood saw far greater value in the steadiness of their commitment to faith, their learning to work toward a goal as a community, and perhaps most of all the ways in which faith worked its subtle and deeply personal changes in the life of each individual in the process of contributing to the faith community. Faith *experience* needs participation, time, and reflection to be fully claimed and understood as one's own. This was a chief reason for his support of the so-called Nevius System. Underwood wrote,

> This land of Korea as far as Mission work is concerned is in a marvelous way the exponent of the self support system that is known as the Nevius System, and in this land in the Presbyterian Mission it has been carried to an extent that I believe has not been equaled in any Mission field. I believe that it is the plan that should be followed and that only by this plan can a strong work be started in a comparative short time. . . . Dr. Ellinwood has written to me asking me to write a history of our Presbyterian Mission in Korea so as to have it for the Pan-Presbyterian Alliance that is to meet in Washington in 1900. I shall endeavor to show in it how the use of this system has so materially affected our work. I am more and more convinced that it is the plan that should be followed the world over. We have one difficulty to encounter and that is that our sister missions do not see eye to eye with us in this matter, and it is no easy work to carry out such a system with other missions right alongside of you working along other lines and following the very opposite policy.[42]

Nor did Underwood apply the principle to church-building only. Although he did not hesitate to share such valuable commodities as Western medicines and Western knowledge freely wherever needed—during his honeymoon trip alone to northern regions of Korea he and Lillias saw and cared for some six hundred patients—he understood that for the mission programs and services to succeed in the long run they could not be made to continually depend on the largesse of mission offices in America to keep them going. While he never sought to make money for the mission from the sales of quinine, agricultural implements, or his tracts and the weekly *Christian News*—despite the potential short-term gain for the mission from such income—he did constantly seek out ways to recoup the cost of their purchase, transport, and distribution to make the programs

---

42. Letter to Thomas, August 1, 1898; see p. 187 in this volume. See also chapter 1, p. 15 and n27.

a *self-sustaining* part of the mission, frequently discussing the process in detail with Thomas and others.[43]

One might call this the spirit of the entrepreneurial Christian, one who understands the strengths and weaknesses of both modern commercial economy and the assumptions of human character underlying it enough to intelligently work the system without falling victim to motivations of self-interest or catering to the self-interest of others. Underwood moreover understood that establishing the mindset and infrastructure needed for these principles and processes to saturate deeply into a society took time as well as patient, unwavering guidance. What set him apart from many fellow missionaries in this regard was that he did not fight for quick justice, solutions handed on a plate, or independence in name only. From the many occasions when Underwood took the long-term work of building up of cultural and social *infrastructure* to be as important and in keeping with the more short-term efforts directed at staving off immediate threats from foreign powers or gaining immediate benefits of church growth, we may read in them an implicit third principle of "right" in which he differentiated between rightness to be practiced by individual persons and those to be wrought by God through the workings of history in the long term. He exemplified the kind of faith in which one lets God unfold history as *He* wills, thereby *freeing* the human creatures including himself to simply do what is right at any given moment rather than compromising that right in the name of some "greater" good of one's own discretion.

This to Underwood seems to have been no small privilege of Christian faith in the confusing, fast changing contexts of Korea in which old and new values, worldviews, and ways of life all clashed against one another and with his own. In a sense it was his answer to the "constant remarks that we hear on all sides" of "No one to lean on, no one to rely upon, no one to trust in."[44] Though he enjoyed the trust and friendship of the King and Queen—indeed he came to be regarded as a figure of some necessity and security to them both—he did not abuse the fundamental humanity of the relationship or his privileged position by trying to parlay it into benefits for the mission much less his own person. Despite their many confidential conversations, for example, he professed to Thomas he still found it "very difficult" to find a way to broach the subject of Christian faith during such meetings. This was most clearly not for lack of will on his part. Underwood was only too aware of the "tremendous good" a Christian ruler could wield for Korea; it had been a large part of his reason for trying to get the Prince

43. See, for example, the letter to Thomas, August 1, 1898.
44. Letter to Thomas, June 12, 1896.

"to America and to putting him under Christian influences."[45] But for all the potential gain to be had by prodding the King toward becoming Christian, to persuade him to conversion by enticements of its benefits political or otherwise, or to make "giving ear to Jesus talk" a condition of their friendship, would have been to do a grave disservice to the mind and dignity of the King, to the basic humanity of their friendship, and most of all disservice to the power of the Holy Spirit to render the change of heart when and how God willed his history.

By the same token, although Underwood counted himself personally beholden to the King and Queen for their generosity, friendship, and trust, and in turn did not fear to stand guard to protect them from the potential violence of " pro-Japaners," the being beholden did not extend to trying to influence political affairs beyond his position as a foreigner and a missionary despite the King's frequent requests for his advice. Early on when Korean law forbid foreigners from engaging in proselytizing, Underwood abided with the law and did not try to "talk Christ" even during his many medical missions unless specifically asked by individual patients of their own volition. When asked by the American Legate to promise not to proselytize or to baptize anyone during his trip to northern Korea in 1889, instead of complying or refusing outright he redefined the meaning of "proselytizing" to something he could work with, then crossed the border into Manchuria to give baptism to those who had long been preparing for the sacrament at risk to their lives.[46] Similarly, when he criticized certain missionaries in Korea and Japan such as Allen, Loomis, and Gale on various occasions he did not necessarily question their Christian motivations as much as their overstepping their proper boundaries as human beings in the name of Christian greater good. With his *Christian News* as well he sought to establish basis for absolute trust: "Its general news, its firm stand for truth and justice regardless of position and party, its [firm] and practical scientific notes all are tending to make it a necessity to all parties Christian and non-Christian, and thus a weekly tract goes into hundreds of heathen homes and already in several cases direct conversion has been the result while not a few have been led to say that they did not know there was so much good in Christianity."[47] The reward of such trust was to be able to write Thomas how the King asked him on a visit to the Palace "whether I was going on a 'preaching trip.' To us such remarks from the King of Korea

45. Letter to Thomas, August 1, 1898.

46. See his letter to Ellinwood of the Presbyterian Mission Board, May 26, 1889, in In Soo Kim, *Rev. Underwood's Missionary Letters*, 762.

47. Letter to Thomas, August 23, 1897.

before his officials has no small meaning. A few years ago the fact that we are missionaries was only mentioned under one's breath."[48]

It is with above points in mind that we should read Underwood's following dispassionate comment written as late as June 17, 1898:

> I think that it must be acknowledged by all that the best government that Korea has ever had [in recent years] was when the Japanese were in power. The Japanese were Orientals and knew how to manage these people better than anyone else that has ever tried it. They knew well what this people needed and where they were lacking and it was with this knowledge that they set to work. They were far from perfect and made some awful blunders, but as far as the people of this land were concerned they did attempt to see that Justice was meted out to the poor people and the laborer was assured of the result of his labor. Today the country is without law of any kind and "might makes right" all over the land. What the end will be no one can at all see but I feel sure that as they are at present things cannot go on and either another power must step in or the people will arise and there will be a period of riot and anarchy in this land. It is a little ominous when way off in the interior you find people discussing the French Revolution and saying that that is the only hope for the country.[49]

It cannot have been that Underwood supported the Japanese or any other people's annexation of Korea in principle. But what the above paragraph shows is his primary concern for building up an infrastructure for justice and for civil order as the basic first step in the right direction. If that could only be gotten more effectively through temporary rule by another people, Underwood seems to have had sufficient faith in the long view of history— as given in the bible, for example—to think it was a viable even if not the desired means to an end.[50] Too, there was the solace and assurance of a better future—a truly independent, enlightened future in his mind—to be had

48. Letter to Thomas, June 12, 1896.

49. Letter to Thomas, June 17, 1898.

50. Underwood was of course a foreigner from a powerful country, to a great extent able to count on the basic protection of his person and rights despite the very real dangers of illness, exhaustion, accidents, ignorance, and even the occasional fear and malevolence he voluntarily risked as a missionary. This fact cannot and should not be discounted in understanding his operative mode. However, neither can that express the whole or even the main of his fundamental identity. During his final illness he famously wished to be buried in Korea—this despite the fact that "Korea" had formally become an annex to Japan six years earlier on August 22, 1910. His wish was granted only in 1999. See chapter 1, pp. 17–18.

from the enormous headway being made by and for the gospel throughout these difficult, unsettling times. And so it was that in a single long letter written on August 1, 1898, Underwood could on the one hand complain,

> Everything is so childish and the Koreans from the highest down are just like so many babies. It reminds me of when we as children would be playing and something was done that we did not like we would say "I won't play any more if you don't play my way." It will be a long, long while before Korea can govern herself aright and how I wish that she should ask help of old England.[51]

And on the other hand he could exult, "Work goes on well and if the politics do not interfere the next few years will see some wondrous changes in this heathen land."[52] In a letter to Dr. Elliwood of the Presbyterian Mission Board dated only a few days later he similarly wrote, "You will hear good reports from all parts of the field & in fact in Korea at this time the only thing that all looks bright is Mission work."[53] Indeed, Underwood attributed much of the growth *to* the difficulty of the times. The period between 1894 and 1898 was among the busiest in Underwood's ministry in terms of what was getting accomplished, and despite concerns about the political crises or the Prince's visit to America the bulk of his letters describe his missional activities and his enthusiasm and well-founded hope about the gospel's progress among the Korean people. Underwood wrote repeatedly to Ellinwood of the Presbyterian Mission Board during this period, literally begging again and again for more workers to be sent to Korea because "the field is so ripe for harvest," comparing it much more favorably to both China and Japan.

Witnessing Neo-Confucian Rightness at Work, and the Maturing of the Vision

Then in early November of 1898, Underwood witnessed an event that over time would fundamentally change his understanding of the workings of justice and civil order among the Korean people—and with it, I would argue, his approach to the mission in Korea as well. In a letter begun on November 8, 1898, Underwood described the progress of events:

> The last few days we have been on the very verge of a popular uprising. The people are waking up to the fact that they have

51. Letter to Thomas, August 1, 1898.

52. Letter to Thomas, August 1, 1898.

53. Letter to Ellinwood, August 5, 1898, in In Soo Kim, *Rev. Underwood's Missionary Letters*, 912.

some rights and in a dignified way they are insisting upon them. The King has yielded to them, but some of his advisors thought best to try and stop what was going on absolutely, and got the order for the arrest of 19 of the peoples [sic] leaders. They were arrested one night, [and] when it was learned the next morning some 30 thousand people gathered on the street and big square and in a dignified way sent in a request that as the leaders of the people had been arrested and the leaders had only done what the people had asked, they too might all be arrested. For some four or five days this crowd with bonfires etc. have continued night and day waiting to be arrested. They in a quiet way simply say that if they have done wrong they are ready to die and there they stay. The leading stores and merchants have all stopped business and closed their doors on the plea that if they have no rights they might as well die of starvation as oppression. They have in the main been quiet and orderly. The only thing that they have done that might be said to be wrong was that when a company of soldiers was sent to disperse them and the order was given to prepare to fire they rushed up and disarmed the soldiers but nothing more, and then gave them back their arms and let them go. There they still are camped, and there they say they will wait and die if they do not get justice. I tell you the fact that we see these people are getting a little backbone is most encouraging and as we see this we feel that there is some hope for this country after all if only the outside countries will keep hands off and let them work it out for themselves. They have waked up to the fact that they have some rights and that if they can only stick together they have no little power.[54]

This was not the first time Underwood had observed a popular demonstration by the Korean people. He would have seen the demonstrations against Japanese domination of Korea during the course of the Sino-Japanese War, for example. But he had easily attributed that to sentiments of nationalism or a kind of instinctive defense against potential infiltrators from outside more than reasoned outrage against injustice itself. This time around, however, when he saw the thirty thousand demonstrate peacefully against a wrongful action by their own monarch, he had to recognize and understand the situation differently. As discussed in chapter 2, what he witnessed on the occasion was a deeply embedded essence of Korea's Neo-Confucian culture—what in fact may be understood as an important precursor to the civil disobedience of Gandhi and Martin Luther King Jr. What characterized that act of civil disobedience was its absolute and spontaneous commitment to civility

54. Letter, November 8, 1898. See also chapter 2, pp. 77–80.

almost to the point of "impartiality"—a concept highly significant in Neo-Confucian thought.[55] As a word it denotes a sense of public-mindedness or commonality, and in fact the word was used as a contrasting term to "private" as in "private gain." According to "On Understanding the Nature of Humanity" by the great Sung Neo-Confucian scholar Cheng Hao (1032–85), one of the most celebrated essays in all Chinese of literature,

> Essentially speaking, the way of humanity may be expressed in one word, namely, impartiality. However, impartiality is but the principle of humanity [i.e., of humaneness 仁]; it should not be equated with humanity itself. When a person puts impartiality into practice, that is humaneness. Because of impartiality, one can accommodate both others and oneself.[56]

Rightness and impartiality, then, may be described in *pedagogical* terms as above to facilitate understanding and recognition, but they cannot be defined or bounded in analytical terms because in doing so we would necessarily lose sight of their *fundamentally dynamic* nature (much like the workings of the Holy Spirit). It is perhaps with that context in mind that we can better understand Underwood's venting in frustration to Thomas only a few months earlier, "The land is without law of any kind and 'might makes right' all over the land . . . either another power must step in or the people will arise and there will be a period of riot & anarchy."[57] That might well be so, until—as Underwood witnessed for himself that November—the ethos of rightness dependent on the deeply within reverence for "Hananim" comes to the fore, to place whatever matter at hand beyond questions of external proprieties as codified in terms of rites, legalities, or even natural rights. He witnessed the spontaneous, entirely non-violent coming together of 30,000 people in readiness and even willingness to be imprisoned and possibly put to death—neither willing to compromise what they believe is right nor willing to hurt others for the sake of demanding that right. Without negating the real differences in orientation between Confucianism and Christianity, this widespread ethos of this rightness may have been a key—if as yet unrecognized—factor in what Underwood called the extraordinary fertility of Korea for Christianity. Later, in his *Religions of Eastern Asia*, Underwood would intimate this simply in terms of how "in the Korean concept of Hananim there is even less anthropomorphism than is seen in the Jewish ideas of Jehovah":

55. For my discussion of Neo-Confucian "rightness," see chapter 2, pp. 76–81.

56. *Er Cheng yishu* 15:8b, in De Bary and Bloom, *Sources of Chinese Tradition*, 1:695.

57. Letter, June 17, 1898.

Even the conception of their lesser deities is far superior to that of the other nations of Asia or of Greece and Rome; and we believe that this is largely due to the fact that they have been able to conserve so much of their ancient henotheism, and have held their ideal of God in so lofty a plane, that even I their backsliding polytheism they have not yet reached the point where, like other lands, they have altogether lost their first childlike reverence, and degraded Him to the level, or below it, of themselves . . . the high ideal of Hananim has much modified what would otherwise have been a doubly degrading influence of Korea's polytheism; and while the level is not higher than might be expected under the circumstances, we find that the Korean in the high ideal of his Supreme God, which has been, shall we say, providentially conserved for him, has had an anchor which has kept him from drifting still farther, and it is probably to a great extent due to the strong hold which this ancient faith still has upon him that he accepts Christianity with such phenomenal readiness.[58]

What Underwood discovered, in essence, was that above and beyond any established doctrines or teachings of Confucianism, Buddhism, Daoism, or any other ism including shamanism, the Korean people continually referred and reverted back to the idea of "heaven" or "hanŭl" as the final resort. Underwood's gradual understanding of this "hanŭl" as the source and hope of rightness, as witnessed in the "sacrificially peaceful" appeal for justice by the gathering of over thirty thousand people, led—among other things—to his finally assenting to the term "hanŭnim/hananim" (i.e., hanŭl-nim, where "nim" is an indicator of both reverence and intimacy) as a legitimate and even preferred name for "God" to "Chŏnju" (from Chinese "T'ienchu" or "Lord of Heaven" coined by Matteo Ricci). In hanŭl and hanŭnim Underwood had in effect discovered the "*basso ostinato*" or recurring bass line of Korea. An important point of note here, however, is that just as "impartiality" in Neo-Confucian thought is only the principle of humaneness which remains a meaningless abstraction until put into practice as humaneness, there is very little "doctrine" regarding Hananim in Korea except in the recognition and practice of rightness. It was not necessarily "childlike" reverence but the deep-seated understanding that rightness in Hananim, especially as mediated by Neo-Confucianism, is at least *ultimately* not a matter of "negotiation" via such means as building temples, sacrificing to images, engaging in rituals, etc.[59] Indeed, in seeking after rightness one's ac-

58. Underwood, *The Religions of Eastern Asia*, 132.

59. Indeed it is possible to understand the absence of such ready means of

tions are not necessarily or even usually organized in terms of affecting the most immediate practical, effective, or efficient change toward the desired end. The actualization of change itself is entrusted to Hananim; the focus of rightness is in the longing to somehow be a person who manifests even a little of the Heaven-endowed dignity of human moral "nature," and the existential gratitude that engenders in one's deepest being.

In his "Outline History of the Korea Mission of the Presbyterian Church in U.S.A.," written at the request of the Presbyterian Board and included as part of his letter to them dated July 1899 (i.e., some eight months after his witnessing of the thirty thousand civil demonstrators, and six months after the last of the letters included in this collection), Underwood writes almost nothing of Korean spirituality; it is quite literally an account of the works undertaken by the mission described in very factual terms. He also famously held out against use of the term "Hananim" for "God" until as late as 1904. In short, it was not a case where witnessing the peaceful demonstration by the thirty thousand Koreans led to immediate, radical, and systematic change in his understanding of Korean spirituality or of missiology. The "discovery" of the inner workings of an Other was not so simple—precisely because for Underwood it entailed more than mere knowledge to be used, however much for the "benefit" of the mission, but rather the discovery of broadening himself. It is one thing to note, as other missionaries did, the ready availability of "Hananim" as a term allowable for natives use for "God"; it is a very different matter for a missionary to find the way to an understanding whereby *he himself* can *equally* relate to Hananim *as* God in the full re-cognition of who God/Hananim is, which is interculturation. By the time Underwood gave his lecture at New York University in 1910 his maturation in this process is much more clearly evident.

Conclusion

The synergy between Korea's underlying ethos of rightness and Underwood's long-term vision for a Christian Korea led to the explosive expansion of Christianity in Korea as in no other modern mission history.

---

negotiation as giving rise to the widespread experience of "*han*" 恨 both individually and culturally in Korea. Rachel Chung has described it as the gamut of feelings sensitized to long-held desire of ideals in face of the continual postponement of their gratification, and especially as "grief of a finite being holding itself together under the demands of an infinite universe" and "a profoundly Neo-Confucian spirituality" centered on the "experience of suffering through sacrifice and humaneness to the very end, to come out its 'other side.'" See Chung, "The Song of the Faithful Wife Ch'unhyang," 365–66. See also Andrew S. Park, *The Wounded Heart of God*, esp. 15–17, 20–21.

This, however, is not to argue that it was the only or even necessarily the most ideal of synergistic combinations with the gospel. Every civilization, country, culture, possibly even every individual may each have their own different and distinct cultural, spiritual, and/or psychological "*basso ostinato*," which the mission and missionary must be sensitized to hear. As a musical term "*basso ostinato*" refers to a short recurring melodic pattern in the bass line—literally meaning "obstinate bass" in Italian—such that it not only forms an underlying repetitive motif of its own, independent of the more obvious melodic lines at top, but by continuing to function at the same time as the harmonic outline necessarily modifies or conditions everything happening above it in the music to its terms.[60] In the 1970s the Japanese political scientist and theorist Masao Maruyama (1914–96) used the term to describe the phenomenon in Japanese political history where, despite its "topnotes" such as Confucianism, Daoism, Buddhism, and including modern ideologies such as liberalism, constitutionalism, anarchism, socialism having been imported from abroad since ancient times, each of these ideologies underwent a subtle but notable modification after arriving in Japan. He noted a distinct and recurring similarity of pattern in the nature of these modifications each time, and it was this repeating pattern or hidden undertow he likened to *basso ostinato*.[61]

My purpose in referencing Maruyama's apropos use of the musical term is threefold. First, by borrowing his articulate analysis from a discipline outside of missiology I wished to reinforce, as an issue, how far beneath what we usually consider the culture or character of a civilization its more meaningful, *conditioning* character may be buried. For missiology this ought to impart some sense of the enormous challenges and responsibilities required of missionaries in terms of the training, effort, and sympathy needed to begin to "understand" another's culture, be it that of a person, community, or civilization. It could not have been an easy or immediately obvious matter for Underwood to see that a strong, shared consciousness of rightness ran beneath the chaos of political factionalism, social upheaval, abject poverty, general ignorance about the world, and many superstitious beliefs.

Secondly, without attempting to establish a parallel *basso ostinato* running through the whole of Korea's history, or conversely to present a history of Christian missions in Japan, I thought the essay a useful reminder of the variety and distinctness of cultural dynamics regardless sometimes of their

60. This is in contrast to the more musically common "*basso continuo*" in which the bass simply supplies whatever harmony the melody above it requires.

61. In brief, Maruyama identified "the separation of the level of legitimacy from the level of actual political power" to be the recurring "Japanizing" element in Japan's political or governmental history. See Maruyama, "The Structure of *Matsurigoto*," 27–43.

geographical proximity. This not only speaks to the issue of the gospel itself speaking to different needs among different peoples to become meaningful, but also of the constant element of surprise and discovery toward mutual if subtle "calibration." Underwood's evangelism in Korea was not so much as an actor or a reactor, but as part of a mutual and ongoing "interculturation" process in which both parties deepened their understanding of the gospel's power *in relation to and through* one another. If we take Maruyama's analysis of Japanese dynamics at face value it will not be difficult for the thoughtful reader to imagine Underwood's missional approach being received differently in Japan, for example, than in Korea, thereby subtly shaping in turn Underwood's subsequent thoughts and actions, and so on back and forth.

Finally, as important as it will be to learn to recognize, understand, and to work with the *basso ostinato* underlying each mission context, what needs equal emphasis is that, what allowed Underwood to hear the underlying *basso ostinato* of Koreans in spite the din of Western and Japanese imperialisms in the late nineteenth and early twentieth centuries was the purity of his long-term vision for a Christian Korea. A long-term vision—the kind that places its hope on what will happen long after one's death and not in expectation of any "fruits" to oneself or anything attached to oneself in the process is fundamentally humble, selfless, and antithetical to all that is imperial. It points to trusting God to have a plan for the people—in this case the people of Korea—independent of what the missionary's own wishes, beliefs, sensibilities, thoughts, and/or interests might be. Clearly, learning to distinguish between the two is an essential aspect of interculturation. Inter-denominational cooperation and coordination such as we saw in Underwood and Alexander Waugh is therefore also integral to and an extension of this non-assertion of self in mission work. Long-term vision implies trusting the people to have *within themselves* and in the arc of their history those qualities leading to how God envisions them to be, thereby understanding the missionary's own role in that relationship to be no more than that of a midwife, rather than of a mother giving birth to a continuation of her DNA albeit also an independent being. The constant identification with the limited role of midwife may be the foundation of the genuine *civility* we find in a missionary like Underwood.

If in outward terms one sees few features that separate Underwood's mission activities from those of his predecessors and contemporaries, the inner dynamics of his work as described above nevertheless distinguish his achievements and set him apart as a model for missions and missiology in the twenty-first century. Like those before him, he studied the local language and culture, shared as much medical and other scientific knowledge as he could, expounded the gospel, translated the bible and printed hymnals; founded churches, schools, orphanages and Christian societies; and trained natives for the ministry. To the extent that he could, and felt to be legitimate, he engaged in Korea's politics. He even emulated principles laid out by another, in his case those of John L. Nevius. All of these activities had been by and large basic to the work of missionaries throughout the nineteenth and twentieth centuries. But by the light of his long-term vision and its corollary of inter-denominational cooperation, they were made to mean something extraordinary and different.

Yonsei University offers a good illustration of this point. At first glance Underwood's founding of Yonsei might seem to conform to numerous other mission endeavors across the world to build schools and offer education as part of the "progress" represented by the Christian gospel. But an important point of departure with Yonsei was that Underwood specified it to be an institution for advanced secular learning as well as seminary education—one, moreover, where the secular program focused not on training technical workers but rather on providing highest levels of learning in entrepreneurship itself. Underlying the vision was Underwood's recognition that people of faith must also function in the world as it is, i.e., not merely as its docile employees but as its leaders and fully developed human beings with visions and ideas of their own to contribute to the world community of the future—this in 1915 if not earlier in terms of his planning. In singling out business and entrepreneurship as subject of advanced education Underwood was in important ways also addressing Chosŏn Korea's long-held culture of contempt toward the merchant class for its "profit-mindedness." Of the traditional four classes in Neo-Confucian Korea—*yangban* (comprised of civil and military gentry), farmers, artisans, and merchants—*sang'in* or those engaged in trade and commercial ventures were held in such low regard that the word "*sang-nom*" was a commonly used pejorative to refer to those ignorant of ritual propriety or lacking in proper human feeling. Adhering to Mencian warning against profit-mindedness as ultimately bringing about the downfall of states, Chosŏn government had long repressed commercialism on principle and by policy.[62] Over time, however, this had the effect of merely driving commercial-mindedness underground where it carried out its activities hidden from view and increasingly divorced from any sense of public or social responsibility. In bringing profit-mindedness out of the shadows into the light, redefining it in terms of modern entrepreneurial leadership, and involving it in the shared responsibility of building Korea's modern infrastructure, Underwood was extending the capacity for

62. Mencius opens his eponymous book with a sharp criticism of and warning against profit-mindedness. It has been understood as functioning as a "thesis" for the rest of the work.

Neo-Confucian ethos of rightness to a class that had long been disenfranchised from such self-respect.

As a missionary Underwood saw his job as not only planting an enclave of Christians in Korea holding themselves somehow set apart from the rest of Korea, but as paving the way for the highest and best Christian Korea, supported also by Korea's *basso ostinato* of Neo-Confucian ethos of rightness. Significantly, the first president of Yonsei was Oliver R. Avison (1859–1956), the Canadian Methodist medical missionary whom Underwood had recruited in 1892 to take charge of Korea's medical mission and of whom Lillias Underwood described as "from the first, Mr. Underwood's most sympathetic and efficient co-worker and adviser, who stood at his side in every difficulty and shared his cares and toils through twenty-three years of service. . . . I do not think a life of Mr. Underwood could be written with either his brother John [Thomas] Underwood, or Dr. Avison left out."[63]

This leads to what is in my view one of the most important principles of "interculturation" as I define it—that of the mutuality of transformation and enlargement beyond the immediate actors at hand, to the more homebound Senders of missionaries. It was not in the general purview of late nineteenth century mindset to ask in what ways Westerners could or should be changed by their encounters with the East, nor for those in the East to seek to change the West. But for those actually open to learning not only "about" the East but to the kind of learning Confucius talked about where one begins to "embody" and be transformed in one's own ideas and thinking by what one observes, the opportunity was and continues to be there. We are not privy at this time to the many letters Underwood's family must have sent back to him over the more than thirty years of continuous exchange. Even so, we are able to get a sense of the changes in his family back in the United States through their involvement and investment in the mission. At the very least their view and knowledge of what must have been a previously unknown country was vastly expanded. But much more than that, they became involved in appealing to the American government for more support and awareness of the plight in Korea, in becoming the proactive hosts and protectors to various visitors, students and political "refugees" from Korea, and as primary "investors" in Korea's future by funding missionaries beyond their brother and seeing unconditionally to the completion of Yonsei University even after his death. In that sense, Underwood's mission represented the transformation not only of the one physically sent to Korea, but equally importantly of the Senders back home who supported him throughout the endeavor (to what extent the Presbyterian

63. Lillias Underwood, *Underwood of Korea*, 114.

Mission Board that officially commissioned him was willing and/or able to be, themselves, transformed by him is beyond the scope of this book). Unlike Roland Allan (1868–1947), whom Lesslie Newbigin praises for never staying more than a few months or at most a couple of years in any one field of mission in an effort to not impose "his" way of faith,[64] the descendents of Underwood "became" Korean, either spending their lives in or maintaining close ties with Korea over the course of five generations.

Through this analysis of Underwood's letters I hope to have opened the door to many more studies in which interculturation—understood as the mutuality of meaningful transformation and regeneration—is made a new and central standard for the evaluation of missions and missiology both past and present. Without brushing aside the overwhelmingly imperial historical context to which Underwood had been born and under which he necessarily fashioned his mission, these personal letters to family show his richer, more frank, and nuanced attitudes toward all that was happening in Korea, while also providing insights into how he might respond to some of contemporary missiology's most urgent questions. The issue of separating the gospel from its historical encasing in Western cultural and political imperialism, for example, is one with potentially huge ramifications in multiple fields from theology and history to sociology and pastoral psychology, to name just a few. But if anything, what I hope to have shown through Underwood's example is that the issue is not always best served—much less resolved—by engaging in yet more analyses of the various insidious ways in which imperialism still operates at large.

Would it be possible instead, as Underwood's family and social education had done, for pedagogy to focus on teaching/learning to recognize the seeds of "imperialistic" desires within each and all of us as part of the human condition, to thereby learn also to limit and restrain it within oneself?

Would it be possible to orient our motivation in the classrooms less toward knowledge of *what* the various Christian denominations believe in terms of their commonalities and differences, and more toward understanding the *patterns* by which human associations and institutions tend to come together, develop, and break apart? In that way, instead of being invested in any one of them as an absolute value, or conversely conceiving of global Christianity merely in terms of more or less passive pluralism, could we not be empowered to continually and dynamically engage in the mutuality of interculturation across shifting and multiple boundaries?

---

64. Newbigin, *Gospel in a Plural Society*, 146–47.

Could pedagogy be reconceived to help Christians understand world history less as a history of "the Church" in the world and more as a history of Christians working toward a Christian world, as Underwood had done?

My main purpose in writing this book has been simply to introduce the Underwood letters that follow by way of providing some historical and personal context. To do so, it was found necessary to show Underwood to be a particular product of his disposition and time, shaped by his family, social, and institutional education, but in important ways also by what he learned through Neo-Confucian Korea. If in undertaking this project I have also succeeded in small measure at pointing to the centrality of pedagogy in determining the future of missiology and therefore also of Global Christianity I am grateful to Underwood for providing the inspiration and the opportunity.

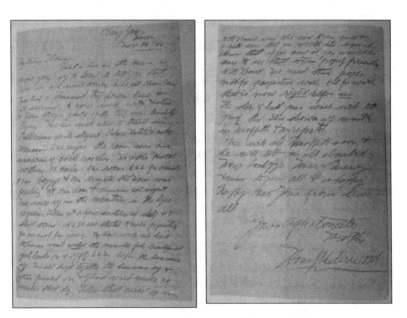

Underwood's first letter, written to Helen, en route on the train, Dec. 22, 1884

Letter to Thomas of Nov. 1896 (sample of Underwood's handwriting)

[New Series No.6.]

I said in my letter No. 5 nothing of any serious nature came up.

About the paper they seem to be more at ease and I think that things will go along better now. About all the other affairs they are now straightened out and all will go well and I have arranged to turn all the Quinine business over to/others and this has been done in such a way as to continue the work that was going on as a result of it and at the same time to relieve me of all work and responsibility about the matter.

THE PRINCE has never come to Korea yet and I do not know when he will. From a political point of view all out here is very much mixed . The last few days we have been on the very verge of a popular uprising. The people are waking up to the fact that they have some rights and in a dignified way they are insisting upon them .

The king had yielded to them but some of his advisers thought best to try and stop what was going on absolutely and got the order for the arrest of 19 of the peoples leaders. They were arrested one night and when it was learned the next morning some 30 thousand people gathered on the street and big square and in a dignified way sent in a request that as the leaders of the people had been arrested and the leaders had only done what the people had asked, they too might all be arrested. For some four or five days this crowd with bonfires etc have continued night and day waiting to be arrested. They in a quiet way simply say that if they have done wrong they are ready to die and there they stay. The leading stores and merchants have all

Letter to Thomas of Nov. 8, 1898

Chapter 4

The Early Letters of Underwood from Korea, 1884–1898

Brief Notes about the Letters in This Collection

THE LETTERS INCLUDED WITH this book are private letters by Horace G. Underwood that have been in the possession of the Underwood Family, never before published or even known about, until 2013 when they were gifted by the Family to Underwood's alma mater, New Brunswick Theological Seminary. The collection is comprised of twenty-four letters in total, of which twenty-two are written by Underwood between the years 1884 and 1898 to members of his family, beginning with the one dated December 22, 1884, while on train to San Francisco to take the ship that would take him to Chosŏn Korea. Of the remaining two letters, one is written by Lillias Horton Underwood to her sister, Hannah Horton (Letter 11); the other, last in the collection, is from 1974, making mention of the manuscript about Lillias Underwood by another sister, Leonora Horton Egan.

Thirteen of the letters were handwritten (4–7, 9–10, 12–17, and 22) while the remaining eleven were typed—presumably on an Underwood typewriter. Sample facsimiles of each type are provided.

> Letter 1: December 22, 1884, to Helen Underwood, while on train to San Francisco
>
> Letter 2: February 6, 1887, to Fred Underwood, from Seoul
>
> Letter 3: July 25, 1887, to Fred Underwood, from Seoul
>
> Letter 4: October 11, 1887, to Fred Underwood, from Seoul
>
> Letter 5: Undated, late November or early December, 1887, to Fred Underwood, from Seoul
>
> Letter 6: February 27, 1888, to Fred Underwood, from Seoul

Letter 7: April 29 through May 2, 1888, to Fred Underwood, from Anak in Hwang-hae-do, Hwangju, and Pyongyang

Letter 8: May 29, 1890, to Thomas Underwood, from Seoul

Letter 9: January 11, 1895, to Thomas Underwood, from Seoul

Letter 10: August 2, 1895, to Thomas Underwood, from Han River

Letter 11: November 29, 1895, from Lillias Horton Underwood to her sister Hannah, from Seoul

Letter 12: February 20, 1896, to Thomas Underwood, from Seoul

Letter 13: May 29, 1896, to Thomas Underwood, from Cheefoo, China

Letter 14: June 12 and June 17, 1896, to Thomas Underwood, from Cheefoo, China, and Seoul respectively

Letter 15: November 14, 1896, to Thomas Underwood, from Chang-yun, Korea

Letter 16: August 21, 23, and 28, 1897, to Thomas Underwood, from Han River

Letter 17: October 26, 1897, to Thomas Underwood, from Cheefoo, China

Letter 18: June 17, 1898, to Thomas Underwood, from Seoul

Letter 19: June 20, 1898, to Thomas Underwood, from Seoul

Letter 20: August 1, 1898, to Thomas Underwood, from Seoul

Letter 21: November 8, 1898, to Thomas Underwood, from Seoul

Letter 22: December 5, 1898, to Thomas Underwood, from Haijin, Korea

Letter 23: December 28, 1898, to Thomas Underwood, from Seoul

Letter 24: July 13, 1974, from John Thomas Underwood to Philip Egan, from Centerport, Cape Cod, U.S.

The Letters

Letter 1

ON TRAIN. Dec. 22nd 1884

Dearest Helen,-

Thomas left me only a little while ago and I thought I would start a letter to you expecting of course two or three from you for this one. It has turned out very nicely, as doubtless [you] have already heard, that the party of Japanese officers who were to have been on the ocean with me are on the same train and in the same car going to San Francisco with me.

I shall leave them at Ogden while I go to Salt Lake City but I shall meet them again when I get on the Steamer at the end of America. One of them is Mr. YOKOYAMA'S (whom as you will remember, I met in England) partner, but I have not seen him yet as he is a little indisposed and has been in bed all day. The interpreter is a Swiss and a very nice fellow, he has travelled almost all over the world and is therefore quite a good talker. Just at this moment the Minister of War, who is a thick set broad shouldered fellow though rather short for his breadth is taking his after dinner siesta (If a broken and disturbed sleep in a Pullman car can be dignified by such a title) & a party of seven others are hard at work? [sic] over a game of cards[. T]hey seem to enjoy them very much and I am told by their interpreter that no matter how much they get beaten they never lose their temper and it does certainly seem as if those who are beaten enjoy their defeat as much as their opponents.

They do their counting by means of little shells and keep on playing as if wound up to go forever; the interpreter is try[ing] to while away the hours by diving into the pages of a novel and here and there as I glance down the car I can see the head, the top of the book, the toes of two feet, the tassel of a cap, or the fingers and elbow of some arm which warn me that there are more in the car than those I see and remind me of "Roses born to blush unseen;" and now and then a not far off rumbling (shall I call it a music or a discord) reminds me that the Japanese have a "hymnology" distinctively their own.

As I look outside I see that we are going over a section of country that is remarkable not for its mountains, not for its plaines [sic], for neither its beauty, nor its homeliness; for neither its literati, nor its poets; (we just passed the stations Hawthorne & Emerson) but is remarkable for its entire lack of anything that is remarkable. Now I suppose you will say "why is it that Horace can't write a decent letter? He might know that I wouldn't care for such stuff as that."

Well the truth is Helen I can't and never could. Now you need not take pity upon my weakness and say you do like this letter for I sha'nt believe you if you do.

Now I must stop my nonsense and get to business which just >now< chances to be the closing & signing of this letter of which you I am sure you will be very >glad< & wish I had done it long ago. Love, kisses, & a merry Christmas to ALL with Lion's share for yourself.

YOUR LOVING BROTHER
HORACE GRANT UNDERWOOD

Letter 2

Seoul, Korea. Feb 6th. 1887

My Dear Fred;-

I want to sit down and send you a few words about Korea and the things out here. I had intended to write you a long letter by the last mail but I was unable to do this and it has already been some time since that mail left and it will probably be still some time before she does leave.

When she does leave I shall leave with her as the mission have voted me permission to go to Japan and I am going to avail my self [sic] of that permission at once. I have been feeling a little worn out of late but now that it is decided that I take a run to Japan the very thought has straightened me out. I do not realy [sic] need the changes but then I have thus far been sick every summer that I have been here and I think that by going now and taking a rest I shall be able to ward off this difficulty this summer. Then it is settled that I go to Japan and the very next steamer, the one that will take this letter[,] will take me to Japan. There I will see Oltmans and Demarest whom I knew in New Brunswick and spending about a week there will at once push on to Yokohama. I am going to try and look into the school work and I think that now that I have had a little experience myself I shall be able to look up the matter much more thoroughly than when I passed through Japan on my way here. I am also going to try and take a copy of the gospel of Mark to have it printed there and will then try and find out about the cost of printing a phrase book [i]n Korean. I shall spend most of my time in Yokohama and am looking forward to my visit with Dr. and

Mrs. Hepburn as much as to anything else. They are a fine old couple and it does one good in every way to see them.

I suppose you have seen from the letters to the girls that I have been having a very good time out here and that while I have a good deal of work to do it is not all work and no play at all. We have as I have told them a good deal of society here and it is of the best a fact which you can see from the list of those who were at my dinner.

I was giving to the girls a sort of diary of what I have been doing and I will take it up just where I left off with them. I suppose that you will be surprised to hear that I have commenced to learn to skate. I have not been doing remarkably well at it and have been the source of amusement an[d] but [sic] of ridicule at more than one of the skating parties.

Mr. Hunt of the customs has had a rink made in his grounds and it is open to any one [sic] any day that there is skating.

During the week between Christmass [sic] and New Years we had a good deal of skating there and things were quite lively.

Through Miss Ellers we had an invitation to the Palace to skate on their pond which is very large. A good sized part[y] went and we had a very good time till the snow came and stopped us. When we stopped we went to a reception room where there were cigars and cigarettes for all who wanted and in a little while Min Pansa, one of the highest men in the kingdom[,] asked me to announce that Supper was ready. We then adjourned to another room where we found a table laden with delicacies.

It was a foreign dinner and there was nothing Korean on the table. During the meal the King and Queen were in an adjoining room separated only by paper doors and they continually spoke through the doors to Min Pansa giving him messages to the company[,] which messages he then asked me to translate into English. We had a very pleasant time but the journey home

(2)

was not at all what we could have wished as the snow was coming down very fast and it had already become quite deep and neither my horse nor chair had been sent for me. This I found out afterwards was owning[1] to the fact that my servants did not expect us to start for home till quite late instead of which we started quite early. Each of us had an escort of two soldiers to see that we got home safely.

---

1. This may be an error for "owing," however, according to the Oxford English Dictionary, usage of "owning" to mean "attributing (a thing) to some source," is rare, but legitimate (s.v. "own" usage 3.d.). This may be a usage Underwood was familiar with.

I have not been doing very much in the skating line since this night but only the day before yesterday we had a sort of petty ice carnival and there was skating by moonlight on the rink which was also lit up by lanterns and there were fires to keep the feet warm and then there was chocalate [*sic*] and tea to help keep the inner man warm. It made a very pretty sight and there were a good many there. I look my little boy round and he had a very nice time. All the foreigners here make so much of him and he is liked by all. He is a very nice little fellow and is as bright as a steel trap. Some time ago I decided that it was too much to ask the foreigners to remember his Korean name and that he ought to have an English name. I did not know what to call him so I decided to ask him. I only did it in fun and rattled them over at a pretty fast rate never thinking that he would be able to get hold of one and then asked him which he thought best. He astonished me by answering at once John and thus he is called now.

On New Years Eve all the Foreigners of Seoul (about 50) were invited to Judge Denny's to see the old year pass out.

A large company was there and just as the old year passed away we rang all the bells that we could find and the whole company joining hands sang "Auld Lang Syne."

We did not get home till quite late and it was about 3.30 when I got to bed. On New Years Day I could not help thinking of the last New Years that we spent together and I did have the audacity to picture to myself the sight that Thomas and I saw from the window of Mr. Harrison's study. I wished that I could see you tipping over the buggy at the lane near our house but above all did I wish that I could be at home again and running over the same route with you. There was but little time allowed me for dreaming however for after I had received a note or so I had arranged to go off for a skate and meeting.

The rest we had a very good time. I took lunch at Mr. Hunt's and as soon as this was over got my horse and went round to make calls with Mr. Hunt and Mr. Huldurt.

It was then quite late and to start out at that time although we all were well mounted it took all our energies and some very short calls to get round and finish up as it seemed to be the order of things not to call after 6 in the evening.

On the whole I had a very pleasant day of it.

We enjoyed the week of prayer very much but we felt that we did not have the Spirits [*sic*] presence as we had it last year.

There was not that feeling of nearness to God and of Gods [*sic*] nearness to us that there was last year. And as I speak of this we feel that we have as a community the Spirituality that we had last year. We seem to be degenerating

and we need the prayers of those who are at home that in the interval of studying the language we may be kept from turning into all head and no heart.
This is the danger that we feel and we have to st[r]ive against it. I am in great
hopes that my trip to Japan will be a benefit to me in this respect and that my
intercourse with those who are in Yokohama will do me good.

(3)

Now I have only time to say a few word[s] more and say good bye and
I feel sure you will say that two pages of fools-c p [*sic*] ought to have been
enough without my starting on a third. Pardon my saying so much but then
you can think how you would be dunned and bother[ed] by my talking were
I to come home for this is not a tith [*sic*] of what I have to tell.

It was very good of you boys to remember me as you did at Christmas
time but it was altogether too much. You have already done so much that
this only makes the debt of obligation the heavier. Very many thanks.

Tell the girls (and this is for you also) that the last mail brought no letters
at all from home. Everyone else had plenty but poor me had not a letter. I
know I ought to write more than I do but there is only one out here and I tell
you that to a fellow out here letters from home cannot be valued.

One gets to look and watch for them and when after three weeks
watching there is nothing but papers one feels like throwing them away. I
am sorry that Ethel is having such a hard time of it and I trust that long ere
this reaches you she will have fully recovered her old strength and will be
making rabid strides toward real strength and robustness.

I had meant to have written to her but I have not as yet been able to.
Give her my love and ask her not to wait for me to write to her, but to sit
down and let me have a line.

I want to know about business and all such particulars. I have not heard
from you for a long time and I do not seem to be going to. I hope when I come
back from Japan to find a whole host of letters waiting for me. I shall try and
stop the letters on their way by but I am not sure that I can.

While I am gone I am going to lock up the house and Dr. Heron is going
to look after things somewhat. He is going to attend to my horse and Mrs.
Heron has been so kind as to insist that little John shall be sent up there. I did
not know what to do with him and had in fact serious thoughts of taking him
along but then when Mrs. Heron made this kind offer I accepted. I thought
that there might be some difficulty when I go to Japan if I took the little fellow with me as I had invitations for myself but not one of them had asked me
to bring a baby along too and although he is a good deal more than a baby
there would have been a good deal of bother with him.

Trusting to have a good long letter from you by the next mail, thanking you again for your generous Christmas present I am

Your Affectionate Brother

Horace G Underwood

P.S. I do not get very good results with this ribbon in the copying book. I think the trouble is with myself and would be glad if you would send out a clear minute lesson on copying.

H.G.U.

Letter 3

Seoul, Korea July 25th, 1887

My Dear Fred;-

Many thanks for the good long letter which you summoned up courage to write me on May 19th. You say that you intended writing me for a month past, but that you had not been able to do so and although I am perfectly willing to excuse you, under the circumstances, I want to tell you that there is a place that is said to be lined with "good intentions" and I hope that hereafter you will not only have the good intentions but that you will carry them out.

On the day before my birth day I got a batch of letters from home which made it very pleasant indeed. At the same time however I had a letter from the Board in which there was no hint at any desire at all to investigate the matter or any sign of willingness to take back their former action of deciding without any investigation and they simply said that if I insisted in my resignation they would accept it. I had intended writing copies of all correspondence and sending them to Thomas but the mail goes a day oones [sooner] than I thought it would and I shall not be able to do so. This in part took away from the enjoyment of the following day but then the batch of good letters that I got from your folks counteracted a good deal the effect of the Boards letters. I have the blues at times and then I am good for nothing. I feel the need of some one to whom I can go for advise and counsel.

I hope the Canada branch is doing well and that Spen is getting along nicely. Of course there will be I suppose a good deal of extra expense in connection with it and that it will be some time before you will see the returns coming i[n] as fast as you would like but I suppose they will come in good season. I am glad that you like the things that I sent and that

(2)

some of the photos have turned out well. I am glad that you saw Mr. Booth and I think that you found him a very nice man.

He is as you say a live active man and is doing well in Japan. Everyone likes him there and he seems to be just in his place in the school where he is.

He is a good talker and although he is not quite as much a success as a preacher, he makes a fine pastor and has I think just found his place. His wife also i[s] a fine lady and I wish that the girls could have met her. I am glad to hear about the good times that people have at your house and think that some day I will come over by electricity and see how you are and you know as your daytime is our night I might leave h[ere] at Sunset and reach there in time for breakfast, spend the d[ay] with you all and get back here in time for breakfast and work the next morning. A good scheme, do you not think so.

Many thanks for your photo. I don't t[h]ink that you have changed at all. I have only changed in one particul[a]r, so I am told, have grown more homely and ugly than ever. I am going to try and take my picture and send you a copy so that you may see what I am like. I think that I shall have one picture taken in my summer costume on my poney [sic] but I am not quite sure. Many thanks for the instructions with reference to copying and I will now try and do better.

We are as you will have heard from the girls down at the rive river and we are having a very pleasant time indeed. All the people in Seoul envy us and in this hot season when the thermometer registers 98 in the shade and 128 and 130 in the sun we are very fortunate to be down here where we can get a breeze now and then. It must be remembered too that this is an Eastern Sun and that it effects [sic] one much more than a h[ome] sun does. We went up to Seoul to church yesterday but there

(3)

were only three foreigners besides the Preacher there.

Rather slim i[s] it not. I do not think that we are going to have any cholera this year. The winter was I think severe enough to kill off all germs and if this was the case with cae [sic] at the ports we can be free. Last year it was supposed to have come in from Japan through the port on the South.

We thought that we were going to have a famine because the rains have been so scarce but now the immediate danger is over and it begins to look as though the crops will d[o] well. You know rice is the main article of food in Korea and it needs a great deal of water to grow, in fact it has to be planted in paddy field or shallow ponds and if the rains dont [*sic*] come no rice can be grown. I hope the time will soon come when upland rice will be introduced and then they will not be so dependent upon the rainy season. As far as rainy season this year we have as yet had none. We have had rain by the week at a time but this is very different to what it wa[s] two years ago when we hardly saw a ray of sun-light for six weeks in succession.

But I must close this Epistle and will try and write to you sonn [soon] again. With much love to all I am

Your Affectionate Brother
Horace G Underwood

Letter 4

Seoul Korea October 11, 1887

My Dear Fred:

I am over at Mrs Devry's & Mr Hulbert & I are in the guest house. It is only a little after two so I thought I would drop a line to you & ask how you all are & tell you what is going on out here. First then politically we are in a muddle. China is putting her hand in work that does not belong to her & it is not easy to get the matter straightened out. You know Korea made treaties with other powers at the advice of China, thereby, at least as far as her treaty with the United States is concerned, making herself virtually an independent power. China not only allowed this but virtually advised it. According to treaties she was to send ministers to the other powers but up to this time she has not done so as she had not the funds. Now it is determined to send representatives to all the powers with which she has treaties. She sent one to Japan & appointed others to America etc. The one to America was already to start when China orders not & threatens war if the man is sent. This is rather uphanded but the poor king could do nothing but hold the man back. He is so weak & has been so in the habit of leaning on China that he does not know what to do & could only stop the Embassy. He says that it shall go & we are waiting anxiously to see what will be done.

(2)

The decision in this matter will settle once & for all the position of Korea. If the Embassys [sic] do not go or if they go only after asking China's position[,] Korea is a vassal power but if the king will but say go without awaiting decisions from China, Korea will be independent & China dare not go to war. Some Koreans side with China but they are very few & most of them say that it is too late for China to say anything now, that the time to have spoken was when the treaties were made do. What one gov't will do we cannot learn & there is so much tampering with the wires that nothing can be learned by telegraph. The telegraph lines are run by the Chinese gov't. Russia & Japan will both insist upon Korea's independence and I do not see but that the United States must do the same. We all hope for [?] independence as this is such a bad [?] —even in all China's work. 2nd Socially out here things are as pleasant as ever. Though I could not get round early I managed to get to Tennis before it was all over & had a couple of sets. I do not play well as I do not have much time to practice & then too as we have some crack players here my poor playing shows up rather badly. I am laughed at a good deal about it as also about my skating but I can stand this. I do not know whether I shall go in for skating next winter or not. It is such a pleasant pastime & then it makes so many pleasant gatherings that I think I shall go in again.

(3)

There is one thing about it I have only a very poor pair of skates & although you will tell me of the "carpenter & his tools" I know that if I had better I could succeed better. They are a pair of second hand ones that came from China. In a little while the divisions will begin here again. I was [at?] Mrs Devry's to a little informal dinner on Saturday last with Mr Hulbert, Miss Merrill & her brother. We spent a very pleasant evening indeed & broke up at about 11. Then last night there was a sort of a card party at Mr. Gilmores but all did not play. There were Mr Hulbert, a Mr. [?], Mr Merrill & his sister & myself there. It made just a nice little number[.] We are not without our pleasures in this benighted land. We are all of us continually saying how fortunate we are. In Nagasake [sic], Japan, there are just about as many [ladies?] as here & they are all divided into cliques while here we are all one. It makes it very pleasant indeed & all of us seem to think that if anyone has a visitor all the rest must try & see that he has a good time. Now & then we have riding parties & go a little way into the country. 3rd Climatically, we are having splendid weather. Korea is noted for its climate any how but our fall weather is something unsurpassed. Every one here speaks of it & all who are fortunate enough to be here at this time of year carry away a fine impression of our weather. The whole year here is good with the exception of the one or two months of rainy season. Then it is bad & we almost need boats to go around in.

(4)

4th As to work among the Foreign residents here. We have the regular Sunday services at 11 o'clock alternating between the Episcopal & a non-liturgical service. On the Liturgical or Episcopal Sundays Mr Hunt play[s] the [organ?] & on the other Sundays Miss Merrill, who is a thorough musician officiates. I have the regular work of decorating the church with flowers every Sunday & I find a great deal of pleasure in it. Last Sunday I used wild flowers entirely except 4 bright red dahlias. We have here a very pretty pink dog daisy & we had a sort of pillow of those with a round bunch of bright yellow with Chrysanthemums in the centre. On each side were vases with fancy [roses?], daisies & dahlias. It made a very pretty effect. By the way our wild flowers here are very fine indeed & there is not a month in the year but what you can find a host of varieties that are perfectly charming as to color & odor and shape. I think that I shall have to work up my bottany again & set to work & classify them all. It would be delightful work & I am sure that it would not be too easy a pastime.

5th Go to work among the Koreans, things are [booming?]. The work is going forward faster than we can keep pace with it. On all sides we are finding enquirers. I ought to go out into the country but my school work hinders me. I am hoping to take a trip

(5)

to the northern province soon as there are a number there that are desirous of Baptism. If I could give over my school work to other hands I could find more than enough to keep my hands full in real missionary work. I cannot go north purposely for missionary work & therefore think to take medicines with me & do medical work all along the road. I should enjoy such a trip very much indeed & I know that a good deal of good could be accomplished. We have as I have told Thomas bought a place to use as an evangelization centre for our work [?] men. The work opens up for women & we are going to do the same for [this?]. I have myself bought the house but I expect the missions to take it from me as soon as we can have a meeting here. We expect to put a Korean woman there & have women meet there right along. It will also be a very good [freedom?] for a girls school. I do not see how I am to look after all this but the work must be done & as the ways open we must enter. If the mission does not take up this work for women I shall either hand it over to the Methodists or else try & raise the funds outside. I think that this can easily be done. The orphanage is going along nicely & we are soon going to start a new school. Here also we see an open door & although we do not see far it is our duty to enter as the door is open. Thus the work goes on & there are almost we might say "added to the church daily if such as shall be saved."

(6)

I suppose you will think this is a queer way to write a letter but I thought I would be more apt to tell you all by doing it in this way. Now as it is fast approaching midnight I must think about closing this already too long epistle. I am glad to hear from your last letter about business being so well & that all things are going along so nicely. I hear also about your 13 girls. That is rather many & as they would not go to Utah with you & as the Edmunds' bill has become a law I would advise you to confine your thoughts to one & settle down. Rather strange advice for a bachelor to give, but since I heard of the 13 I have been feeling quite anxious. How is Helen getting along & Hannah & Becca. You must keep me posted. Don't forget Thomas also. I cannot imagine why you all [hang?] fire so. Now with much love to all & hoping that you will excuse a letter which tells so much about myself & surrounding [?]

Your Affectionate Brother
Horace G. Underwood

Letter 5

[undated- November or early December 1887]

My Dear Fred:

It is [6?].20 am & having retired last night at 12 I am up now to just drop you a line. The mail goes tonight & if I do not write now I will not be able to write at all. As you know from my last letter I have been away in the country. I was away for almost a whole month & did nearly 1000 miles. on horse-back & on foot. You may be sure that after being away from every-thing foreign for so long when I turned my face Seoul-ward I did not let the grass grow under my feet. I was about over 350 miles from Seoul & did the whole distance in 7 days. It has never been done before in less than 11 days & every one [sic] had told me that I could not possibly do it in less than 12 so you maybe [*sic*] assured that the folks were all very much surprised to see me at the Thanksgiving Dinner at Mrs. Scranton's. It almost pays to go away to have such a hearty welcome when you get back. It was so pleasant to feast that I had been missed & to have them all give me such a hearty shake of the hand & tell me how glad they were to see me. The Thanksgiving dinner was at Mrs & Mr F. Scranton's this year & all the Americans were invited. We sat down 20 in all. On Christmas I expect to give the Christmas dinner. I have got to do it for, following the Underwood plan, last year as before they had all gone I asked them all for this year, though I did not for a moment think that there would be so many more to be asked.

If all come that I will have to ask there will be about 28 though of course there will be some that cannot come. I shall decorate the same as last year & shall have to make my table in the shape of a cross. By doing this I shall be able to seat them all. The dinner will not cost very much as I have not forgotten the ways & means of giving a good dinner cheap & then my garden has yielded me all the vegetables that I will need, my greenhouse gives me all the flowers & I have some of the fruit from my garden & then too Koreans have been sending me presents. By a little manipulation you see that a dinner can be given without very much cost & as far as the waiting on the table is concerned it is the custom out here for every guest to bring a "boy" or waiter with them. This makes things very easy indeed. I am going to have a Korean paint some menu cards so that each lady will have one. They cost but a little & make such pretty souvenirs. They have been designed by Mr Hulbert & are two Korean dragons facing each other & their tongues running out into the initials. Their long bodies go down on both sides of the page ending in arrow beaded tails. In the center will be "Merry Christmas '87" & "a la Korienne" down below. Tied to this with a little piece of Korean silk cord will be the menu card which will be decorated with butterflies & flowers. It will I think look very pretty & I am glad that I am where such things can be done so easily. How one thing leads up to another. I had started in with the intention of telling you about work here etc & what I was doing but my trip led me to the Thanksgiving dinner & this to Christmas. Since I got back I have been so driven that I have not had time to know where I stand. I have a tremendous pack of unanswered letters to answer & cannot find a moment to sit down & write a line. I have not yet had time to balance accounts for November & as treasurer this ought to have been done by the end of Nov. I am now lecturing in Korean on Natural Philosophy & Chemistry for two hours every day & these lectures must all be prepared beforehand. I have been asked to translate a tremendously long document for the government. They have no one that can do it & so have come to me. Of course I feel honored that they should ask me ~~but~~ &

~~woul~~ feel that I must do it but I would much rather as I am so busy, that they had got it done somewhere else. If it were Korean into English it would not be hard but it is a semi-legal official document of 12 newspaper columns of printed matter to be put into <u>Korean</u> & it is no easy work. Then I have my teaching at the orphanage to attend to & almost all the business of the mission. This you see is entirely outside of the real Christian work that has to be done. At times as I think of what is to be done I almost feel that it is no use trying. Then too there is the work of house-keeping. You do not have this for the girls do it & then too your servants understand your ways & customs but out here they do not. I manage to keep my house so that it is just liveable & that is all. You want to know why I do not get some one [*sic*] to [put?] with it but how am I to get anyone if there is no one here. You boys have such a host to choose from that I have a great mind to get you to take the commission from me of getting one & sending her out to me. I do not know whether your taste would agree with mine or not but if you were to take the girls into your confidence I might be willing to risk it. It is ever so pleasant having Mr. Hulbert boarding &, at present, realy [*sic*] living with me. He is such a jolly fellow. He will be in New York next Summer & I want you all to see a good deal of him. We have quite lively times on the whole & he to use his expression wants to know "if we tooo [*sic*] cannot make Rome howl." I do not know whether you have heard this college phrase but it is quite expressive. Now I want to state a few facts about our needs here. The orphanage is enough for any one man to run. The hospital medical school cannot get along without two. Mr. Hulbert is helping just now but he would rather not as he is so busy himself but only does it to help me out. Then we are to start a new school, a sort of public school in the spring. One man cannot run it. It <u>must</u> have <u>two</u> men. For all this I am alone. How can I do it? I cannot & did I have the time to teach in all these places the strain of the responsibility is more than I can stand. I do not know

(2)

how we are to wake up the Presbyterian Church. As far as I am concerned as I can now use the Korean, my <u>whole</u> time ought to be given to <u>direct Christian</u> work. The way is open & there is work enough in Seoul alone for two or three men, if they could speak Korean, to spend <u>all</u> their time in <u>direct</u> <u>Christian</u> <u>work</u>. This is to say nothing of the work in the eight provinces where it has already started. The seed has been sown & without watering by man has already begun to germinate, in many places is ready for the in gathering but there is no one to go. As I think of this at times, I cannot contain myself. I cannot sit still. I feel almost that I ought to pack up, rush home, & spend a few months preaching a crusade to be fought with the "sword of the Spirit." At the same time I realize that such a thing cannot be done as the work ties me down here. The way for work is <u>wide open</u>, the room for men is plenty & I cannot understand why it is that we have been left alone for so long. The work that has been done is also glorious. Who would have thought when I left New Durham three [years?] all but 8 days ago that before three years had passed there would be a regularly organised Presby. Church in Seoul Korea of [25?] members with a doz[en] more applicants for Baptism. Who would have thought that in the Hermit Nation Korea whose valleys and hills had been so lately made to resound with the cries of those who were dying for their faith, before three years were up. Missionaries would be accorded the position they have today, that they would be on intimate terms of friendship with the officials of the highest rank & this too when we were known to be missionaries.

A <u>wonderful</u> change has been wrought in this land, thanks be to God for it[,] but is the <u>Church</u> at home going to take advantage of it or not. These facts have been <u>repeatedly</u> sent home but for some reason or other they have been kept from the public. Why I do not know. I have made up my mind that they ought to be presented to the people of the Presbyterian Church & I am going to ask you & Thomas to help me get them there. You have already done so much that it is almost am imposition to ask you to do more but I simply want to make the proposition & if you for <u>any</u> <u>reason</u> <u>whatever</u> do not think it a good one, or do not feel that you have the spare time or the spare money that it will take to carry it out, then I want you to tell me so.

The proposition is this. I will write a long letter, circular letter to the Pastors of the Presbyterian Churches, stating, what has been done, what were the prospects three years ago, what they are now, what can be done today, the doors that we open & showing what the Presbyterian Church has done & what she ought to do.

Now I want to know whether you will have such a letter printed & sent round to all the prominent ministers of the <u>whole</u> Presbyterian Church in the United States, I to furnish you with a list. There are in the Presbyterian Church today nearly 6000 ministers & the prominent ones will be from 4000 to 5000 in numbers. You see it will be no small undertaking & I hesitate the more in mentioning it as the brunt of the real work will fall upon you. It will also cost no small amount for the postage alone is a big item. I have thought a good deal about the matter & see no other way of letting the <u>whole</u> Presbyterian Church know the facts. Now I want you to think over this matter & I do not want you to do it because <u>I</u> ask it. If you feel that, had such a request come from some other source for this sake of this cause of the Missions, you would not have done the work, <u>do not do it</u>. I do not know whether this plan is [as?] good. It came to me in this way. I was thinking that if I could only be home & talk to the churches (and I would want to talk <u>night</u> & <u>day</u>) I could stir them up. Then I thought why not write & taking down the list I saw the number. I have not the time to write 5000 different letters nor have I the means of manifolding in this way here & then too the cost of postage from here is so great.

Thinking this the idea of asking you to assist occurred to me & I decided to do so. I <u>know</u> it is a <u>great deal to ask</u> but as I have said before do not look upon it as a request from me but consider it <u>simply & only</u> as a suggestion of a way in which good may be done & then act on the line that seems best. With our present force, the work <u>cannot</u> go on. We <u>must</u> either be reinforced or take a backward step & [retrench?]. Are we to do this? Is the church going to go back when the way is wide open? She has been asking that the way be opened up & now that it is open wide is she going to order her men to retreat. This is just what it amounts to. To do the work that is <u>here</u> & to do it well we <u>must have at least</u> 4 new men before late in the spring & then there are the eight provinces.

But I must close. I cannot send this letter now but I will try & send it with a list by the next mail. If you do not do this & can use the letter in any other way do so. Do what you think best. Many thanks for that $100.00 that came to me last mail. I think to use it in starting a public library on a small scale when Christian books can be read. I do not know yet. I have not written this on type-writer because I have not had the time to clean it since I got back. [In haste?]

With much love to all

Your affectionate brother
Horace Underwood

Letter 6

Seoul, <u>Korea Feb 27th 88</u>

My Dear Fred:-

I want you to read the opening to my letter of this date to Thomas for it will apply equally to you. It was late for you to write & I hope that henceforth you will make it right by not keeping me so long without a line. It is as you suggest lonely out here but its ten times more so when one does not get a line from home. Many thanks indeed for your kind & realy [sic] extravagant Christmas present to me. It is very good of you boys to do so much for me & I only wish that I could in some way do a little giving back. I do not like all the giving to be on one side.

I am glad to hear that business is doing so well & can well imagine what the work of watching a building going up is as I have had so much of this kind of work to do here but I have had to be my own architect & also to teach the Koreans how to do much of the work that they have done. It must be annoying to have Andrew & Wadsworth doing as they are. But it will all work well in the end. I was as you know back in Seoul long before Xmas & as you know also long ere this had a jolly good time. I had a grand dinner & everything

(2)

went off well but this is all old news so I will not enlarge [upon?] this[.] I have already told the rest how glad I am that you all had such a good time.

Many thanks for your kind advice about marrying but I shall feel inclined to say "physician heal thyself." I have now come to the conclusion that I am cut out for an old Bachelor. I am getting bald & gray hairs are showing. By the time that I come home, not only will I be a regular "bear" in manners but an "old Bach" in every way.

We have just had a three weeks vacation. During this time, I have done a little hard work at Korean, one week was the Korean week of Union Prayer & during the last week I took a run into the country.

We wanted to go for a hunt, Mr. Hulbert & I, so we let it be known & obtained an order from the Foreign Office ordering the magistrate & people of the village of Pochun to show us every attention & provide us with professional hunters to take us to such places as would be likely to have some game. Mr. Hulbert went down on Friday but I could not go till Monday. It was about forty miles from Seoul & by leaving early in the morning I got there before dark.

Everything was done for us to make our stay pleasant. We were entertained at the magistracy & the

(3)

entertaining extended to feeding our horses & all our servants. Dr. Scranton joined us on Tuesday night & although we did not get any game to speak of, we had a royal good time. We wanted an outing & we got one with a vengeance. We stayed out till Saturday night. We had Korean hunters with us when hunting & they presented a strange appearance with their match-lock guns & several yards of fuse wound around them all which they unwound as it burnt down ready at any moment to put on the powder & thus fire their gun. A gun that would go off without fire was to them a marvel & a "repeat-ing["] rifle was more than they could understand. Instead of coming home the way we went, we came back by a different road & thus were enabled to see one of Korea's famous temples. It has been fine in its day but it is no lon-ger what it was. It is sadly in need of repairs but if they would but do this it would be fine[.] The temples however of Korea are nothing to those of Japan & China. You know Buddhism was outlawed & so the temples have gone to ruin. Everywhere we see signs of the fact that Korea is a country without a religion & hence the need of presenting the true faith to them before in their haste for a faith they accept one that is not true.

(4)

We did not see any large game at all till on our way home when a deer bounded across our path. We got some ducks, pheasant, rabbit, quail, & other small birds[.] But I must close. It is already [morning?] & I must have a few moment [sleep?]

With much love to all & many thanks again for your Christmas pres-ent[.] [I remain?]

Your Affectionate Brother
Horace G Underwood

Letter 7

Anak, Whang Hao Do
Korea
April 29th /88

My Dear Fred:

I thought I would sit down & drop you just a line from this place. You will see from the heading that we are now among "the sons of Anak." They are not "giants" by any means nor did we feel ourselves "grasshoppers" in their presence. I reached here this morning at about 9 having got up early & came 40 li or about 15 miles. I was at [Sein?] Chun & did not want to spend Saturday there as I knew that Mr. Appenzeller would be here. We have now been away from Seoul for nearly two weeks & we find it very pleasant to have each others company. We are finely treated here. As soon as I got here this A.M. I sent in my card to the magistrate & he at once sent me a present of chickens, beef, eggs, pork & clams. In a little while he came to call. He came in style with blowing of trumpets, beating of drums & playing of flutes. In front of him were soldiers who went ahead ordering the way to be cleared. Then came the musicians blowing their trumpets & playing a weird tune on the flutes, keeping time with the peculiar Korean drum beating. He himself rode in a chair of carved ebony or imitation. The chair was open & over the seat was thrown a tiger skin as the sign that he had reached the

(2)

rank of "champion" & was entitled to stand among those of the 2nd rank before His Majesty. He also had an enormous umbrella carried over him. He was a very pleasant man, tall, well built of 56 years of age. He seemed very intelligent & asked a good many questions about America & other foreign countries. We had some tea prepared for him but we had not enough tea cups. We had one tumbler, one jam-jar & one tea-cup & saucer. It was not the most stylish tea set but then the magistrate would not know but that it was the latest style. We gave him the tumbler because it was glass & the largest. He seemed to enjoy it very much. In the afternoon we went to call on him & to wish him good bye.

Whang Ju May 1st /88

I did not have time to finish this at Anak. The magistrate was very kind & sent ahead & ordered boats for us at the ferry. He also gave us an escort of 2 mounted [Changgo?], a sort of internal reserve officer; 2 Sariang, a sort of soldier, & 2 pogio, a sort of policeman. These men escorted us to the river, ordered rooms cleared for us & saw about us getting to the boats with our loads. Had it not been for them we could not have crossed at all. We took our lunch the other side of the river. As the room was small & neat we at once remarked upon its neatness. It was plain mud walls & clean paper windows: but then the mud was smooth & neat.

(3)

[Pyeung Jang?]
May 2nd 1888

Your letters you see can only come in driblets. Well my trip comes to a sudden end. The King through the Foreign Office has invoked Mr. [Drismore's?] aid in stopping us doing Xtian work. We do not know that we ought to obey or not but to decide this point we have come to the conclusion that we will return home via [Hameury?] & Wousan & have sent word that we stop work from here. I do not know how to write about it. I feel almost like a coward for turning back & yet it seems the only course. I feel that as a minister of the Gospel & a missionary of the cross it is my duty to go forward even though to do so I must waive my rights as an American citizen. I shall think & pray over this on my way home & you need not be surprised to hear of my starting out again.

But I must close with love to all.

Your Affectionate Brother

Horace G Underwood

P.S. Have just decided to follow advices of gov. but to continue the trip as Americans [simply?]

Letter 8

Seoul, Korea. May 20th. 1890

My Dear Thomas;

Once more we are back in Seoul and are getting ready for work anew. Our trip to Japan has we think done us both much good in many ways and in none more than in giving us an insight into the work as it is done in other fields and by other missions.

We have indeed seen much to learn in such a ripe field as Japan but this has not been to us the only experience for while we were in Japan we met missionaries from every field in the world which you may well imagine would be a great benefit. The books are now done and as they were to be sent direct to you I suppose that you will have seen them before this. I hope that you will like the get up of them and that they will please in every way. I should very much like to have any suggestions that you may have for there may be some things that ought to be changed. Now that we have got back I am going to ask the mission to permit me to spend most of my time on the work of translation and at the same time I am going to work on a larger and more complete dictionary. Of course the one as now put out is as it claims to be very concise but there are I think enough words for all practical purposes.

A larger work is needed and I shall put in what spare time I may find in working on this. I can carry on to this work as I go along with the work on translation.

I find work quite as ready as ever and the need for men quite as apparent. I do not know what is the matt[er] but if we only had more men there is a host of work that can be done. I have just heard again that our board are not going to send us any more men for some time to come yet. If this is so we will have to work all the harder but I do hope and pray that the men may be forthcoming. As soon as we got back we opened up the boxes that you were so good as to send. How good of you to remember us so. The piano lamp is a beauty and helps wonderfully to light up a room as well as being such a handsome ornament. The Lord is too good to us. We have every thing so nice and comfortable now and in fact the whole house has we are afraid too much of an air of refinement and comfort.

The Bible is a beauty and will be a great help. I pray that I may ever try to follow its teachings

I shall use that copy entirely in my work of translation as there are such good wide margins on which I can put any notes that I may want to. We tried the cake at on[ce] and hung up the pudding for a special occasion. John was delighted with his things and at once commenced to play with his toys. He is getting to be quite a big boy and professes to be a Christian and I realy [sic] believe that he is trying to do what is right.

We have been very busy since we got back with a sort of house cleaning. You may imagine how dirty every thing would be after a house had be[e]n shut up for six months. While we were away some one got in and took off quite a few of our things. We cannot imagine who it could have been but it seemed to be someone who was acquainted with the values of things as they took [o]nly cut

(2)

glass and left the other. Then there were a lot of other small things. Lillie says it was because we prize them too much. But then we have a host of good things left and as they did get in and did not take all that we had we ought to be thankful. While we were away the people did not keep the greenhouse fire properly and as a consequence most of the flowers were dead but they will soon pick up again.

When we got back we found that Mrs. Hulbert and Mrs. Bunker had come in and opened up and had a lot of flowers around and that every thing was made to look as homelike as possible. Mrs. Hulbert and Mr. Moffat were at the house waiting for us with a cup of tea and some cake. We went up and took dinner at the Herons and I hope that all will be right in that quarter.

Work here in Seoul has been going along very well especially among the women. This latter has been due to the untiring efforts of a Miss Davies who was here with her brother but whose brother has died and now she is returning to Australia. I do hope and pray that she may be led to come back again as I do not know of any one who has in any way been nearly as successful as she has. All the women like her and if she would only stay a fine work might be done. We went to one of our out stations on Sunday and found the people quite glad to see us. We had a very good time and trust that some good was done. The service on Sunday was very well attended and although at times I felt a little embarrassed in preaching it soon wore off and I got along alright. I cannot tell you how glad we are to be back with what we love to call our people and we hope and pray that in some way or other the Lord will use us. We are going to extend our work in several directions and sow all the seed that we can and in as many places as possible get the ground ready. I think that before the summer is fully here we will have another preaching place and if we do we will have a Sunday School if that is possible.

But I must be closing and sending this down to Chemulpo or it will not reach you by this mail as the mail has already closed in Seoul. Lillie was so glad to get all the things and would have written by this mail but she has been so busy and then too she has not been as well as she might have been. She has not been sleeping as well as she should for the last few days but with a little care this will be alright.

With much love to all

Your Loving Brother

Horace G. Underwood

Letter 9

Jan 11th /95

My Dear Thomas:

I had meant to write before but ones hands keep full. The Xmas box arrived about 4 weeks before Xmas & we could hardly wait for the day to arrive. I cannot describe to you all the joy & pleasure there was in opening it and now before we get a word off to you about it comes your Christmas letter containing the check on London for £25.00. I do not know how to thank you. It fairly took my breath away. I had been out at a prayer meeting (the week of prayer) & when I got in & found your letter I was speechless.

I do not deserve one half of all that I get. I was only that very day thinking what a helpless & inefficient servant I was & how unworthy of all the many favors that I had received when your letter came. It was awfully good of you. I do not know yet what we shall do with it but we will certainly be able to do a great deal with it. I think I may buy some books but this is not yet settled, or I may get some harness for my mule. This will be two small things & the balance will go to my summer house. I wish you could have been with us Christmas morning & seen us open up the box. We had been up till almost 12 the night before trimming the Xmas tree & the house & filling Hollies stocking. He thought his was too small & begged one of his mothers which according to all proper rules we hang by the chimney. He woke up the next morning before 5 & must get up to see his stocking, so I quickly ran in & lit the fire in the fire place (you know it burns wood & lights up in a minute) & we all went out. Hollies stocking was full. We had had the Chicago & N.Y. boxes all brought into the Parlor in front of the fire place on great sheets & with the lids all loosened so that it did not take us very long to find out something about what was in them.

You may remember what a time we used to have opening the box from England well it was the same only more so with us. We knew of some of the things in the box from Chicago but we had not read your list so as to have all the pleasure of the surprise.

What a fine box it was & how you have laden us all down. I was just a few days before talking over things with Dr. Airson & wondering whether we did not have things too nice & then came that box from 99 St. James Place to add to our nice things. The silver [salva?] is just as pretty as it can be & altogether too fine for missionaries. At present we have it in the parlor as it seems too good for use. Then that book of Pictures of the

(2)

World's Fair was very fine & we enjoyed it very much indeed. The greatest disappointment of all was that we did not see the [mamoth?] battle of Underwoods inks. The whole fair while a financial success & in the point of beauty & size far in excess of anything else that was ever put forth did not seem to be a place where directors etc. were anxious to show honor & honesty.

Lillie as perhaps you have heard has been almost constantly at the Palace of late. The Queen has showered her with favors & hardly seems able to do enough for her. She asked to see some pictures of America & while we hated to do so, yet she had been so kind & good to us that we sent her round the World's Fair book. It was the only book of the kind that we had & we felt sure that you would be glad that it was so well used. She was charmed with it & thanked Lillie for it with a great deal of enthusiasm & said [s]he had enjoyed it immensely. We had no other book of pictures that would have been good enough to send but that one with its beautiful leather cover seemed just what was right.

As soon as we were through this we all dressed & had breakfast. Then all the servants & their relation came in to prayers. We sang "Hark the Herald Angels Sing" in Korean, read of Christ's birth & then when prayers were over we all went in to the tree where there were eggs, oranges, pheasants, for all, caps for the men lined [to?] cover their ears & cloth for the women & ribbons & fruit for the boys. Hollie took charge of these & dispensed them to all who were there. All day long presents were coming for Hollie. We send celery, cauliflower, cabbage, pumpkins & persimmons (all from my garden) with compliments of the season to those who had no garden.

At 430 [sic] we sat down to Xmas dinner, the old [slandtys?] Scrantons, Appenzellers, Hulberts, Airsons, Mr Baird & Mr Pauling; (Mr. Pauling is a good, spiritual man, a baptist but a free-will baptist who is just out here) & Hollie & Helen Hulbert sat at the table with us. We had a fine time & all those who were there were invited to be present at Xmas dinner next year. Just as they left, all the children of the families were found to be coming in & we all set to work to amuse them. Hunt the thimble, Hunt the slipper & a host of games were of course in vogue, when the little ones went in for cake [ito?] & then came out to a Christmas tree. We had a fine time & with all the children it seemed much more like a good old Christmas than if we had had only old folks.

I wonder if Lillie has told you about her trips to the Palace. She is quite intimate there now & I almost feel that I ought not to remain seated in her royal presence. The queen was sick & sent for her. Lillie had an old open wicker sedan chair, in which she road [sic] to the Palace[.] They took he[r] right in to the Queen's apartments in her chair. This was a great mark of favor. One day when she was leaving the Queen looked out & saw the old chair Lillie road [sic] in

(3)

& that afternoon she sent round her own chair as a present to Lillie. It is a very handsome chair, of course, & is covered over with blue silk plush & trimmed with carved brass & lined with brocaded satin of a light green color. A very nice note came with it. The day before she had sent her a Christmas present of cotton goods[,] silk goods, screens for windows & mats.

Just as new years came round, another present of 30 pheasants[,] 15 large fish, 3 bushels each of chestnuts, walnuts, pine-nuts & Korean dates were received so that we could have a good feast on our new years. This was not their new years & showed a thoughtfulness that in these troublous & warlike times we had not at all expected.

In the mean time they had asked Lillie to take Hollie & to him they had been just as kind as they could be. The King took Hollie in his arms, held him on his lap, kissed him & setting Hollie on a chair got down on the floor in front of him. The queen too held him on her lap. In Korea if the King ever in fondling the child of a noble should take hold of the child's hands, it would ever after have a piece of white paper around it as a sign that the King had touched that hand & that no one else must grasp it.. we have not yet wrapped up Hollie's hands nor do we think that we shall do so.

Then on new years eve came that which completely capped the climax in a present from her majesty of $500.00. The way the interpreter put it was so nice, and although they sent it as a personal present yet Lillie thought we had better use it in the Lord's work. They distinctly said that it was a personal present & said perhaps Lillie could purchase a pearl with it.

Lillie has been to the Palace two or three times since & has now sent her, at her request, a full set of her under clothing & night wear. I do not know what Her Majesty will do with it but should not be surprised to get a commission to get some.

The great traveller & writer, Mrs Isabella Bird Bishop is here in Korea now, & Lillie asked whether the Queen could see her. No answer was vouchsafed & Lillie felt that perhaps she had presumed too far but on Saturday the interpreter Major Gi came round with the announcement that the Queen would give Lillie & Mrs Bishop an audience on Sunday. It has generally been considered that the day set has to be adhered to but Lillie very boldly suggested that when her majesty was sick & needed her she would go any day or any time but that she hardly thought she could go to an audience on Sunday & while apologizing for her boldness asked that the day be changed to Monday which was

(4)

done & on Monday last Mrs Bishop & Lillie went to the Palace where they had a most enjoyable time. The King, crown prince & Queen were all dressed up in style & received them in the rooms of state, a large reception hall [lined?] all round with yellow silk. After the formal part of the Reception was over, they ordered chairs for Mrs Bishop & Lillie & had a long chat at the close of which they were ushered into another room where a regular course banquet was served to them & the first ladies in waiting[.]

Her Majesty told Mrs. Bishop that she had only consented to give the audience because Lillie & her majesty were such great friends & had asked it. She on several occasions referred to Lillie as a doctor & to her pleasure in being able to sit down & chat with her.

Lillie has on several occasions been able to talk with the Queen about Christ & the Gospel & she has most willingly listened to all that has been said. She is a very bright & intelligent woman, with a great deal of character. She has a mind of her own & if she could be won to the truth she would be a fearless advocate of it & what a power she would be. [Pray?] for Lillie that she may be given words to say, the opportunity to say them & that this entrance may not be without good results. Work goes on about as usual with us all here & the war has made little or no break in our work. Our meetings have been fully as well attended as ever & in some cases they have been increased. The street Chapel services have been more loyally attended than ever & it is our hope that this will be of a great deal of good. We are going to increase their number as fast as we can. Books are in as great a demand as ever & a goodly number are steadily being printed & a large quantity are being sold.

Miller is pushing the school work & all goes on well there, Airson is steadily increasing the number of patients at the hospital & is winning a good name by his skill, enthusiasm, & kindness. He is just the man for the place & I do not know where another like him could be found. I have seen a number of missionary doctors but have not seen one who so thoroughly was both out & out missionary & good doctor enthusiastic in his profession.

Politically all seems quieting down. I am sending by this mail a copy of the *Korean Repository* where you will see a list of the new cabinet & their 1st secretaries or vice ministers[.] No 2 was in America for a number of years at school. No 3 was one of the progressive men driven out of Korea in 84. No 4 is the man you supported in Washington. No 5 is an old friend of mine, quite an enlightened man who has been bold enough to assert his independence of custom & come out in foreign clothes. No 9 is the old man whose picture I had home who was so intimate with me.

(5)

No 10 was the first Korean minister to Washington a man of a good deal of force of character. No 12 is the man whom Fowler brought down to your office several years ago. No 13 is a man I taught English who was secretary of Legation at Washington for some years. No 18 is a bright, intelligent, active young Korean who has spent several years in Tokio [*sic*] Japan. No 19 is a former minister to America, the one whom I met in Washington when I was there. No 21 is the father of a Korean who is now a Methodist missionary in China.

This makes a pretty good cabinet. The men are all young & here is I fear one great difficulty. They need badly a balance [wheel?] & I fear they have not got it. What they will do remains to be seen. The country is all quieting down, the rebels are routed & disbanded & we hope for quiet times now. When all is over this whole country will be open to us & then we must be ready to go in & take the land for Christ.

Mr. Soh called on me & Shane called on him. He desires to be remembered to you but I fear much his Christianity is not of much weight[.] I do not think it was a heart matter. If he had been soundly converted it would have been different.

Now a little business. I suppose I have a little interest money. I think it is over a year since I drew last. I have been sending an order to London to J.T Morton of 107, 108 & 109 Leadenhall street for a years supply & have told him to draw on you for the amt & as far as the interest will go use it to pay his bill. If the interest is not enough let me know how much it lacks & I will send an order on the Board to cover the same. J. T. Morton's bill will be about £25. It may of course run a little over perhaps be even over £25. as prices on sugar & butter vary so but he is a good Christian man, a great supporter of missions & he will do the right thing I feel sure.

Now a word about myself. I am much better, I think I shall take a little trip into the country in a week or so & this will set me up. The stay at the river was a great help & I have been much better ever since. My appetite is good now & that is half the battle. Lillie's Rheumatism has been so far much better this year than last, thanks to a good heater and a tight house.

I have now arranged to make the house even tighter by double windows. These will do for our summer house when we come to build it & next winter we can put in more double windows here. Our house is a beautiful even temperature & as all

(6)

the rooms are about the same, we seldom have the thermometer above °64 Fahrenheit. We could if we wanted have it very tight but we find this is all that we need. Our coal is fast running down & we must get in some more wood. Mr. Sill, the American minister has promised to let us have some coal & this will of course be a great boon. We do not know how much he can let us have but every little will help. We could make out without wood but it does not get up as much steam as coal nor does it last long when put on.

About the Board's action with regard to my appeal, it was not an <u>answer</u> at all to my appeal, the members of the Mission felt it to be <u>adverse</u> to <u>them</u> as it did not uphold their course. Nothing was said about it at the annual meeting so I think I had better let it drop.

The hymn-book has quite a good deal of use & will I think gradually have more & more. It will hold its own but I am awfully sorry to see the row it stirred up.

Now I must close. My letter is already too long. Give my love to all at home. Remember me to the friends in Laffayett Ave, Church etc.

Your loving brother

<u>HG Underwood</u>

Letter 10

The Firs. Han Kang. Aug 2nd/95

My Dearest Thomas:

The last mail that we have had from America was you kind letter of May 17th which contained your generous gift to the work & to myself. It reached here on the afternoon of the day that I had to start off for Chang Yun in the country & when I opened it neither of us could restrain the tears that would come when we saw again how good & kind you were. We do not deserve all that you do for us & I do hope & pray that God will enable us to use all these things that come to us, for His Glory & not for self.

Now I am down here at the river for half a day. Hollie is sick & this called me from that city & that is how I am down here[.] I must go in at daylight tomorrow morning.

I just this moment was stopped in letter writing to put up some Cholera medicine for a patient who is at a village about ½ mile further down the river. There have been several deaths there already & now they are after medicine. But let me go back a little & you will know what I have been doing & how I have been spending my time. On the 27th of June we had a day of prayer & fasting for the work here in Seoul & for the manifestation of the power of the Spirit among the missionaries & among the natives. The prayer was held at our house here. All who could come, came & we had a blessed season of prayer & Bible study. In the afternoon word was received that Rev Mr. McKeyin who had been doing a grand work up in Chang Yun all alone by himself was dead. It was an awful blow. I felt that a brother was gone. An earnest worker who proved himself a good soldier of the cross was gone & what was the meaning of it. Word came to me. I was for a time speechless. In broken sentences I announced the news & said that I must at once start for Chang Yun. I went to Seoul & learned to my horror that Mr. McKeyin from the effect of a sunstroke had gone crazy & had taken his own life. It was an awful shock to us all & Dr. Wells & I made arrangements to start straight off to the place to look into all the details & to uphold & strengthen the little church that was there. It was only about 200 miles but it was 5 days journey there. We had a good deal of bustle getting things ready. We had to get horses & packs ready & start off bright & early. It was while we were getting ready on Thursday that your letter came & I cannot tell you how it effected [*sic*] us to see how kind & generous you were. You had already done so much for us. I could not believe my senses. I though there must be a figure too many & yet the writing was plain. I read it. I read the letter. I re-read it & re-read the letter. I had Lillie read it & still could hardly believe my own eyes. Such a noble & generous gift demands prayers that we may use it aright. That for the work came just as we were needing it. It is wonderful how God has watched over the work & sent money just as it was needed. Reading Müller's Life of Faith I was very much struck with the way in which carried on his work & in the same way he has provided us with money just as it was needed. I was all out of money for the various independent work that I have on hand, for tract, dispensary, [itinerative?] practices etc.

(2)

I did not have the money to pay the next month's wages of the people employed.

It was March 1st that I paid out the last of that money. Lillie asked why I had not written to you. I said I had been led I thought simply to take it to the Lord. On March 21 or 22nd I received a letter from a stranger in Chicago whose name I had never heard in which he enclosed $100.00 gold saying that he thought it probable that I had various schemes outside of Mission appropriations & if I had to use the enclosed for the same. If I had not to turn it into the General miss. Funds. Just before this the shelter funds were all gone & a note came from two young girls in San Francisco who heard me speak there on my way home, who were preparing now for the Foreign field, who hoped to come to Korea & had sent this out. Thus the God of our Fathers takes care of & watches over us.

We went down to Chang Yun. I wish I had time to tell you all about the trip. Wells is a fine fellow. I wish he were independent so that he & I could be associated. He works hard & is willing to endure hardship. Of course he is to go with Moffett to [Pyey Yang?] & he will do fine work there. We took books & medicine. At Songdo I sold 10,000 cash worth of books & preached to great crowds. Haijin the capital of the next province also took a goodly number of books. On the whole trip a lot of patients were treated & much preaching was done. It was bread cast upon the waters & it will not return void. We got to Chang Yun & found out all about poor Bro Mr McKeyin. He had got sun stroke, had gone crazy & had shot himself. It was a great shock to his congregation.

We stayed there about a week, had meetings every day[,] baptised some & had the Lord's Supper. We left there in a boat & after sailing about for 8 days we reached Seoul.

Here we found that Cholera had broken out. You remember how it was in 1886. Now how will it be. A good deal has been done. Measures have been taken to stomp it out & I am in this. Dr. Wells & Lillie & I have charge of a Cholera inspection office & Cholera Hospital at the "shelter." We have had about a hundred cases reported & several cases in the Hospital. The inspection work does most good. We go round to houses[,] disinfect, instruct, give medicines & thus try to stop its progress. I have been busy at this. I had a bad attack of Diarrhea for a day & Lillie feared it might develop into Cholera but I pulled round O.K.

Now the money you sent came just in time, for I have to ask & wait for reply from no one about funds, I go ahead & do what is needed. If the good will pay back afterwards, well & good if not we must do what we can to save the lives of these people.

They have a central office in the city & a large fort has been fitted up as a Hospital & all that can be done will be done. I was up there when word came that Hollie was down sick. So I came as quick as I could. I go in at daylight tomorrow.

We shall fix this house up a little now. We will paint the outside, make it tight & build a chimney so that we can use it as a retreat even in

(3)

winter where we can get away from the bustle of Seoul to do some quiet book work.

With the money from England I shall send for a bicycle so that I can get around to do my work. Several have them here & it is found to be a great saver of strength & time. I wish you could run down & see this place. You would not find a very fair mansion but a beautiful site with lovely views that change every moment almost because of the clouds & sky as they are reflected in the water.

But I must be closing. I cannot tell you how much we enjoyed that sugar, it was better than any we get here & the flour & the butter. The latter was the best that we have had in a long while. We found we could not use it all before it would spoil so we sold some & Lillie has it on one side as <u>butter money</u>. Then later still came that birth day box & what a box it was. That umbrella came <u>just</u> as it was needed. Mine was broken & now I have to be out so much in sun & rain in this inspection work that I do not know what I would do had I not got it. Thanks ever so much for it.

Then those lovely suits of clothes for Hollie. How good & kind & thoughtful of you. I cannot tell you how pleased he was with all that was sent.

Called to another Cholera patient. Must close this. Love to all in great haste Your loving Brother

HG Underwood

Letter 11

[Lillias Underwood to her sister Hannah.]

Seoul, Korea, Nov. 29. 1895.

My dear Hannah

We received your nice letter (the first which has come for a long time) the other day and thank you so much for all the trouble you have taken to get all those things for us; indeed it must be a great deal of bother, and I assure you we appreciate it. The list on the other side looks very tempting; we try not [to] allow our minds to dwell on it till Christmas. Indeed, you all send us too many nice things. We have enjoyed the nice things that came in Horace's birthday box. The orange marmalade was certainly the nicest we ever tasted. Even I, who can not [eat] ordinary marmalade liked that. You ought to try it yourselves, if you have not yet–Gordon & Dilworth's I think it was. I am glad the two suits of clothes are soon to be here as Horace is just fitting out a couple of refugee Koreans in two suits of his clothes. He is getting them off to China for safety. By the way I'm afraid we were deceived in that. I'm afraid he is a cold blooded murderer who really plotted to destroy the queen before he left and is rejoicing now in her death. By the way, a secret, don't tell, but the queen is alive. She escaped from her enemies that night in the dark, donned a soldier's clothes and went out with the palace guard when they were driven out by the Japs and found shelter in the country. She is expected to take shelter here in our house for a day or two at least–poor little queen. How I pity her! The king has been in danger of being murdered ever since. We have sent him food repeatedly. Horace has been almost the only one whom the king could trust to carry secret messages and it has been with the greatest difficulty he could get even a

(2)

word in private with his majesty–frequently he has written messages on his cuffs at odd minutes. Night before last some of the king's friends attacked the palace in order to arrest the conspirators and release the king, but the attack failed. The king was greatly frightened and called out "Call the foreigners." Mr. Hurlbert and Dr. Avison were at the palace at Horace's request with Horace, as they expected the attack and feared for the king's life, should the conspirators become alarmed. As soon as shots were heard they rushed to the king's apartments which they found surrounded by a heavy guard, bayonets were crossed in front of them but Horace pushed them aside and hurried in followed closely by the two others, and they remained by the king all night. To-night we are getting a Korean general off to China who has been guilty of trying to help his king in time of sore distress. A poor woman whose husband has just been arrested for leading in the attack the other night has just left us. We seem pretty deeply mixed up in politics but how can we help it. All these years the king has loaded our Mission and ourselves with kindness–suddenly he is plunged in the deepest distress and calls on us for help–it is pitiful to see how he depends on a few poor missionaries. Our American Minister has asked Horace to act as confidential interpreter and go between, and has asked other missionaries also to stay with the king (or near him) at nights, as witnesses, knowing that the ruffians now controlling the palace would be reluctant to do any open acts of villany [sic] upon the king with foreign witnesses. It is gossiped around here that Dr. A.[,] Mr. H. and Horace sat by the king pistols in hand all night. They did nothing of the kind. Though they had revolvers concealed on their persons for their own possible protection, they were never shown and they simply stayed with the king as witnesses and to give him moral support, that too

(3)

at the request of the American Minister. Now, to change the subject, looking over your letter, I see you say I asked you to get frilled shirts for Horace. Either you misread the letter or I was crazy or asleep when I wrote it. I never dreamed of such a thing for him–and Hollie has plenty of them–I would not buy such a thing for him. I may have said tennis shirts, or flannel shirts, but I can not think what else it could have been. But my servant is rather impatiently waiting for this letter. I am nearly distracted and so is Horace. The queen's stopping place is known to the man who was arrested today and he will probably be tortured to tell all he knows. Be glad you are in America.

love to you all from us all

Your sister Lillie

Letter 12

Feb. 20, '96

My Dear Thomas:

Your three letters dated Dec 19, Dec 28, & Jan 10th all reached me about the same time. I was very glad to hear from you & to see a copy of the paper you sent. It is as you say annoying in the extreme to have these things said but it is a whole lie out of whole cloth. I do not know how Col. Cockerill came to write it for he had seen me & I thought he knew better, perhaps he heard it harped upon so much by the Japanese papers that he thought it was all true. As you say it is best not to answer them at all. I had nothing whatever to do with the attack, & knew nothing about it till a few hours before as the enclosed account will tell you I have not plotted at all. I have on more than one occasion been sought as interpreter & perhaps these things have lent color to the statement that I was in the plots. I have felt a strong sympathy for the King & when he has asked my advice I have not hesitated to give it. I have cared for no one, been outspoken against wrong & those who do the wrong of course do not like it at all. They have tried to injure me & to get me out of the way but I do not mind what they say. I knew when I saw the lies that were cabled to Japan that they would go further. About Cockerill's letters & his reference to you there are only two ways to acct for it. He was at our house & as he spoke of its comfort I said yes, my father-in-law in Chicago & my brother in New York have done their best to make us comfortable. He was surprised at steam heat in Korea so I said a present from my brother. I feared he would think [they[2]] were all out of Mission funds. When the Prince was to be gotten out of the way he was in the plans & had to be consulted & I said that the prince should be sent to you. Thus you see he may have got ideas about a wealthy

2. MS seems to read "then."

brother in New York. Now all things are changed & Japan is ousted for the present unless she declares war which I hardly think she will. Now if war is to be declared she must take the initiative & this she hesitates to do. She is trying to stir up sedition among the people, is circulating all manner of rumors but whether the people will believe her or not I cannot tell. We still live on a volcano & what the end will be we cannot foresee. This much we do know that as a result God's work will go on much better.

(2)

He will over rule it all for good & make His Glory to appear.

We were in the country when this change was brought about. We hastened home. His Majesty ordered an escort to go for us so that we should be in no danger but we did not need them. Everywhere we were recognized as Europeans & not Japs & everywhere we were greeted as those who were going to change things & save Korea. All whom we saw seemed glad of the change in this city & looked upon Russia as Japan's friend. People that were rising in mobs against the Japanese & the pro-Japan government at once began to disperse. Their work was done & there was nought else for them to do. The people everywhere seemed pleased.

We got in on Monday night & early on Tuesday His Majesty sent for me. He was most kind & gracious, cleared the room of all who were there & asked me to tell him plainly all I thought. I had quite a long talk with him about affairs in this country & made one or two suggestions all of which he ordered to be carried out at once. He told me to come whenever I wanted to but I shall be careful not to push myself forward. I shall go when I am called or if urgent demand exists ask for an audience. May God guide me in aught that I may say & in some manner open up the way for me to speak of Christ to His Majesty. It is a very hard thing to do but may God show me how. All the present cabinet seem most friendly to me but it is not a strong cabinet. It has ma[n]y weak [points?]. There is hardly a strong man in the cabinet & what is needed just now is a strong man. A strong & brave arm is needed just now & the man has not been found. There is one man who is strong & brave & could do the work here but he has such a host of enemies. It is [Rvnd?] Pak who is now in Washington. I do not know whether he would be allowed to come back or not. He certainly is fearless & would work for the interest of his country but Russia does not trust him & I do not know how His Majesty feels.

The present cabinet are most of them afraid for their lives & unless they get over this I do not know what will happen.

With reference to Kate Redpath's salary it is now paid up to now Feb 29th of 96. I think you will find this is so if you look up your check stubs. She has been so paid & has given me a receipt to that date. You sent out the money & I paid her. She has not been very well of late but is better now & relieves Lillie of no small amount of work. If it were not for her Lillie could not do all the Missionary work that she does.

(3)

About coal & the vessel.

1st If it has not been sent get consign to me & then when it gets here I can make whatever arrangements are best with the shipping houses in Chemulpo.

2nd Though no cargo of any amount can be gotten here, I have no doubt but what a full cargo can be made up in China or Japan.

3rd I have already written you at length about amounts of coal & oil & stoves etc.

4th If things have not yet started & there is time when this reaches you can you send for me one doz cane seated chairs. Not the cheapest something that will do for bed-room or dining room. Let it be a chair with a brace as they soon go to pieces out here.

Now one other matter[.] Hale has not yet sent me a statement of acct with you. I fear I am terribly in your debt & would like to know the truth. I have not had a statement of account in two years.

My letter has already assumed too great a length but I must not close without telling you of the success of our work. The very uneasiness of the people is causing many to seek Christ. God has been harrowing the hearts of the people & they seem ready for the seed. In both Chang Yun & Koksan we had most delightful meetings with the Christians who are there and a fine work is in progress. In Chang Yun it has been of several years standing & it looks as though it had sent its roots right straight down into the ground. Whole families have taken Christ & the sentiment of the whole village is Christian. It was a blessed privilege to spend a week with them & their families. All the way down we preached[,] sold books & dispensed medicines. We must make some arrangements for the carrying of our medicines better than we have.

Everywhere we were received well & everywhere people were willing to hear what we had to say. We sowed seed, God will bless it.

Your Christmas box was opened when we got back. What a host of things you sent us. The tears came into our eyes as we thought of how kind you were to us. The only thing is that you teach us be extravagant with all these elegant things. The rubber coat is just what I needed. Mine was all worn out & no good at all. In fact it seemed almost worse than useless & I was going out without a rubber coat at all. Now I shall be able to keep quite dry & comfortable. What a host of other elegant things you all sent. What with tea kettle & chafing dish for our table & dinner wagon we are almost if

(4)

quite as swell as they make them. I tell you what[,] we are stylish & when our table is all set it does look so fine.

Lillie looks elegant in that lovely cape. It quite outshines all out here & with the hat on too there will be no one to equal her. May we be kept from clinging to these things & be enabled to keep our thoughts on things above. What a time we had opening those boxes. I tell you we enjoyed it & we thus had two Christmases instead of one[.] You should have seen Hollie. How he jumped & how delighted he was. He could not contain himself & he says every now & then, "It was just like Christmas when we opened the boxes[."]

I expect the Prince will soon be walking in upon you. He is the King's son & though not the heir will I feel sure come to the thrown [sic]. He desires a good school education & a military one after it. I hope & pray that with his education he may by all means get Christ. What a change it would work in the land if its King were a genuine Christian. The King will I believe pay back all expenses incurred. I shall go to him in a few days to ask his will about the matter & shall see what he has to say.

Now I must close. With much love to you all, with many thanks for all the lovely presents & a prayer that God will bless you all.

Your affectionate Brother

Horace G. Underwood

P.S. If Lillie sent you a copy of this slip, please send this to Chicago to her folks.

HGU

Letter 13

Beach Hotel
Cheefoo, China
May 29th '96

My Dear Thomas:

Here we are for a week for so at Cheefoo. We have been here just a week & had expected to return on the same steamer we came on but Lillie is so poorly that we shall wait over for one more steamer which will keep us here about 10 or 12 more days. Neither Lillie nor I have been well for some time. Lillie was working too hard. She had three weekday catechetical classes or rather Bible classes, three native services to attend every Sunday & two if not three days a week at the dispensary. This with all the other household affairs was rather much, then too the late disturbances in Korea have been the source of considerable anxiety to Lillie & when the Queen was murdered it almost seemed to Lillie as though a relative had been fouly dealt with & the whole affair has been rather trying on her nerves. She did not seem to have her natural vitality & I thought an entire change of air & also a change of scene where for a week or so she had entirely different surroundings would do her good. Then too my old nervous chills & headache & nausea were back & I thought that a run over here would set me up entirely so we got permission from the station & came over here. We are very nicely situated[,] have two splendid front corner rooms facing the beach & the hotel keeper very kindly & generously[,] as it is the opening of the season & he has so few guests[,] provides us with two rooms at the same price as one. Lillie's Rheumatism has been made worse this spring than any time since we came back from America & she is not at all strong.

Almost the slightest effort tires her & she gets out of breath & heart palpitations from simply walking up stairs. Since she came here she caught a bad cold that has settled on her lungs & every day she has several degrees of fever. We are however dosing her up & hope to pull her round. Add to this just now quite a severe blister started on her foot that shows a tendency to ulcerate. You see, "it never rains but it pours," is true again. She has been laid up ever since we have been here but she can lie on a lounge on our piazza & watch the water & hear the surf.

(2)

I am now trying a new remedy that is <u>old</u> in the old country but new out here. It is called "acetopathy" or Acetic Acid cure. It consists in the application of

Acetic Acid to the proper nerve centers on the spine & to the part or parts of the body effect [*sic*]. By this means the circulation is stimulated[.] I have for a long, long while felt that Lillie's whole trouble was a weak heart & poor circulation. If this only can be stimulated sufficiently I believe she will be <u>well</u>. Whether this can be done or not remains to be seen. I am now giving her a treatment every morning & it certainly has a soothing effect for almost as soon as the treatment is over & sometimes <u>while</u> I am giving it she falls asleep. I am feeding her on Melius food & dosing her with Fellows Hypophosphites. For myself I am taking the latter & am much better for it.

Hollie keeps very well & is enjoying the sand & sea very much though it is too early for him to take any sea baths or even to paddle. The water is too cold. We did hate to leave Korea just at this time but it did seem as though it was the best thing to do. We shall go right to our river house when we get to Seoul & hope that we shall have a cool summer there. It is a beautiful place & as cool as cool can be. We will both as far as health will permit carry on our work in <u>Seoul</u> from the river & I will have my teachers & literary helpers down at the river with me. I have been doing a good deal of printing & publishing of late. Some of the tracts are in their 20th thousand. There is just now a good deal of willingness to hear & to read & we can easily dispose of our books. The hymn book of which I printed a 2nd Edition is all out & a new or third edition is now in the press. It is no small gratification to find that this book which was so much spoken against is so well received. There are two others now in the field but mine still holds its own & finds a good deal of favor. A large number of these tracts are for free distribution & those that are sold do not quite pay for the cost of the paper so that there is from a financial point of view quite a loss in this tract work but that is what we expect in this work. The funds that you have sent me have also gone to provide extra writers & literary workers & [to?] buy Chinese scriptures & tracts. You told me to let you know when more would be acceptable. I am about out of such funds. I provide 1/10 of my salary & income for this & this too is about used up. Now there is hymnbook to be reprinted. A lot of tracts out of print & some new ones now ready. If you have funds for charitable purposes to spare they could be well used along these lines & I feel that the investment would most certainly be of great benefit in the work here in Korea. I have underway & I hope most sincerely to have it quite far along before this summer ends

(3)

an annotated New Testament in Korean. I think very seriously of having it printed by the photograph process that is coming into vogue in China[.] If this is done I want to have it struck off in three facsimile editions at once. This is simply done by changing the position of the camera. Of course an annotated New Testament will cost a good deal to print but when it is once ready the money will I feel sure be forthcoming. I think I shall first try one or two of the Gospels & see how they take. I believe they will take well. They will have references & perhaps a map or two. It will meet a felt want among these people. In a country where customs are so dissimilar with the bible without note or comment is in many place[s] absolutely unintelligible. The new bottles for new wine does not appeal with any meaning where stone or earthenware bottles are the only kind used. The parrable [*sic*] of the sower loses almost all its meaning in a country where all the sowing is done in drills with the utmost care because they would never let any fall where there was a rock or on the road. In a great many such places a note or two just of explanation seem almost a necessity. I am now preparing this & hope to have some of the books ready this summer.

Now there is another matter I want to speak about. Do not understand me as asking it! But if you are ahead on the Lord's acct & would care to take up another worker in Korea, there is Mr. Kemner who called on you at your office & brought the Bethlehem shell home to you. He is expecting to resign from the Bible society. He does not know what he will do but he is a good practical man & one whom I should much enjoy to have associated with me in work. I could do a good deal more if I had an associate. Those that come out from the Board are each given separate work but if you cared to take him up as a missionary he would be I think a most wonderful help[.] [A]s it is I do not get to the country to my out stations as often as I should & he & I could so divide work that it would be more than two men working separately. He is a good scholar. If you see fit do not send any money till I send word for I do not know that he would accept. Just let me know & what offer to make if any & for how many years. I suppose he would have to have the same as a married missionary man of our mission though this is less than what he gets from the Bible Society. He has a wife who is a good helper in his work. He is a good [practical?] business man[,] has practical [printers?] knowledge, is a good scholar & would be a great help in the publishing line.

(4)

I am still as time & opportunity afford carrying on my dictionary work & when the time seems ripe, if it is needed I shall publish mine. Mr. Gale's is only Korean-English & is I think not quite full enough. Time will show whether another is needed & if so & mine is ready I shall publish. I asked Gale to [invite?] but he declined. I could have cut him out of rushing into print but this I hardly thought best & as he was wanting to go alone I let it be. It will be as well in the end. Then too I have been busy on Christian books & this has been increasing my vocabulary & I will get out a much better one for the waiting. I had 6 books & tracts in the press when I left Seoul & this is quite as important if not more so than dictionary though I carry on this work at the same time. My dictionaries & grammars have sold fairly well & I shall have to reprint one of those I think in a couple of years.

A Now as to my acct. with you I have not had it for an age & have not the faintest idea how matters now stand. I do wish I could have a statement. I have not had one for at least two years if not more. My debt will get so big I do not know what I shall do. Please have Hale send me a statement so that I can see about settlement.

B Please take $25.00 from our bank acct or 30 or even $35 if necessary & buy a wedding present for Leonore & send it on to Chicago from us. This will I fear be late but we had expected to send something from here but the parties are not going who could have selected it from Japan.

C) Take $100.00 & send it for the Armenian sufferers for us. It is what we desire to contribute & draw it from what you said was to our acct in the savings bank.

(D) If you at any time hear of a good investment for the small balance now or when it has grown somewhat invest for us.

Work in Korea goes on well. All is most promising & we feel sure that a big work is before us. North south east & west reports well & we feel that much will be done during the present year. Everywhere we get a quiet & attentive learning & you know what this must in the end mean. You know well that when they begin to listen results must follow. Mr Moffett has doubtless sent you word about his work up there & it is the same all over where the work in Korea is pushed. Our work in the country I will write to you about more fully while I am here. Mail goes soon & I will send this

(5)

on & add more before we leave Cheefoo.

About Kate. Mrs Airson has been very sick near to death's door & we sent Kate down to help them. This has shown that with the work that Lillie has, it is very hard to get along without Kate as she has to leave Hollie all alone so much.

Kate tried to get a place at the British Consulate but did not succeed. She desires very much to stay on & if you are willing to continue your kindness in this matter we would like much to keep Kate with us somewhat longer. Lillie's work takes her out a good deal & Hollie is rather young still to leave all alone.

As far as government affairs go all seems fairly going on. Nothing of note has happened. The King is now free to go & do & rule as he sees fit. Russia leaves him entirely free.

He is very kind to me & I have seen him quite often. I can go & see him whenever I want & he seems determined not to forget the little that I have done for him. In a great many ways he has shown his interest & I have to go & see him & bid goodbye every time I go to the country & call again as soon as I get back.

The present officials are not all that they might be but things will come round O.K. The Japaners are entirely out & what the end will be we cannot definitely see. The King needs advice & if he can get this from a reliable source I believe things will go on well. The people love their King & I believe the whole country are glad that he is at the Russian Legation.

The Second Prince will <u>not</u> come to America just now. His majesty has called him back to Korea & of course he must obey his Father.

But I must be closing.

I have just heard that Dr. Allen has proposed to the U.S. Govt & also to a Mr. Hunt that they negotiate direct with the board in N.Y. for the purchase of the old girls school property & out to the road for $3000 Yen or about $1500 Gold.

1st This is twice the size of Girls school (proper) as they desire a straight line to road. It is worth a good deal more than <u>$3000.00</u> Yen. If the board is going to sell for that I should like to be allowed to buy it. It would be a good investment for me.

2nd It cuts out nearly all <u>my</u> garden. They ask for a <u>straight line down to road</u> & this cuts off nearly all of my garden which is hardly the fair thing. I will write at greater length but feel that

(6)

a halt should be called before any transfer is made in New York where they would not know what this "<u>straight line to the road</u>" would include. Now I must close. I will write more by next mail. Love to all from us all & especially to our Brother Thomas.

Your Affectionate Brother
Horace

Letter 14

Cheefoo June 12, 1896

My Dear Thomas,

We will be leaving Cheefoo in a day. Our boat is due today & we shall I suppose start for Korea tomorrow. It has been a good rest for me & I feel that shall be able to do more work when I get back for this charge. Hollie has had the "Chicken Pox" while we have been here & was indoors for about a week. Lillie I regret to say is no better & has been quite low ever since we came here. I don't know just what the matter is but her cold hangs on without any let up at all & she does not gain strength. She is very weak. But a little exertion tires her. She cannot walk a couple of blocks. I hope when we get back to home & home comforts, she will then feel the benefits of the change of scene & air that she had had in Cheefoo.

She had had several severe attacks of heart palpitations & difficulty in breathing. The doctors all say that there is nothing that is organically wrong & while this is a great comfort the time when the attack is on is not easy to be born. I do not know whether a longer stay here would be of any benefit or not but we have our work to do & must get back to it. I shall try & get Lillie to rest this summer & be ready for more work in the fall. I wish we knew what would build her up. I have started her on Fellows' Hypophosphites but she still has no ap[p]etite & I am feeding her on Mellin's food & milk. I also gave her an Acetic acid treatment every night which I hope will tone her up. It does help her at the start & if we can only get it to cure her.

We will be back at our work in but a little & oh how Korea needs workers just now. The war, the murder of the Queen, the constant upheavals that we have had here so far in no way hindered our work but [we[3]] rather have shown the people that they have no one on whom to rely & made them this more ready to receive Christ. "No one to lean on." "No one to rely upon." "No one to trust in": are the constant remarks that we hear on all sides & are they not then ready to hear of Christ in whom they can trust on whom they can rely. The Missionaries strong trust on the side of right

3. This word seems to look like "the," but "we" makes sense in the context.

irrespective of [party] has had a good effect upon the natives & I hope its effects are now being seen. The King & the high officials of the [highest?] class all know that we are [always?] to be counted on on the side of the right that we should of right before anything else & that the word of the missionaries is believed. Though this must not be generally told around. I saw the King one morning & told him of some wrong doing of an official & one of the favored ones at that but the next mornings official Gazette announced the removal and degradation of the official. This is simply a sign of the confidence His Majesty places in the word of

(2)

Missionaries. I have been quite [mutual?] with His Majesty ever since he has been at the Russian Legation. He wished us bon voyage before we started & told me to be sure & call & see him as soon as I got back. When I took my last missionary trip his majesty asked me weather I was going on a "preaching trip." To us such remarks from the King of Korea before his officials has no small meaning. A few years ago the fact that we are missionaries was only mentioned under ones breath.

Yours of April 18th came [to hand?] a few days ago. It went up to Seoul and was forwarded from there over here & hence the delay.

About the vessel. The only reason that hereto-fore no sailing vessels have gone direct to Korea has been that there has not been a cargo load shipped there at any one time & the only reason against going direct to Korea is that they have [never?] gone. As you say it's a "new field" & the people hesitate to go. There are charts of the Chemulpo Harbor [published?] [by our?] U.S. government. I think after the surveys of the U.S. [Stewardship?] Alerts.

Korea is a new place & they do not care to go but with [a] U.S. gov't chart I do not see why they should not go about cargo, there would be no cargo from Korea. She would have to run up to New [Chway?] & get a cargo of beans or bean cake for Shanghai. Then go on [berth?] at Shanghai for a cargo home. That is what the oil vessels do. Japan & China have been opened for years & there is a good deal of trade & that is why they all go to China & Japan.

About Airsons goods[. I]t was as well that Mr. Horton sent them as he did as part of this order was Dr. Airsons House building Hardware & he was in need of it at Seoul. He had not calculated aright for it. If the vessel should reach Chemulpo as late as the end of Nov. it would be alright.

Seoul. June 17/96

Dear Thomas,

Here we are back again & I must send this off to catch the mail at once. I had hoped to have sent it off before but was hindered. We had a bad trip of it over & were rather tired but feel much better now. Little is still very weak & I shall get her down to the [river?] as soon as I can. The doctors in ~~Shanghai~~ Cheefoo all said that Lillie ought to stay there all the summer but I could not leave my work all that while & Lillie could not well be kept at a hotel all that while so we came back & I shall try & get her to rest from work all the summer. This will be hard to do as she is right in

(3)

in the "swarm" of work & she finds it hard to keep out.

Yours of April 23rd re Young Prince just to hand.

I am very sorry to see what Loomis has been doing & saying. I ought to have known better than to have entrusted anything to him. He is a <u>half cracked</u> individual & I should have known he would make a muddle of it but he knew the young prince & I thought as he was in with the Japanese officials he would be best able to get the Prince out of their clutches.

The prince is a bright and intelligent fellow. He stopped with us & he was anxious to go to America. When he said that he was willing to work his way to America & to go steerage if he could only get to school I said that I would pay his passage & that you would see to & help him in his studies I thought that it would work for the good of Korea if one who is destined to play a prominent part in the government could be brought up & educated under Christian influences. Then the Japanese got him over to Japan & have held him since. I wrote to Loomis about what should be done.

But when the King was free I thought that he should decide what his [sire/son] should do. I have talked the matter over with his Majesty & he desires that he shall first of all come back to Korea. Now when His Majesty says this I have nothing to do but abide by his decision.

About the 3000 Mexican dollars I believe that the Prince never saw the money & that he was charged this simply to hold him in Japan [but?[4]] we could never pay this & so I wrote to Mr. Loomis.

I never gave Mr. Loomis permission to <u>draw on you</u>. I told him I would see about his getting to America. He volunteered to draw on you but I did agree to this at all. Mr. Loomis is queer & if he gets an idea into his head as a good one he is apt to think you suggested it as a good one. I have never drawn on you & I would not for a moment authorize another to do so. You did when I was in America say I might draw on you & I sold a draft on you to Mr. Ohliger but I certainly would not unless some great

4. MS blotted.

(4)

contingency arose. At that time Mr. Ohliger was coming to America, wanted money in the U.S. It was a saving to him & a saving to me to take his money here & the building you & I had talked over it at the South Gate was for sale. I then bought & got the money from Ohliger.

The Prince was given directly to understand that he would have the economical & in fact while we volunteered as much. There may be excuse for him in Japan. The then government sent him to Japan as an ambassador, gave him 1000 [?] & promised to send him 70,000 more at once. Now he may have spent 3000 [on?] in preparation for his official all round the world trip. I do not know but if a man goes to a country with the promise of $70,000.00 he will be apt to live differently from what he would if he went as an object of Christ. Of the promised $70,000.00 they never sent a cent & after a month or so of dilly dallying withdrew his papers but provided him with no means to continue his journey or to return. I do not know what the 3000 was for. I have been told that he was cheated & on the other hand some have said that he never had the money but that the debts were manufactured to keep him in Japan.

However, this may be the King having decided that he is to come back [to] settle the matter. If he should come go to America, I should think Dr. Ellinwood could find some scholarly [Godly?] minister would be willing to undertake his education at the start somewhere in the country.

So much for the Prince. Now we must await developments.

About stamps. I did not think you cared for them at all or I would have sent you some before. I do not remember ever having a request for some. I send herewith 10 sets. They are at present only used for internal postage & as yet this is in a very poor, limited & unsatisfactory condition but little by little this will be righted.

Politically things do not look at all promising. Things do not go along well & I do not know what the result will be. Corruption & abuse of power are on all sides & there does not seem to be much chance of righting matters. Just now the conservative element is in power but it will not be for long. There may be apparent backwards steps but Korea cannot go back now. She has gone too far forward already & then apparent backward steps are but halts to get breath for another rush forward. It has been this way in every land & it must be expected here in Korea. Things cannot go on all smoothly here and be all rough elsewhere. The great difficulty just now is a capable head. There is no capable head in the present government & I expect that the Prince who was in America will have to come back & take hold ere things will go forward at any great rate. I shall try & see His

Majesty this afternoon & pay my respect to him. He told me to be sure & come & see him as soon as I got back.

I wish much that the Queen were alive that she might guide & direct the King. Russian Military intruders are now on their way. A good honest Britisher is the head of the Finance& has hold of the Purse strings which is a big point gained. An American has been hired to superintend road making & sanctions arrangements. An American syndicate has agreed to & has been authorized to build a railroad. A good smart Electrician a Dane has been employed to superintend existing Telegraph lines & construct more.

(5)

All this means progress & we welcome it gladly but this is not all by any means. We need more. We have a fearless paper in the native language that calls itself "The Independent." It is edited by Dr. Jaisohn a naturalized American Citizen, a Korean nobleman that has come back to Korea. The paper is very bold in speaking for the right & takes up everyones cause that writes a complaint. It has done much good & will do much more if the editor is allowed to live. Koreans are not slow to put a troublesome man out of the way & as we see his boldness we fear somewhat. He is courageous & comes out on the side of the right at every step. He was a cousin of Pom K Soh's but made a very different use of his [time] when he was in the US.

Yours of the 30th of April also came to hand at the same time, about the Anti Toxine. I am almost sure its receipt was acknowledged. There have been a great many things lost in the mail the last few months. A great many of our Mission letters have now reached home & complaints do not come from but one quarter. On all sides we hear things. However it reached us in a busy time I think in the midst of Cholera & it may not have been acknowledged through I feel almost certain that a letter was sent about it. The Anti Toxine came to hand as well as the two books. The latter have been of a great deal of service. They were up to date books & have been read & studied by several of the physicians with a great deal of interest as well as profit. Nothing on the books gave us the faintest idea as to whether they were sent [by the?] company or to whom thanks, if any, should be sent. We have been very glad of the books & the anti toxin & will find the books a source of continuous benefit.

Yours of April 30th to Lillie came [duly?] to hand just at the same time as yours

(6)

of the 25th. You have doubtless ere this received our letters from Cheefoo about Kate.

Lillies health is poorer & as she has to be away from home so much for her work it will be a great help to us if you will allow us to keep Kate on. This was explained in my letter about 10 days ago or perhaps it was 20 days ago. How time does fly.

We are in the midst of our rainy season here in Korea. It has come earlier than usual & means that we will have a pretty hot summer but it is a very good thing for the city to have its annual cleaning before the hot weather comes. It needs it badly enough & it has rained almost more this year than most years. One periodic deluge has in part swamped our house. We had to move the dining table twice to get away from the drops & then had to put a [tumbler?] on the table to catch the drops. All over the dining room floor we have pots & kettles & in one corner of our room it is sopping wet. Lillie awoke one morning, the first of the hard rain to find her clothes all wet. These things do not bother us so much as they used but at the same time we do not have much enjoyment in finding so many leaks. Our thought is that as some have had their house all washed away we ought to be thankful to have even part of rooms that are all dry. We do not now have to wear our waterfrocks & use umbrellas in the house as in olden times but with Korean tiles it seems almost impossible to be without leaks at all.

But I must close.
With love from us all to you all
Your Loving Brother

Horace G. Underwood

PS: Hunt about the furs in that box. Not a word has been said about the furs. Were they spoilt. We fear much that they must have been as you say naught about them. We tried to pack them well and sincerely hope they reached you alright.

Horace

Letter 15

Chang Yun
Korea
Nov 14th /96

My Dear Thomas:

Just a line as the mail is now going up to Seoul to tell you that we are all well down here at Chang Yun. We had a pleasant trip down here &

it seemed to agree well with Hollie & Lillie though parts of the trip were decidedly trying. We are not able to travel in Pullmans or to stop at "Palace Hotels" & ["A]stor Houses." One night the room was one swarm of cock roaches. No other Hotel within 10 miles. One room is 6 x 6 for ourselves & our baggage & our bicycle, the horse was feeding at our door & munching all night. We were up in the mountains in the [tigee?] region. Lillie got a few snatches of sleep & I slept some. At 2:30 we started to make preparation for our next day's journey. By hard work we had the houses food cooked[,] the men all fed, breakfast [got?], loads on & off by 6 a.m. before the sun was up. We all kept together till sun was up & then pushed on & by hard work made 30 miles that day. Lillie slept curled up in her Korean chair which is a frame with a level bottom about 2ft. square. How she managed it I do not know. I walked on & kept my eyes open for pheasants[.] I saw lots of them but only got one shot & got a fine fat cock pheasant which we enjoyed very much. Down here there are lots of pheasants & ducks & game but I shall be too busy to hunt any. Perhaps I shall have some time over on Saturdays & may be able to get in a shot now & then.

This church here is our banner church. Last year they built anew their church at a cost of $400 in money besides wood & labor which were largely given. This year they have doubled the size of their church all this at their own expense. Now they need a bell & a large one that can be heard a long way off & I think the Lafayette Ave Presb Church should have the privilege of giving it. This church is the first church in Korea that built its own building & now at their invitation our training class for [helpers?] meets down here & they leave a large part of the expenses of the class. They deserve a fine bell & I should think the Lafayette Ave people would be glad of the privilege. I enclose a letter to Dr. Greggs about it which you can forward for not as you see fit.

We shall reach Seoul about [Dec?] 15 & then about Jan 1st I think we will have another class there[. A]lmost all of our work goes on [well.?] Especially in this province north & south things are most progressive. All over the province churches are springing up. The harvest is ready but where are the laborers. How can we train them & what shall we do with them all. We are asking for a large number of workers this year & we must have them. Mr. Bishop's letter

to the Board was to be sent to you first & I felt sure that you would like to see it. I knew that if you saw it you would be sure to see that it was properly presented to the Board. We need then people not for prospective work but for work that is now right before us. The story of last year's work will tell you of this. It is shown up mostly in Moffett's & my report.

You will see Moffett soon & he will tell you all about it.

Now goodbye Merry Merry X-mas to you all & a happy happy new year from us all.

Your Affectionate Brother
Horace G Underwood

Letter 16

Han Kang, Seoul
Aug 21st '97

My Dear Thomas:

After the longest illness that I can ever remember having I am up & around again though I have not got my wanted strength & but little work soon knocks me up. I am quietly resting at Han Kang & will not do any work till I get to feeling strong & well. Mr. Speer & Mr. Grant are both of them here & we expect them to arrive in Seoul from the north tonight or Monday. Our annual meeting will begin at once & whether I shall attend all the meetings will depend upon how I feel. I do not know but what my long sickness & enforced vacation may not in the end do me much good. I wish much that Mr. Speer could have made a longer visit in Korea than he has, for I fear that with but little knowledge he will think he has a great deal & that will not be as good for us. I want to have a long talk with him about the Educational policy of our mission as also about the self support-ing aspect of all of our work especially that in connection with our Seoul station. We have made a strong steady effort along this line & have we think so far worked it out well. We were a long while at the Airsons & they were very good & kind to us [&]we owe them a great deal. As perhaps I men-tioned before we think the typho-malarial fever was largely due to some bad drainage around our house. This we will at once try & put to right. My cement floor in the cellar has cracked & lets in water. I think that this can be easily fixed as also an outside drain that does not serve its purpose very well. We shall all stay here till this can be fixed or else take a trip to the interior in the interest of mission work & fix it when we get back. We had been back here for some days when the boxes from New York arrived. They took a month all but a few days to come from Chemulpo to Seoul. Will not our railroad be a welcome to us. It is now underway & the leveling etc for the road bed is well underway. It will be finished as far as the Seoul river by winter & will be running by next summer. Then we can make the journey in a little more than an hour & such boxes as these will come by rail almost to our very door. It is American capital that is doing this. Well, after the month's voyage on the river these things reached us & as Mr. Miller was here he opened the boxes while I watched from the lounge. When he got the lid off however I was not to be restrained & sat up & pulled the things out. It was very kind of you all to remember us so

(2)

often & I cannot tell you how we appreciated all the things. Hollie was still in bed & we sent the things all into him one after the other how he exclaimed over the things & what a joy they have been to him. Most of the things on the side that we opened were for Hollie & as they were taken in he hollered out "I believe the whole box is for me." "It is all Hollie." "Hollie," "For little Horace." The things to be cut out where [sic] a great joy to him & kept him busy & quiet while he had to be in bed. He is a dear good little fellow & complains very little while he is sick. I am well stocked with socks & have discarded my threadbare ones entirely & with my new slippers look quite stylish. My study will look altogether too Elegant for anything when I get my beautiful curtains that Helen & George sent hung up & in fact I feel that all my things are almost too good for me as it is. A missionary from Japan wrote & asked to be entertained at our house. We welcomed him most cordially, tried to have things nice for him & he, while being entertained at our house, talked about how fine our house was & from house to house criticized & found fault with everything as too good & fine for missionaries & yet we noticed that he seemed to enjoy the comfort of the house & the quality of the food that he had. It is needless to say that he will not be invited to stay with us again.

Lillie & all of us were delighted with her things & it is realy [sic] awfully good of you all to remember us in this way. The oh's & ah's that were sounded as the box was opened & the various things were exposed to view were beyond count. The "pocket-pistol" that Lillie had ordered for me was a fine one. I have never seen as fine a one & the only difficulty is that it is so fine that it may tempt me to use it too much. That would be disastrous.

Hulbert helped me out while I was sick, on the "Christian News" & now I have taken this work back. We have a special for His Majesty's birthday which comes on Sunday but is celebrated on Monday. One paper will come out on Monday three days ahead of time & will be accompanied by His Majesty's portrait as a supplement. This is the first time that such a thing has been done in Korea & it was only done with the Express & special permission of His Majesty. We will also have a special service in all the churches on Sunday & a grand mass prayer-meeting on Monday at 3 PM.

I shall not be present at these meetings though I have had to arrange & prepare tract[s] & see somewhat about the meetings.

Monday, Aug 23rd '97

The special number of the Christian News is meeting with much favor & the supplement that is only given to annual subscribers has been swelling our list

(3)

not a little & the last few days quite a little money has been coming in. Our list of annual subscribers is about 600 though the money has come to hand for about ½ of these. The balance are all well guaranteed & we are hastening up the payments by only giving the supplements to paid up subscribers. The paper is already doing no small amount of good. It is uniting our church members, is a good medium of communicating between churches & church members as well as between the missionary & his friends & adherents. In addition to this it is steadily working its way into the homes of those who are not Christians. It's [sic] general news, its firm stand for truth & justice regardless of position & party, its [firm?] & practical scientific notes all are tending to make it a necessity to all parties Christian & non Christian & thus a weekly tract goes into hundreds of heathen homes & already in several cases direct conversion has been the result while not a few have been led to say that they did not know there was so much good in Christianity. All this is an advance & when it is remembered that His Majesty & his household see it every week & that it goes to every magistracy in the country we have strong hopes that God will use it for good in the conversion of many many souls. I have hopes that before the year is out we can run up to at least 1000 prepaid subscribers. We do not yet know what we shall do about Christmas & next King's birthday but we shall have some other supplement for then. I am sending you under separate cover a few copies of His Majesty's picture. Will send more if you desire.

Re. salaries. In your last letter you ask about salaries. I answered but as some letters go astray will answer again. As you knew at the time, our salaries were reduced to $1350.00, about 2 ½ years ago & they were left at 1350.00 till May 1896 when without any word to us they were reduced to 1250.00.

Now there is one other matter about salaries. Do you pay the whole 1250 for Lillie & I. On looking over the report of the "woman's board of the north west,["] I see that Mrs. Blair is down as still paying Lillie's salary which will be 400 or 450 per year. If this is so it is not right of the Board to receive the full 1250.00 from you. Do not let it be known that I have called your attention to this but it should be looked into. We of course get only the 1250.00 & that is right but it is not right (if this is done) to take full salary from you & 1/5 from Mrs. Blair as well.

Now I have a proposition to make. You propose a trip to Europe for a rest. The same results

(4)

can I think be obtained at less cost. If you will take the 400.00 from our salary now overpaid & add to it $200 more it would make $600.00 with which I could hire an assistant who would relieve me of a great deal of my work & thus relieve me of much of the nervous strain. There is a man out here now who has a knowledge of Korean & is a good Hebrew scholar. It is Mr. Pieters, a converted Jew. I do not yet know whether he would come or not but I do know that he will not long remain where he is. I have broached the subject with him but of course have made no definite offer to him. He is single & gets from the Bible Society for which he now works a little less than $600 gold a year. He could help me in a great many ways. If he could not come perhaps I could get some one else but at any rate a helper would be invaluable to me. Mr. Pieters could help on the paper, on tract work, in translation, he could assist in country work, see Koreans who come to see me & relieve me of a great deal of minutiae that is so trying. I could tell him to see that a thing was done & he would see to it. He has been on the field here at work for the Bible Society for three years &it is because I know him that I think he would be of more use & better than a new man whom I did not know. Of course I realize that he would not have a knowledge of shorthand such as a man from elsewhere might have but this would be almost counter balanced by his knowledge of Korean. Then too not to be too modest the possession of a phonograph would easily do away with this difficulty. Perhaps you have forgotten but you asked me once whether I could use a phonograph in Korea & at that time I said I did not see how it would be of any use. Now however it is different & if you have that amount of the Lord's money on hand a Phonograph would be of great use for my editorials & articles for the paper etc etc. I have to dictate to Koreans who write very slowly indeed (though faster than my Korean) & you can realize what a tremendous saving it would be. There is no shorthand for Korean. My necessary Korean correspondence is very large & steadily growing, I have to correct abuses & send as it were pastoral letters. Sometimes a general letter will do & then again the abuses differ & particular letters must be written. You can readily see at a glance of what immense value

(5)

a phonograph would now be under these circumstances. When I was home & when you spoke about it before, the circumstances were different. I did not have to prepare 4 or 5 whole pages for the newspaper each week, nor did I have the immense amt of correspondence in Korean that I now have. If I had it & Mr. Pieters I would use it for House correspondence as well.

We have been wondering whether you ever got my long letters, an oft begin one, that I sent you from Yokohama, Japan. It was begun in Seoul, continued in Cheungfu, & posted in Yokohoma. Lillie sent a letter & it was never received. We were so shadowed & watched that we fear our letters were taken out of the mails. Of course we could not prove this but we know that special messengers were intercepted & their letters opened & read & that some letters we posted in Yokohoma never reached their destination. We also know that during the war letters were opened in transit & their contents copied, published in Japan & criticized before the letters even reached their destination in Japan.

Concerning the Prince: As I have not been able to go see his Majesty I sent your letters to Mr. Brown the King's advisor & have as yet got no definite answer. I shall try & see him tomorrow so far as to send something definite to you. I know that originally it was not the King's idea that the prince should not at the first handle his own money but that arrangements should be made for him. I will try to enclose definite instructions tomorrow.

Aug. 28 '97

My Dear Thomas,

Mission meeting has begun & we are in full swing but I keep out of it all I can. I read my report which I shall have printed & send you copies. This Paper Your two letters dated July 8th & July 21st both arrived in same mail & contents note. That of July 8th with enclosure reached me O.K. & I will send you a detail about her account by next mail. I want to answer your other questions & to send this by tomorrow's mail. You have with this check paid [rog?] up in advance. Your last check was in adv. & I put balance out to interest so that I had paid her I think £4 above what was due her Feb 29th. I have not books here but I think that after I pay her £21 she will be paid up

(6)

to Aug. 29th & if this is so I shall put this £29 this left to interest for 6 un [sic] @ 5 ½% per annum & pay her for another 6 months then. I will let you know definitely.

About the house, His Majesty <u>told me</u> in person that he did not desire us to move & that he wanted me next to him. Of course I do not know whether he told the truth or not. I wrote you before about Dr. Vinton's place. I do not want the place to go to the King as it looks down on our place & would make our place untenable. The Mission here will never consent to sell our house but they might consent to sell the Vinton's after they have moved. I wish you could stop this if it comes up without a full correspondence with us by letters. The <u>cable was</u> not sent by me[.] Mr Miller & I were the Corr. & he sent cable in my name without a word to me though I forward this sale of that part. A piece of property had been put up for sale, put on the market by our mission. The King expresses a desire to buy, we could not but sell.

<u>Re Prince</u> I have sent again but no answer & will urge the cabling of money to you at once for Prince. Will write as soon as I can get further word from Palace.

<u>Re stoves</u> Vinton has been away. Will send further word but think you had better not be bothered.

Re. Miss-carriage of letters. I do not know that any of your letters have gone astray as yet but our letters home we know have been tampered with. I think now that the Prince is in U.S.A. perhaps we will be let alone.

Now I must close with best love to you all. This is the first letter I have written without a nervous tick so I am improving.

Your affectionate brother
Horace Underwood

P.S. I have written Teele to get me some 1000 pictures for X-mas no of paper. He may draw on you for $20.00 on my acct. H.U.

[Memo on verso of included table list of mission stations.]

Thus you will see I have 17 stations to see to with the supervision of 84 weekly service & practically a church of 1000 members & 2000 adherents. Also six day schools & 7 S.S. to see that there are people to carry them on properly. There is my weekly paper. I have spent almost 4 mo. of daily meetings of Bible [News?] Corr. & printed [an] addition to Bible last year once a million pages of tracts etc. Then too five [?] & book shops & the Mo Ha Kwan Shelter. Propose lesson leans for all these as well.

Letter 17

Cheefoo China
Beach Hotel
Oct 26th /97

My Dear Thomas:

Since writing last we have returned to Nagasaki & thence to Shanghai China where we were detained about a week then up the China coast to Cheefoo where we now are. The whole trip has done me a power of good. I have not only regained my normal weight & lost flesh but have exceeded all previous records in this line & weigh now 148 lbs. Hollie too has much improved & is eating well & rosy & fat. Lillie has not done as well as I had hoped. She looks fairly well & strong but has terrible attacks of dyspepsia & at times her Rheumatism is quite bad. I do not know what should be done but a good deal of success has attended the use of the Electropoise out here in the east & I am thinking of getting one to try & see what can be done. If Lillie could only have her health again she could do so much more work with & for the Koreans. Ere this reaches you, you will have received copies of my last report & I feel that we indeed have a great deal to be thankful for. Here in China work does not wear the cheerful aspect that it does in Korea, the numbers are not so great, the people are not so willing to listen, nor when converted are they as willing to help on the work by their own labors as are the Koreans. This is I think largely due to the plans that we have adopted in Korea from the very start. Here other plans have been followed & as a result other harvests have been reaped.

The attitude of the people is of course to no small extent a result of their nature but the view with which they take hold of the work & the way in which they are willing to suffer sacrifice for the cause is to a large extent the result of the plans & methods that we have used & followed from the start. We have worked along what are commonly known as the [?] methods though we have been a little more strict on the [?] side of the question. Here we find that the [?] method is not much in vogue & I think the results show that it would have been wiser to have followed them.

We expect to go up to [Lung?]-Chow-Fow where Dr Matee has his college & see that before we leave for Korea. We shall probably leave here on Thursday the 28th. If we go we will have to ride in a _shensa_ a sort of litter that is slung on poles which are hitched like the shafts of a wagon to two mules one in front & one behind & thus you jog along. Jog is just the word for it is indeed jog, jog all the way. We shall stay there for a couple of days & be back here in time to take our steamer for Korea one week from the coming Saturday. I hope then that we will be back to do some work to make up for our long absence.

With much love to you all,

Your affectionate brother,
Horace G. Underwood

Letter 18

(No. I)

Seoul, Korea. June 17th/ 1898

My Dear Thomas;-

Your three letters previous to May 2nd. and covering a period of about three weeks all reached me by one mail the other day. You see that I am trying the new type-writer and as you will see I am not yet quite accustomed to the upper & lower cases but this will come in a little while. The machine is a beauty and is the admiration of all that have seen it. I have had a number of inquiries as to price and also as to whether there would be any reduction to missionaries. The tabular stops are a fine thing and we have already found that they were of great use. It was an example of this that made the treasurer of the Methodist Mission here come round and ask what it would cost for him to get a machine like it. Then too everything if right before you and you can tell all that you have written without lifting up the case which is a wonderful help to amatures [sic] and writers like your humble servant.

RE. PRINCE: I went and saw Mr. Brown as soon as your letters reached me and let him have that part of your letters that referred to the Prince. It was not a fact that he had had a cable from here ordering him to come home but it is generally supposed that he did get a cable from the rebels in Japan who, it is supposed, knowing that the Russian has at present relinquished his hold[,] are concocting some plot for the overthrow of the present government and if they could get hold of the young Prince it would be a pretty good card. It is a pity that he heeded any such cable for the chances are that he will be degraded

(2) J.T.U. NO.I

AND THIS WILL BE NO SMALL AFFAIR TO HIM. I regret much that his trip to America should not have had a better result but the whole difficulty was with the way in which he was sent. I objected to Mr Pak from the very start and I think that the whole difficulty came there. Mr Pak was a Romanist and of course was anxious to keep the Prince from under the control of Protestants. I feared this before we started and referred the matter to Mr. Brown (who is hardly a nominal Christian though he cannot be said to be anti-Christian-), but he seemed to have a good deal of confidence in Mr. Pak & I could do nothing. I had a long talk with Mr. Pak & he talked so straight forwardly that I was fain to believe that all would be right. Then too, if Mr.

Gale talked to the Prince as he talked publicly on the steamer about his affairs, his influence was none for the best. He seemed to think that he should have been maintained as a Prince while in the States, that the amount allowed him from here of $100.00 gold a month was altogether inadequate for him as a prince, that it was a disgrace to the Korean Government to attempt such a thing. If the Prince was talked to in this fashion it is no wonder that he decided to get home as soon as he could. Mr. Gale seems while in Washington to have been very strangely under the influence of the present Korean Minister to Washington. We in Seoul know him well and have known him for a number of years. It might not be politic nor would it be the best thing to say so to his face, but he is generally considered to be a rascal and Prince Min Yong Whan who is also in Washington has proven himself to be one of the best of Korean officials and yet Mr. Gale

(3) J.T.U. NO.I

is loud in proclaiming Min Yong Whan as a rascal and the Minister as a saint. You said in your letter that you would send me full accounts & particulars of the Prince and his affairs so that I could hand the same over to Mr. Brown and I should be glad if I could get the same.

We had quite a time when Lillie got back. Hollie & I went down to Chemulpo to meet her. We wished much that we could have run over to Nagasaki and met her there but we could not well afford this so we contented ourselves with a trip to Chemulpo. Lillie's steamer was late on account of the fogs and instead of getting in at 4 A.M. on Monday did not arrive till 1.20 A.M. on Tuesday. Chemulpo inner harbor can only be entered at full tide and at all other times the ships have to anchor three miles out. Under these circumstances it is not an easy matter to meet anyone nicely for one cannot well stay in a little boat (Japanese row-boat-) three miles out in the open sea all day waiting for a steamer and then too if you do not go out you cannot tell what boat it is till she has reached her anchorage. Just at dusk we were badly fooled. A steamer was seen coming in and as Lillie's steamer was the only one that they were expecting the company told us that it was the steamer. Hollie & I got a boat and road [sic] all the 3 & ½ miles out only to find that it was a Russian steamer. I heard the whistle at 1.20 and went out only to find that they refused to let me on board before the Customs officer came off which they informed me would be at daylight. I did not give up and after a good deal of parleying the Captain consented to allow the gang to be lowered and I got on board.

(4) J.T.U. NO.I

We all got safely up to Seoul and we found that some of the Ladies had been in the house and had decorated it beautifully with wild and cultivated roses and other flowers. The Koreans also gave her a most hearty welcome and tried to make her think she was realy [sic] coming home. The next day the boxes were here and we proceeded to open them with no little dispatch. We do not know how to thank you for all the lovely things with which they were filled. Hollie, and in fact all of us were beside ourselves with excitement as one thing after another was brought out of the box. Hollie looks just lovely in that suit and he takes the shine off all the other boys. Not that he needs any such thing to set him off but when he gets them on he is just beyond description. That gun is just a beauty, it is the finest shot gun in Korea and I wish that I could in some way get to you a few of the wild ducks & geese and pheasants that it will shoot. I had seen only one Parker gun before and it had been shown to me as something that was very fine but it was not nearly as handsome a gun as this. I will be the envy of all and you can think of me when I am in the country as having a good deal better fare now because of that gun. I shall not run much danger of starvation in a country full of game when I have such a gun.

Work goes on well all over Korea wherever the workers are sent and our successes are only limited by our efforts. The idea that it is open in the North and no where else is a sad blunder that quite a number of people have gotten into. I wrote you while I was in the country the last time about the success of the work on that trip &

(5) J.T.U. NO.I

The way in which the people were taking hold and setting to work. They do wonders and are to be commended much but they badly need leaders and as yet these have not been found among them. They will in time be found but it will take some time to train them and this is the work that just now demands our attention. And yet who is there to do this work and how best had it be done. We must show by example how to carry on the evangelistic work and in fact we must, be the leaders.

From a political aspect things are no better than they were & as far as we can see they are realy [sic] worse than they were. I think that it must be acknowledged by all that the best government that Korea has ever had was when the Japanese were in power. The Japanese were Orientals and knew how to manage these people better than any one else that has ever tried it. They knew well what this people needed and where they were lacking and it was with this knowledge that they set to work. They were far from perfect and made some awful blunders but as far as the people of this land were concerned they did attempt to see that Justice was meeted out to the poor people and the laborer was assured of the result of his labor. To day the country is without law of any kind and "might makes right" all over the land. What the end will be no one can at all see but I feel sure that as they are at present things cannot go on and either another power must step in or the people will arise and there will be a period of riot & anarchy in this land. It is a little ominouse [*sic*] when way off in the interior you find people discussing the French Revolutions and saying that that is the only hope for the country.

Again there is talk about the government desiring to buy property

(6) J.T.U. NO.I

and that they desire to buy out the old Vinton property and our house & I am writing to Dr. Ellinwood about the matter. I do wish that in some way it could be settled >by the board< that this would not be done do that we could feel secure in our house. I think that it would be a great mistake to sell our house after all that has been put into it and not only that I do not think the money could repay for the time and physical energy that would be used up in the building of another place. We have little by little put a good deal of time and energy and money into this place and it is just adapted to our work both here and in the country. Dr. Vinton's place is right back of ours and on a higher level so that that too should not be sold as its sale would make this place untenable. Dr. Vinton has left there now and Miss Wambold (whose work is in connection with our Church and therefore in our neighborhood) and Dr. Whiting are now living there. If the Board should sell that place they would have to get some other place elsewhere for these ladies for the Millers and for us. I do wish that something could be done that would settle it that we were not to be sold out. I have been to see Mr. Brown about the prince and also spoke to him as to the intention of the government as to the purchase of our place. He says that he has no definite information on the point but that he has no doubt at all but what the King will want to buy this place as soon as he can lay his hands upon the money to do so but that he (Mr. Brown) does not see for what he can want it or what will be the use when he has it.

About the Prince he says he would be obliged to you if you could send him an account of the moneys spent and the balance left over.

(7) J.T.U. NO.I

He also said do not pay any of those other unauthorized bills. He feels rather badly about the Prince's trip to America and feels that it has been a failure and blames this upon Mr. Pak and also upon Mr. Loomis through whom the Prince received some very poor and ill-judged advice.

I wish that it had turned out differently but we tried to do the best and that is the end of it. I do not know how the young man himself feels and trust that he feels alright though I have heard since he has been in Japan that he complains bitterly about the amount allowed being too small. His feelings on this score have no doubt been no little increased by some of the foreigners who are pitying him and putting such ideas into his head.

Well I do not know but what I am getting to have too long a letter and think that I had better stop. All are well and send love. Hollie and Kate with quite a few others have gone down to our river house to a sort of picnic. Give much love to all and accept a full share for yourself from

YOUR LOVING BROTHER

H.G. Underwood

Letter 19

(BUSINESS LETTER.)

Seoul, Korea. June 20th. 1898.

No 2.

My Dear Thomas:-

I have one or two items of business and thought it might be better if they were in a separate letter.

RE CHECKS:- I had written to the bank in Shanghai several times before I wrote you & at the same time that I wrote to you I wrote them again And had found their answer awaiting me when I returned. They replied that it had been a mistake of theirs, that they had received the check & correcting their mistake asked to be excused for it. Check No. B/C 1952 was the check which I[,] so that I should be surer of getting proper rates[,] had made out to the order of Mr. Fitch for him to place to my account. It is all straight now but it has taught me that I must keep a closer watch upon the bank that I had thought. They could not or would not (I do not know which) find their mistake till I stated that I, had written to find out from the bank on which the check had been drawn & in addition to this they had charged me with making entries in their book.

RE MY ACCOUNTS:- In your last letter but one you said that you would send by next mail a statement of my account with you. Would you draw from my account in the Savings bank whatever is needed up to enough to keep the account open and repay yourself and then let me know how much more I owe you and how the bank account stands. If the two statements could come to-gether I should be glad.

RE TYPE-WRITER:- Since the arrive of my new Type-writer I have received a number of requests as to the price and also as to whether if it

(2)

is sold at the same price to Missionaries. I am also all the time receiving requests for the prices of paper inks etc . Have you such a thing as a price list that you could let me have.

RE MY WANTS;- Of a few things I am entirely out.

Ist. I have no Cyclostyle supplies. I need paper ink & a new roler.

2nd. I need Cobalt Writing Fluid. I have plenty of Copying ink & Egyptian Black. Is the latter good for fountain pens.

3rd. I am out of Lead pencils.

4th. I need the oil paper and proper blotter with instructions as to how to copy letters written with the Underwood ribbons.

I can make a success with the writing ink but fail when it comes to type written work.

These will seem some modest requests but it would hardly do for me to send my orders for supplies to Smith.

Trusting that you will pardon my asking so, much

Your Brother
H. G. Underwood

Letter 20

Seoul, Korea. Aug. Ist. 1898

My Dear Thomas:

I have been watching for a letter from you but I have not received a word since the letter that you sent about the return of the young Prince. I received Mr. Hands accounts, and the draft for the balance which I will hand over to Mr. Brown and I trust that his little trip to America may not have been of no avail. I feel that although we cannot now see the good, ~~that~~[5] good can be brought out of it & at the time it certainly did seem as though providence did point to our doing what we could to get him to America & to putting him under Christian influences. It is known now that it was some of the refugees in Japan that sent to America and asked him to come back. The King was no longer surrounded by a foreign guard and it was thought that now was the time to do something and the Prince was just the man to work with. Of course he would be no better than the present King but those who would put him in power would control and out in the east here if you want to do anything you must have someone of Royal blood.

There is and always will be a great deal of dissatisfaction with the present government. His Majesty insists that He & He alone is the power in Korea and he does not even give any power to any one of His Ministers. He has what he calls a cabinet but in reality he has no cabinet for He appoints his ministers without any regard to their fitness for the positions to be filled and without any regard to their likelihood of their agreeing among themselves. In like manner the so-called Prime Minister is appointed entirely regardless of his political leadings and as a result what harmony can you possibly have and what can you do with such a cabinet. It has been known to have a cabinet in which no two members out of ten agreed and as a result all the different departments were working in opposition to each other so much so that the police and army were working in opposition to each other and as a result the police commenced arresting soldiers and when the civil court ordered them not to do so the whole Police force of the land from the Commissioner of police (a Cabinet Officer) and the high Police Officials down to the sergeants & common Police men all struck on one day, locked up all the stations and for several days you could not find a police man anywhere at all. When such things are possible what can you expect. Just now a prolonged trial is going on in connection with an alleged conspiracy to dethrone the King and a large number of the highest officials are implicated but as to what will be the result we cannot at all say. Right in the midst of the trial everything has stopped. One of the native papers took occasion to criticize one of our judges and one Korean also memorialized the throne: so the judge at once dissolved the court and said there would be no more sittings till these criticisms were stopped. Everything is so childish and the Koreans from the highest down are just like so many babies. It reminds me of when we as children would be playing and something was done that we did not like we would say "I won't play any more if you don't play my way." It will be a long long while before Korea can govern herself aright and how I wish that she would ask help of old England.

5. Both the comma and the strikethrough are hand written in this typed letter.

We are much interested in the war though we only get a few notes here and there and do not know much about all that has been done?

(2) J. T. U.

Our minister has been favored with a few cables so that we have heard of the main features of the war but that is all. On Saturday last we heard that Spain was sueing for peace and were rejoiced to think that the war would be soon over. Rumors about the attitude of Germany have not been very satisfactory and we are anxiously awaiting the next mail to see what will happen. As far as we have been able to learn everything has been much for the honor of the States and the war has brought our country forward in a way that was not at all expected by the Foreign powers. When the war began out here it was by a good many people looked upon as a sort of doubtful affair and it was very freely stated that the U.S. had no Navy and that it would not take long for Spain to show Uncle Sam that she had a considerable job on her hands: that of course in the end the States would win because of her resources. Such was the talk then and now that it has turned out as it has they say "Oh well Spain never had a chance against the U.S." I have been wondering all along how it was affecting trade and how it would affect you and your business. Has it made much difference. I have thought that perhaps it would not make much of a difference as no matter what was done there would be as much need for writing and the use of writing materials.

I have been a little under the weather again and for a time I feared that I was going to be affected the same as last year but a good use of quinine set me up and then a rest has about brought me round again so that I am well but not yet as strong as I should like.

It took some time to get the fever under control but we succeeded in the end and I am now taking quinine at the proper intervals so as to ward off a return. Work goes on well and if the politics do not interfere the next few years will see some wondrous changes in this heathen land. This land of Korea as far as Mission work is concerned is in a marvelous way the exponent of the self support system that is know[n] as the Nevius System and in this land in the Presbyterian Mission it has been carried to an extent that I believe has not been equaled in any Mission field. I believe that it is the plan that should be followed and that only by this plan can a strong work be, started in a comparative short time.

Dr. Ellinwood has written to me asking me to write a history of our Presbyterian Mission in Korea so as to have it for the Pan-Presbyterian Alliance that is to meet in Washington in 1900. I shall endeavor to show in it how the use of this system has so materially affected our work. I am more

& more convinced that it is the plan that should be followed the world over. We have one difficulty to encounter and that is that our sister missions do not see eye to eye with us in this matter and it is no easy work to carry out such a system with other missions right alongside of you working along other lines and following the very opposite policy.

Bible Translation comes on apace and if the printer would only do his part of the work we could have almost the whole of the New Testament printed before the next annual meeting. I was kept in the city quite late this year on account of the meetings of the Board and I

(3) J. T. U.

hope to be able to do a good deal of my own individual work down here this summer.

We enjoy this Summer house very much indeed and in fact if it were not here I do not know what we would do for it has proven that as far as we are concerned we could not stand the summer in our house in Seoul. We had a thatch roof on up to this spring but the winds are so high that it was regularly blown off two or three times each summer and then we had to move the bed about from place to place to find a dry spot. Of course we could not stand this and we were forced to plan for something different and so we had to have the thatch removed and have had a roof of metal tiles put on and a number of other necessary repairs done. Now we are well housed and I cannot tell you what a luxury it is to be able to go to bed without being afraid that before morning you will have to get up two or three times to move the bed to a dry spot. Our place does realy [sic] look very pretty indeed & I wish much that you could drop in and see us. The rains this year have not been as bad as in some other years and much to our delight they have in the main been coming at night.

Lillie has been pretty well since her return but has had several turns of sickness and is not at all strong. I felt that what she needed was some tonic to assist her digestion and was anxious to get her to take some Tokay as it did her so much good before but she would not do so but now for a few days she has been taking a little & she is feeling a good deal better for it.

Kate had quite a sick spell but she has pulled round nicely & has just returned from a little over a week in Chemulpo. Of course this is not the first class place to stop at but then it is the sea side and she had sea air while she was away and also it was a change. We told her to stay a couple of weeks or so if she desired it but she did not care to stay longer.

Hollie had a bad attack of fever which was very obstinate and nothing seemed to have any effect at all till of late the quinine has had a good effect but it seemed no good until we gave him such large doses that its toxic effects were manifest. We had rather a fright about him the other day. He was a good deal better and I had gone into the city and was just coming back. He saw me in the distance and jumped up to call and wave to me. In turning he fell full length on the back of his head. The fall seemed to knock all his senses out of his head & for the good part of an hour he could not recall anything that had happened, how he had hurt himself or how he was in his night clothes, & he did not seem to know that he had been sick. We were naturally rather frightened but ice on his head and bromide and a good sleep brought him round alright though we were very careful to keep him very quiet for a few days. He is alright now and is as well as ever.

The Bunkers have left the Mission and have gone up to the mines to act as accountant for the American Company that is working them but he made arrangements with this company that they should provide him with a Christian helper so that he should have the opportunity of

(4) J.T.U.

DOING Christian work there. He calls it entering upon Independent Mission work and the other day I received rather a surprising letter from Mrs. Bunker referring to some rumors of Mission action that was to affect me. I enclose the letter and have marked it "No I" and have underscored the part referred to. It bothered me quite a little for I could not think of anything that it could refer to & spoke with one or two of my friends but as they did not know anything had concluded that there was nothing in it at all when I received another letter referring to something in a mysterious way (letter No 2 also underscored with red) and it does look as though something is being arranged and as though it aims at me. I thought that as I have heard of this I had better let you know so that you may know that if there is any trouble at the next Annual meeting and my name is mixed up in it you will know that it is not of my seeking and if you think it worth while you might mention it or show this to Dr Ellinwood but this I leave to your judgement. It simply occurred to me that if anything is to come up it would be as well for them to know at least this much beforehand.

I do not know to what it can refer nor on what line the action is to be taken it may be any one of the following;-

A. The Newspaper has met with a good deal of opposition from some members of the mission and it may be that the attack is to be along the old line of opposition to it and yet I can hardly think this is so as some talked over the matter, I have been told, with Mr Speer and in his report he did not condemn it and then no further action was taken at the last meeting.

B. The fact that I do not use the same term for God that they do puts me in a bad way with not a few of our mission and I am very sorry for it. They try to represent that I am alone in this but this is not so as there, are some members of our own mission, a few of the Methodist and the entire English Mission as well as the Whole of the Baptist Mission. The objection by us is to taking the name of the cheif [*sic*]⁶ of the Gods and using that for the true God and in all books etc telling the people that we worship "The Honorable Heavens." The contention is not the same as in China where the bulk of the Missionaries use the term that means "the Supreme Ruler" and where the strongest advocates of this term say that they could never consent to use the term used here and in China it has never been used. In connection to this matter I do not hold for any special term but object to the one that has been adopted by so many and time and again I have asked & urged the other members of the mission to meet with me and in prayer to lay the matter before God and to see whether we could not get to a point where we could agree upon one term but this they refuse and they will not for a moment consider any such plan. They have claimed that I have been changeable and have held to one term and then to another but this has been only with the hope and prayer that we might come to one term on which we could all agree. I hardly see however how they are going to take any action on this question as so far in all missions where there are convictions

(5) J.T.U.

on the matter of the term to be used for God it has been left to the individual to use the term that he has deemed right. It should also be born in mind that they have never claimed that the other terms proposed are wrong or that they give a wrong idea to the Korean but that the term they use will do.

C. It may be in the matter of the Quinine business that is being done. You know that for some time we have been supplying men with quinine so that they by its sale could make a living and at the same time carry on their Mission work with out any expense to the mission.

We thought that thereby we might be able to get people to work & not to think that they had to be paid for what they did for the Lord. So far it has worked well and as far as I have known it has been approved by the Mission. It has been reported from year to year in my annual reports and on more than one occasion it has been commended at an annual meeting. Under these circumstances I hardly think that this can be the matter that is coming up.

---

6. This is likely a typographical error, as this letter was typed by Underwood.

This has grown up little by little. At the start I gave it to the Korean at the exact figure it cost but found that there were items of freight, little costs of transportation local, loss by breakage, losses by pillage sometimes amounting to a considerable amount but which were not discovered till after the goods had been receipted for, the initial cost of starting men etc and that there was considerable loss because I was by mistake in reality selling below cost.

To cover this a few sen per bottle were added to the apparent cost with the result that as a rule we have come out about even.

Up to within the last few months there has been absolutely no profit and what has remained since then has been used to stock the shops with books and a little has been used to cover the deficite [sic] on the "CHRISTIAN NEWS."

D. It may be that they are going to object to my putting the Korean in the way of getting some home implements such as plows etc. At the start they are afraid of the merchants but have confidence in the missionary so I have assisted them in the placing of their orders etc and in the getting of their goods but have arranged with a business firm here to look after the whole affair. I cannot imagine that any objection can be taken to this.

E. The last and only other thing I can think that it can possibly refer to is the trip to Fusan that was taken to look into the affairs of the Australian Mission. After we had gone a telegram was received from Pyeng Yang objecting to the investigation and it may be that this matter is coming up but when the BOARD at home had approved it[, it] hardly seems that they are likely to object.

This is the way affairs stand and I have carefully thought of all the things that could come up and I cannot think of anything else that it can be and yet I do not see how they can object to any of these.

I was glad to hear from Lillie about your new offices and the type writer business. I wish that you could tell me all about the

(6) J.T.U.

BUSINESS etc and I should like much to have a photograph of your new offices. I was delighted to get the pictures of the rooms in the Brooklyn house and to see how things were all looking. What have you decided about the changes preparatory to Hannah's wedding. Are you going to have them made and what is Hannah going to do. I want to be kept posted about all that you are doing and all the changes.

But I must close. In connection with the enclosed letters please bear in mind that they are private letters and that they neither of them know that I am sending them to you. The names of the writers must not be mentioned at all and it must not be known at all that I have sent some these letters to you. >Outside of Board if you deem best<[7]

I hope that we shall hear from you soon. You must not be surprised at delays in the mail as there is only a monthly service to, the East coast now. Can you not persuade Hannah & her beloved that if they get out to California they ought to some over here to Korea to see us and to see this part of the East. Everything is changing and they ought to come out here to see it before the change takes place.

All join in much love to you all.

Your Loving Brother
Horace G. Underwood

Letter 21

(New Series No _6)   Seoul, Korea. Nov 8th.1898

My Dear Thomas:-

Another mail has just come in and I have had a batch of letters but to say the least it was rather a strange medley.

I saw a lot of letters and jumped for them at once and thought that I was going to have a lot to read. The first I opened contained the duplicate Bill of lading for the boxes that have been sent.

The second tha[t] I opened contained your letter No 10 that was written last May and was an account of the Prince Funds for Mr. Brown but long ere this I had received Mr. Hands accounts of the same and had turned them over to Mr. Brown. The third that I opened contained the duplicate invoices for the Lamps and Christmas box that you had sent.

The Fourth was a bonafide letter your letter No 12 of Sept 14th. About these let me remark that No 10 which should have had enclosures in the line of accounts had no such enclosures. They are not needed now as the whole matter has been closed with Mr. Brown but I let you know so that you may know that it is no uncommon thing to have letters that speak of enclosed paper without being able to find the paper's that you say have been put in. These papers that were supposed to have been in letter No. 10 do not matter now as the whole affair is settled and closed.

---

7. Hand-written text and previous underline in red pencil.

I was glad to get letter No 12 and to hear that at the writing you were all well. As far as the affairs that were to come off at the annual meeting are concerned they were all moved over and everything went along nicely. There were some rubs but beyond what

(New Series No.6.) (2)

I said in my letter No. 5 nothing of any serious nature came up. About the paper they seem to be more at ease and I think that things will go along better now. About all the other affairs they are now straightened out and all will go well and I have arranged to turn all the Quinine business over to others and this has been done in such a way as to continue the work that was going on as a result of it and at the same time to relieve me of all work and responsibility about the matter.

THE PRINCE has never come to Korea yet and I do not know when he will. From a political point of view all out here is very much mixed . The last few days we have been on the very verge of a popular uprising. The people are waking up to the fact that they have some rights and in a dignified way they are insisting upon them.

The King has yielded to them but some of his advisors thought best to try and stop what was going on absolutely and got the order for the arrest of 19 of the peoples leaders. They were arrested one night when it was learned the next morning some 30 thousand people gathered on the street and big square and in a dignified way sent in a request that as the leaders of the people had been arrested and the leaders had only done what the people had asked, they too might all be arrested. For some four or five days this crowd with bonfires etc have continued night and day waiting to be arrested. They in a quiet way simply say that if they have done wrong they are ready to die and there they stay. The leading stores and merchants have all

(New Series No.6.) (3)

stopped business and closed their doors on the plea that if they have no rights they might as well die of starvation as oppression

They have in the main been quiet and orderly. The only thing that they have done that might be said to be wrong was that when a company of soldiers was sent to disperse them and the order was given to prepare to fire they rushed up and disarmed the soldiers but nothing more and then gave them back their arms and let them go. There they still are camped, and there they say they will wait and die if they do not get justice. I tell you the fact that we see these people are getting a little back bone is most encouraging and as we see this we feel that there is some hope for this country after all if only the outside countries will keep hands off and let them work it out for themselves. They have waked up to the fact that they have some rights and that if they can only stick together they have no little power. The end is in other hands that our[s] and we need have no fear and yet with what trembling and destination and real fear we watch to see what the finale is to be.

Most of us are pretty well now. I found the trial no small work and do not yet know what the end will be as there is a disagreement. The decission [sic] has not yet been reached. Lillie is about the same as usual and as the winter draws on suffers more & more from her old trouble. We are all going to start for a long trip into the country in a few days and we will not be back till just a few days before Christmas. Kate has not been at all well for some days but is

(New Series No.6.) (4)

better now and the doctors all say that it is nothing serious. She will be up to-day and in a few days will be herself again.

ROUTS TO THE EAST. In your letter you ask about this and I would like to state as follows:-

The QUISKEST [sic] rout is taking all in all the one that you sent by but all these overland routs are rather costly. If any thing is wanted in a hurry it is well enough but if there is time to wait the water rout is the best.

The Most usual and CHEAPEST routs [sic] to ship per S.S. from N.Y. to SHANGHAI. If this is done it should be shipped to me Seoul Korea care of PRESBYTERIAN MISSION PRESS, SHANGHAI CHINA.

This is a slow rout and things take a long while to come that way but this is by all odds the cheapest and in fact ordering any thing from the Board it is the rout used by all our missionaries except when there is special haste needed. It is not a bad plan if the package is not a fill ton to send it to, the Board and to let them ship it out with other goods that are coming. I have been told that there is not a S.S. that leaves N.Y for the China coast on xx which our Board does not have some shipments.

I am sorry to see by the note at the end of your letter that you are having so much in a business way to, worry and annoy you. I can see how trying it must all be. At all time you have our earnest prayers and here is whence help must come. I wish much that I were where I could be of some help but it has been ordered otherwise and I

(New Series No.6.) (5)

know that he who rules the world will help. It is our greatest comfort to feel that the work is not ours, it is His and that He is able and will look after His

Own. You I know are working for Him and are trying to carry on the work for Him and I am sure that He will look after and Sustain you.

But I must be closing. I have to take charge of the Miller baby funeral to-day. Here the end of the trial to-morrow and start for the country the day after. I still have a good deal to do in this house and in the line of getting ready.

Give our love to all and merry Christmas and a Happy New Year.

With much love from us all

Your Loving Brother

HG Underwood

Letter 22

Hai Jin, Korea, Dec 5 /98

My Dear Thomas,

Here we are at Hai Jin. We have been away from Seoul for about a month & will be starting back to Seoul in about 5 or 6 more days. I am driven with work as I have the whole work of the class on my hands as well as special services twice a day in different parts of the city.

A maid has just come in & we have heard that dear Hannah is no longer Miss Underwood but Mrs. Stevens. How we long for letters that will tell us all about it.

I am writing now in a hurry about this enclosure. I have just received this letter on Dec 5th & the amount was <u>due on Nov 20th</u>. The reason they did not get it on due date was that <u>they</u> sent the letter too late. It left Chicago on Oct 21st. Now <u>can you have</u> this straightened out. I did hear in some indirect way from home a long while ago that you were helping out about insurance on Father Horton's life. When Lillie got back she said that she had written you about it & no answer had come. Now I do not know what father wrote to you nor do I know just what you said that you would do but I know it was something kind. I expected to have a word about it from you or from Father but not a word, have I received & so I am realy [sic] in ignorance about the matter.

I am very sorry indeed that you have been asked to do this after all that you have done & the more so as I do not feel myself able to assume the whole of it. I feel that I would have felt almost that we were doing nearer what was right had we assumed what we could of the amount & that the balance of principle & payments go to Leonora. Of course I realize that it is a good investment but one that perhaps I should not undertake if I cannot afford it.

Now if you will pay this amount of 107.40 as it calls for & get this straightened out & then let we know what the full annual amount due amounts to. I will let you know how much I can assume & then either tern the balance over to Leonora or else will get you to advance that amount if you will consistent to deduct all such payments with interest when the principle comes in. I cannot tell you how mean I feel to ask even this after all that you have done for me.

The reason amount does not come to hand on due date is that Company sent notification too late. I enclose Dr Frierson's & Lillie's statements that this came to hand on Dec 5th 1898.

(2)

Of course I do not know whether they will allow this claim about delay but in all justice when the fault is their own they ought to allow it.

While speaking about this & about money matters I have not received a statement of account with you & do not know how my affairs stand. Could you let me know. I must I fear be terribly in arrears. At the same time that I have statement of account with you could I have a statement of bank account.

Well I must stop for a few hours as I have to go to the evening meeting.

9.30 P.M.

We had a very good meeting & there were several enquiries although the night was quite [starving?]. I believe the Lord has a goodly number of Souls in this city for himself. Lillie & I have been holding meetings every weekday & we see a steady improvement in the attendance. Things in Seoul have been rather exciting while we were away but this will be alright again soon. Korea cannot throw off her old ways without a struggle you will see about it from time to time I the Repository. Does it reach you regularly. All seems quiet in mission lives now & I do not know but all with the service.

Now must close. With love to all & lots for yourself. Thanks for what you have done and regrets that we ask more.

Your affectionate Brother

Horace G. Underwood

Letter 23

(No 8)

Seoul, Korea. Dec 28th. 1898.

My Dear Thomas;

The mail has just come in and has brought us a fine feast in the way of letters and news from home. Up to the arrival of the mail one week ago we had not had a line from anyone of you folks in Brooklyn since the reception of your letter No 12 which I had answered in mine to you of Nov 9th so that for over a month and a half we had not had line. Now however you have been trying to make up for bad behaviour and have done handsomely in sending me as follows;)

Letter (unnumbered)	written Nov 16	Posted Nov 22
Letter No 14	"" Nov 22	"" "" 22
Letter No 15	"" Nov 25	"" "" 28

If you have kept your numbering right then there has been a letter lost that was numbered No 11 and was written sometime between No 10 of May 6th and No 12 of Sept 14th.

I began the new numbering in June and have sent you 7 letters sin[c]e then the 7th was not numbered as I had not got my tally book with me in the country.

The Christmas box arrived in good time and was here for a few days before Christmas and how we longed to open it. Christmas coming on a Sunday we were not able to open it till Monday and we all got up early and before a big fire in the Study we soon had the covers off and were diving into the box unwrapping and the excitement was intense. Many thanks indeed for that suit of clothes and that hat. It was

(2) (J.T.U. No 8)

just one of the things I was beginning to feel that I would have to get but do you know that you have been sending me out so many suits of clothes that I have not had a chance to patronize the tailors[,] a thing that they object to most decidedly, but that I rejoice in as they do fit so abominally. I look quite the style and more than one has asked who my tailor was and I have replied that I have my tailor in New York. "Ah" they reply ["]I knew that must be a home fit."

I have to preach in the Foreign Church on Sunday and of course I shall wear my new suit.

Lillie was delighted with her dress and things it is charming. Hollie looks well in that new suit. The brown trimmed with the red and the white belt go so well together. He looks like a regular little man and it fits him so well too. There is nothing like it out here and we are all charmed with it. That boat too that he had to put together. He is nothing if he is not patriotic and the late war has made him think a great deal about war ships etc and he never gets tired of anything in the boat or war line and when it is in a line with both he is doubly pleased. That lantern is quite a contrivance and Hollie never tires of seeing all the things go round and the dogs etc jumping. It is a source of not a little amusement to some of the grown folks as and they make quite a study to find out what makes the rabbit jump up & down. The whole box was a delight to us all and you have entirely used up our stock of adjectives. I feel that we must almost ask you to study Korean so that we can have a new lot of superlatives

(3) (J.T.U. No 8)

with which to express our thanks. Even then we would be unable to express all that we feel. I have now a fine stock of paper and stationary and I shall feel well prepared for Literary work. I have a host of calls for Underwood's Inks so that I am going to get one of the merchants here to send you an order so that they can keep it on hand. We had a quiet Christmas. We had planned to have the friends in as usual and then just a day or two before Christmas came letters announcing the death of Mother Horton and of course we had to send round and tell the people not to come. No cable had been sent as Father had known that we were in the interior and that a message would not reach us. He was mistaken as to this and I wish much that he had sent us a message as it would have been better for Lillie. We had been saying all along that of course she had not gone yet as we would have had a message and then suddenly and unexpectedly came the word that she had passed away. We were expecting a few friends in to help prepare for Christmas that evening and of course had to send to them not to come. We had a quiet Christmas all by ourselves and we enjoyed it very much. The night before we all received some presents from the Korean Minister of Finance.

Politically thing[s] in Korea look strange, every day and almost every hour sees changes in the Cabinet and you do not know from one hour to another what the end will be. History is rapidly being made out here in Korea and no matter what happens there is always a steady progress forward. There are a good many set backs as it were but in

(4) (J.T.U. No 8)

it all we can see that there is a steady advance and the present British Repre-
sentative in his official report to his government said that progress here was
marvelouse [*sic*] and that no country had ever advanced as rapidly as had
Korea. The King is weak and vacillating. Were it not for this I am sure that
the progress would be even faster. As it is with such a weak sovereign the
great fear is that one of the powers that would be no benefit to the country
will step in and practically take over the land. What the end will be we do
not know but as long as god gives us an open door to carry on His work it
is our place to do so. He is blessing us most abundantly just now and on all
sides we see great strides. The work is only limited by our ability to oversee
it. Hannah wrote very kindly about being willing to let me have Mr. Pieters
if I could get him. This I was unable to do but I am writing to her about
another young man whom I can get and if I can have him I feel sure that I
can do a great deal more and at t he same time be wonderfully relieved from
burdens myself. You will see all about the matter in my letter to her.

Now in reply to your queries etc I will number them so that they may
be plain before you.

FIRST RE KATE & HER SALARY:-

It is a long long while since I have received anything from you for her.
Last Spring I wrote you that I had money for her that went up to Feb 29th. I
also wrote you asking you to send to Walter Redpath

P.O. Box 195, Kimberly, South Africa

(5) (J.T.U. No 8)

The sum of £25. (Twenty five Pounds Sterling) to be charged to this account.
I have received no word from you that you have done this nor has Kate
received word from Walter that he has received the amount. If you have not
sent him this could you do so as soon as possible after the receipt of this as
I believe they are in need and I know that Kate is in a hurry to have them
get the money.

After this has been sent it will still leave Twenty-five pounds (£25.) to
pay her up to Feb 29th 1899. >Kate has received word that they have <u>not</u>
rec'd <u>money</u><[8]

2nd RE LENSES. I note what you say in regard to those lenses and I will
proceed at once to collect from Dr Avison the amount that you say you

---

8. This is hand-written in the top left margin of this typed letter.

have charged to my account. I fear that you will find that attending to such commissions as these will be rather burdensome.

I feel that it is too much almost to bother you about my affairs as I have from time to time but it is coming altogether too much bother you about other peoples as well.

3rd.RE PEARLS.

I am glad that you got the pearls at least and hope that they were, not altogether too late. I had written asking you to have them set and to charge the cost of the setting [to] my account. Were you able to attend to this and what kind of setting did you have. I wish much that we could have got them home earlier but this was impossible.

4th RE PAYMENT FOR BELLS MACHINE.

As soon as the bill for Mr Bell's machine came to hand I sent it to him and he has doubtless ere this sent you the money. I

(6) (J.T.U. No 8)

will write him again and will find out how the matter stands and see that the amount is sent to you. I note what you say about ribbons etc and I will let him have some of those that you have sent to me.

5th. RE THE OLD STOVE ORDER

You ask that I send full particulars as to the stoves that were ordered but were not sent.

The stoves were from THE ELY & RAMSAY CO. AND the numbers and marks were from their small catalogue published in 1892 and bound in red paper covers. The stoves ordered were

The NEW ROSSMORE RESERVOIR RANGE No. 8–20 listed at 35.50

THE REOSSMORE COOK No. 7–14 "" "" 13.75

Both were wanted with extra wood fixtures and the discount was 33 & a third, and ten off.

Now let them send the nearest to those that they have in stock. And let the stoves be send whether they give the full discount or not and let them be shipped by the Board in the usual way.

6th. RE FREIGHT VIA TACOMA

I had written you long ago as to the arrival of the B/L for the Christmas box etc but of course had not been able to write to you as to the arrive of the box as it had not come. It came through all right as you know from the first part of the letter but the exact date of its arrival was Dec 17th. It was delivered at my house in Seoul on that day and so you can see how long it took. There were some delays in Chemulpo but they might occur any year so that it is a fair reckoning.

(7) (J.T.U. No 8)

7th. RE YOUR QUERIES ABOUT C O P Y I N G P R E S S.

I have a copying press but NOTHING MORE in that line. I wrote you some time ago about this matter and asked for some of the things that were necessary but above all for directions. I can get good copies with my make shifts in the press of all except of things written with UNDERWOOD'S RIBBONS. I know this is on account of ignorance on my part and I sent a special letter to J. UNDERWOOD & Co about the matter but they never answered except to say letter received and will be attended to. If you have any influence with this firm a line or a job from you might get them to attend to the matter. I will give a list of what I need. I have a Press that will take ordinary letter paper up to 11 & ¾ inches. I need as follows:

1. A letter book.

2. Some oil sheets

3. Some blotters.

4. A damping brush. (I use a sponge to rag now and it often tears the paper)

5. A water pot

6. DIRECTIONS OR INSTRUCTIONS.

You see that I HAVE ONLY A PRESS and need all the apurtenances [sic] that go to make up a copying out-fit.

8th. RE CYCLOSTYLE AND SUPPLIES

When I came out here you kindly let me have a Cyclostyle which has been of some use but which would have been of much more use had I had the supplies. You will doubtless remember that as it was wanted to pack at the factory you told me to take the factory machine and this George gave me and I brought out. I am now entirely out of supplies for this and in addition to the need of supplies I need a new roller as the one I have is entirely worn out.

(8) (J.T.U. No 8)

9th. RE SHIPMENT OF THESE THINGS.

All these things could be sent to the Board and they will send them out to Shanghai to which place they are always sending things and from there they will be distributed and we will get out things in due time. Any time medium sized pkge can be sent this way. It is not the quickest way by any means but when there is not enough for a separate bill of lading it does very well. If the lenses have not yet been sent they might be packed in too.

If Mr Miller (SEE 14th note in this letter) is coming he could probably bring all along with him when he comes.

10th. RE AUDITING COM.

YOUR letters and enclosures were duly received and at the same time and the Auditing Com received word from Mr. Hand about the matter so that that is already now.

11TH. Re WILL AND LILLIES AFFAIRS

It is very good of you indeed in the midst of all you[r] other affairs to bother about these details but we have no one who could attend to it but you. Lillie is writing about details. She does not much like the idea of one of Charlie Egans family being Executor but she will write more fully. I had meant to write all in here but this is a matter that is worthy of a separate letter and it would be as well not to have it mixed up with all these other items.

12th. RE MY INSURANCE.

I have been seeing a good deal in the papers lately about

(9) (J.T.U. No 8)

the troubles in the MUTUAL RESERVE FUND INSURANCE CO. I believe this is my company. Are the troubles of a serious nature and would it well for me to withdraw. I would be obliged if this matter could be looked into. If it is best to withdraw I should like to put the same amount of money in insurance in some other company. I will leave it to you to look into and do to what is best. I had always looked upon it as cheap insurance for the time and had thought it best to keep it going but I saw from the papers the other day that those who were in such a company were apt to be liable in certain ways. I do not know whether this is so or not but I thought I would write and ask you about it.

13th. Re MY ACCOUNT WITH YOU AND A STATEMENT OF SAME.

I should very much like to/have a statement of how the account stands. It is now I think two years since I have had any statement at all. Please draw on my Bank account[,] if there is any money in it[,] all or as much as you will be needed to reimburse you and let me know how the account stands and also how the bank account is.

Some two years back you sent me a statement showing some 700.00 dollars in the bank to my credit at which I was greatly rejoiced and felt quite proud and rich until the next mail brought me a statement of my account with you showing that I owed about all of it to you. I should like you to repay yourself as far as you can and to them let me know how the matter stands. Since then I have received several letters saying statement enclosed and no statement has been enclosed at all.

(10) (J.T.U. No 8)

14th. RE MR MILLER OF HALIFAX COMING TO KOREA

I suppose you know that just as Lillie was leaving for Korea she most generously and kindly offered to support Mr Pieters as my helper if he would come the support to come from the beginning of Oct. The difficulty was as to how Mr. Pieters was to live between the time that he left the American Bible Society and Oct and as the B.&.F.B.S offered him a job at once he accepted it and he is with them still. Since then I have heard of a MR MILLER OF HALI-FAX NOVA SCOTIA who from all that I can learn is just the man. HE was an intimate friend of Dr Grierson's out here who knew him well and who is a very conscientious man and he sai[d]after seeing the work that would have to be done that he is just the man for me. I have sent my letter to MR MILLER in my letter to Hannah. If Hannah's odder is still open would you mind writing to Mr. Miller as well and assisting in settling the details.

But I must be closing. 10 pages is a very fair letter and I fear it is too long. It is now Dec 31st and on the eve of the New year.

I want to wish you a Happy New Year And many many of them
With much love from us all, we are all well

Your Loving Brother
Horace G Underwood

Letter 24

At Centerport, Cape Cod
(90 Ladd Rd.)
July 13th, 1974

Mr. Philip Egan
Box 138, RFD 1
Hudson, NY 1 25 34

Dear Philip,

Thank you for the things you gave us from Aunt Leonora's things when we were there this past Tuesday. Of the ones which I promised to have duplicated and returned to you, the most important is the only one I've been able to take care of so far, but it at least is done. The long, handwritten paper called "Lillie in Korea; and Contributing Circumstances, by her sister Leonora Horton Egan" has been copied and is ready to go back to you. I'm mailing it with this letter.

One minor calamity is the absence of pages 2 & 3. I have put in a couple of blank, yellow sheets in case you come across the pages and want to put them back. If you do, please send me xeroxed copies of those two pages, so that we can have them in our copies too.

The pagination got a bit confused, so I took the liberty of adding a new set of numbers where my numbering doesn't mar anything she wrote.

At some points she erased and re-wrote. The copies do not show this, but the original could probably be recovered in these bits. My own opinion is that we don't want to recover anything that she decided to erase. It could be a mistake she recognized and corrected, or something which for some other reason has no reason to be read. Anyhow, if she didn't want it written, I see no reason to go to any pains to read it.

If you have a chance to read it, her story why don't you use the xeroxed copy I'm enclosing, so that that precious manuscript can be preserved as safely as possible? I do encourage you to read it. The quick look-over I've given it makes me impatient for an opportunity to read it through, myself.

Again, thank you very much for it, and for the pictures and the books as well.

Give our best to Harriet. Sorry to have missed her.

Very truly,

John

I'm at James' place on the cape. He sends regards and his own thanks for his copy of your mother's narrative. jtu

Bibliography

By Underwood

Kim, In Soo, ed. and trans. *Rev. Underwood's Missionary Letters, 1885–1916*. Seoul: Presbyterian College & Seminary, 2002.

Oak, Sung-Deuk, and Mahn-Yol Yi, eds. and trans. *Horace Grant Underwood Papers*. 5 vols. Seoul: Yonsei University Press, 2005–10.

Underwood, Horace G. "Address." *Report of the Twelfth Annual Convention of the American Inter-Seminary Missionary Alliance* (1892) 53–54.

———. *The Call of Korea: Political-Social-Religious*. New York: Revell, 1908.

———. *Korean Spoken Language: I. Grammatical Notes; II. English into Korean*. New York: McMillan, 1914.

———. *Letter to the Board of Foreign Missions of the Presbyterian Church*. July 10, 1884. Drew University Archives.

———. "The Need for Workers in Korea." In *World-Wide Evangelization: The Urgent Business of the Church*, 403–6. New York: SVM, 1902.

———. "A Powerful Appeal from Korea—Letter to A. T. Pierson on November 27, 1887." *Missionary Review of the World* (1888) 209–10.

———. *The Religions of East Asia*. New York: McMillan, 1910.

———. "Twenty Years of Missionary Work in Korea—Address Delivered at the Missionary Conference of the 20th Anniversary of the Korea Mission of the Board of Foreign Mission, PCUSA in Seoul on September 22, 1904." *Korea Field* (1904) 205–10. Condensed and Reprinted in *Missionary Review of the World* (1905) 371–76.

———. "The Unevangelized Millions in Korea." In *World-Wide Evangelization: The Urgent Business of the Church*, 93–95. New York: SVM.

On Underwood

Choi, Jai-Keun. *Story of Underwood Who Laid the Foundation for Korea's Church*. Seoul: Kukmin Ilbo, 2014.

Coakley, John W. "The Seminary Years of the Missionaries Horace G. Underwood and Henry Appenzeller." *Korea Presbyterian Journal of Theology* 47.3 (2015) 59–82.

Kim, In Soo. *Protestants and the Formation of Modern Korean Nationalism, 1885–1920: A Study of the Contributions of Horace G. Underwood and Sun Chu Kil*. New York: Lang, 1996.

Kim, James Jinhong. "Bible versus Guns: Horace G. Underwood's Evangelization of Korea." *Asia Pacific Perspectives* 5.1 (2005) 33–37.

———. "A Copernican Re-evaluation of Appenzeller and Underwood's Mission in Korea." In *Yes! Well . . . : Exploring the Past, Present, and Future of the Church*, edited by James Hart Brumm, 211–34. Grand Rapids: Eerdmans, 2016.

———. "The Significance of Horace G. Underwood in Protestant Mission History." Paper presented at 2nd Annual Underwood Conference, New Brunswick Theological Seminary, 2003.

———. "Underwood of Korea: Crossroad of the Christian Mission." Paper presented 5th Annual Underwood Conference, New Brunswick Theological Seminary, 2006.

Oak, Sung-Deuk. "Horace G. Underwood's Experiments." In *The Making of Korean Christianity: Protestant Encounters with Korean Religions, 1876–1915*, 55–83. Waco, TX: Baylor University Press, 2013.

Paik, Lark-June George. *The History of Protestant Missions in Korea, 1832–1910*. Pyong Yang: Union Christian College, 1929.

Pang, Samuel Y. "The Legacy of Horace Grant Underwood." *International Bulletin of Mission Research* 39.3 (2015) 150–53.

Park, Hyoung-Woo. "A Study on the Coming to Korea of the American Presbyterian Missionary Rev. Horace G. Underwood." *The Journal of Korean Studies* 170 (2015) 53–83.

Sunquist, Scott W. "Underwood's Understated Theology of Mission: Six Themes in the Early Years." Paper presented at 1st Annual Underwood Conference, New Brunswick Theological Seminary, 2002.

Underwood, Elizabeth. "Behind the Portraits: Lessons Learned in the Search for Horace Underwood." Paper presented at 2nd Annual Underwood Conference, New Brunswick Theological Seminary, 2003.

Underwood, Lillias H. *Underwood of Korea: An Intimate Record of the Life and Work of the Rev. H. G. Underwood for Thirty-One Years of a Missionary of the Presbyterian Board in Korea*. Seoul: Yonsei University Press, 1983.

———. *Fifteen Years among the Top-Knots, or Life in Korea*. Seoul: New York: Revell, 1904.

———. "Horace Grant Underwood—Missionary: A Sketch of His Life and Work for Korea," *The Missionary Review of the World* 39 (1916) 902–10.

Works Cited or Consulted

1851 Census for England and Wales. National Archives, HO 107. London: Public Record Office.

Ahlstrom, Sydney A. *A Religious History of the American People*. 2 vols. Garden City, NY: Image, 1975.

Allen, H. N. *A Chronological Index of Foreign Relations of Korea from the Beginning of Christian Era to the 20th Century*. Seoul: Methodist Publishing House, 1901.

Allen, Roland. *Missionary Methods, St. Paul's or Ours?* Grand Rapids: Eerdmans, 1962.

Anderson, Gerald H., and Thomas F. Stransky, eds. *Mission Trends No. 1: Crucial Issues in Mission Today*. New York: Paulist, 1974.

————, eds. *Mission Trends No. 2: Evangelization*. New York: Paulist, 1975.

————, eds. *Mission Trends No. 3: Third World Theologies*. New York: Paulist, 1976.

Appenzeller, Henry Gerhard. "Our Mission in Korea." *The Gospel in All Lands* (1885) 328.

Arrupe, Pedro. "Letter to the Whole Society on Inculturation." *Studies in the International Apostolate of Jesuits* 7 (1978) 1–9.

Bang, Im, and Yi Ryuk. *Korean Folk Tales: Imps, Ghosts and Fairies*. Translated by James Scarth Gale. New York: Dent & Sons, 1913.

Barber, John W., and Henry Howe. "North Bergen, NJ." In *Historical Collections of the State of New Jersey*, 233–37. New York: Tuttle, 1844.

Bavinck, J. H. *An Introduction to the Science of Missions*. Philadelphia: Presbyterian and Reformed, 1960.

Bays, Daniel H., eds. *Christianity in China: From Eighteenth Century to the Present*. Stanford: Stanford University Press, 1996.

Bevans, Stephen B. *Models of Contextual Theology*. New York: Orbis, 2002.

Bevans, Stephen B., and Roger Schroeder. *Constants in Context: A Theology of Mission for Today*. New York: Orbis, 2004.

Biernatzki, William E. *Korean Catholicism in the 1970: A Christian Community Come of Age*. New York: Orbis, 1975.

Black, Kenneth Macleod. *The Scots Churches in England*. Edinburgh: Blackwood and Sons, 1906.

Blaikie, William Garden. *The Personal Life of David Livingstone*. New York: Revell, 1880.

Bloom, Irene, trans. *Mencius*. New York: Columbia University Press, 2009.

Bosch, David J. *Transforming Mission: Paradigm Shifts in Theology of Mission*. Maryknoll, NY: Orbis, 1996.

Braaten, Carl E. *No Other Gospel! Christianity among the World's Religions*. Minneapolis: Fortress, 1992.

Broomhall, A. J. *If I Had a Thousand Lives*. London: Hodder & Stoughton, 1982.

Brown, A. J. *The Mastery of the Far East*. New York: Scribners, 1919.

Brown, G. T. *Mission to Korea*. Richmond, VA: Board of World Mission, PCUSA, 1962.

Buswell, Robert E., Jr., ed. *Religions of Korea in Practice*. Princeton: Princeton University Press, 2006.

Buswell, Robert E., Jr., and Timothy S. Lee, eds. *Christianity in Korea*. Honolulu: University of Hawaii Press, 2007.

Byonghyon, Choi, trans. *The Annals of King T'aejo: Founder of Korea's Chosŏn Dynasty*. Cambridge: Harvard University Press, 2014.

Cannon, Katie Geneva. "Surviving the Blight." In *Inheriting Our Mothers' Gardens*, edited by Letty Russell et al., 75–90. Louisville: Westminster, 1988.

Cardenale, Ernesto. *The Gospel in Solentiname*. Vol. 1. Translated by Donald D. Walsh. New York: Orbis, 1976.

Carey, William. *An Enquiry into the Obligations of Christians to Use Means for the Conversion of the Heathens*. Dallas: Criswell, 1988.

Cartledge, Mark J., and David Cheetham, eds. *Intercultural Theology: Approaches and Themes*. London: SCM, 2011.

Catalogue of the Officers and Students of the Theological Seminary of the Reformed (Dutch) Church in America, New Brunswick, NJ, 1881–82. Albany, NY: Terhune, 1881.

Chan, Wing-tsit. *A Source Book in Chinese Philosophy.* Princeton: Princeton University Press, 1969.

Chicago and Its Resources Twenty Years After: 1871–1891—A Commercial History Showing the Progress and Growth of Two Decades from the Great Fire to the Present Time. Chicago: Chicago Times, 1892.

Ching, Julia. *Confucianism and Christianity: A Comparative Study.* Tokyo: Kodansha International, 1977.

Cho, Sang-Youl. *Arthur T. Pierson Memorial Bible School.* Seoul: Christian Literature Society of Korea, 2012.

Choi, Jai-Keun. *Early Catholicism in Korea.* Seoul: Handl, 2005.

———. *The Founding of Chosŏn Christian College: H. G. Underwood's Vision and Its Realization.* Seoul: Yonsei University Press, 2012.

Chŏng, Yag'yong. *Admonitions on Governing the People: Manual for All Administrators.* Translated by Byonghyon Choi. Los Angeles: University of California Press, 2010.

Chuang Tzu. *Basic Writings.* Translated by Burton Watson. New York: Columbia University Press, 1984.

Chung, Rachel E. "The Song of the Faithful Wife Ch'unhyang." In *Finding Wisdom in East Asian Classics,* edited by Wm. Theodore de Bary, 365–75. New York: Columbia University Press, 2011.

Church of England Births and Baptisms, 1813–1917. Parish Registers. London Metropolitan Archives Collection, AT LMA P69/OLA1.

Church of England Marriages and Banns, 1754–1921. Parish Registers. London Metropolitan Archives Collection.

The Church of Scotland. *The Articles Declaratory of the Constitution of the Church of Scotland.*   https://www.churchofscotland.org.uk/about-us/church-law/church-constitution.

Clark, Allen D. *Avison of Korea: The Life of Oliver R. Avison, M.D.* Seoul: Yonsei University Press, 1979.

———. *A History of the Church in Korea.* Seoul: Christian Literature Society of Korea, 1971.

Clark, Charles Allen. *Digest of the Presbyterian Church of Korea.* Seoul: Korean Religious Book & Track Society, 1918.

———. *First Fruits in Korea: A Story of Church Beginnings in the Far East.* New York: Revell, 1921.

———. *The Korean Church and the Nevius Methods.* New York: Revell, 1930.

———. *Religions of Old Korea.* New York: Revell, 1932.

Clark, Donald N. *Christianity in Modern Korea.* Lanham, MD: University Press of America, 1896.

———. *Living Dangerously in Korea: The Western Experience 1900–1950.* Norwalk, CT: EastBridge, 2003.

Coakley, John W., ed. *Concord Makes Strength: Essays in Reformed Ecumenism.* Grand Rapids: Eerdmans, 2002.

———. *New Brunswick Theological Seminary: An Illustrated History, 1784–2014.* Grand Rapids: Eerdmans, 2014.

Coakley, John W., and Andrea Sterk, eds. *Readings in World Christian History: Earliest Christianity to 1453*. New York: Orbis, 2004.

Coakley, Sarah. *God, Sexuality, and the Self: An Essay 'On the Trinity'*. Cambridge: Cambridge University Press, 2013.

———. "Prayer, Desire, and Gender: Re-Thinking the Doctrine of the Trinity for Today," *Proceedings of the 12th Horace G. Underwood International Symposium*. Seoul: Saemunan Church Press, 2019.

Cobb, John B., Jr. "Beyond Pluralism." In *Christian Uniqueness Reconsidered: The Myth of a Pluralistic Theology of Religions*, edited by Gavin D'Costa, 81–95. New York: Orbis, 1990.

Coe, Shoki. "Contextualizing Theology." In *Mission Trends No. 3: Third World Theologies*, edited by Gerald Anderson and Thomas F. Stransky, 19–24. New York: Paulist, 1976.

Coleridge, Henry J. *The Life and Letters of St. Francis Xavier*. 2 vols. London: Burns Oates & Washborune, 1921.

Cone, James H. *God of the Oppressed*. New York: Orbis, 1975.

Confucius. *Analects*. Translated by D. C. Lau. New York: Penguin, 1979.

Conn, Harvie M. *Eternal Word and Changing Worlds: Theology, Anthropology, and Mission in Trialogue*. Grand Rapids: Zondervan, 1984.

———. "Studies in the Theology of the Korean Presbyterian Church: An Historical Outline, Part I." *Westminster Theological Journal* 29.1 (1966) 24–57.

———. "Studies in the Theology of the Korean Presbyterian Church: An Historical Outline, Part II." *Westminster Theological Journal* 29.2 (1967), 136–84.

Corfe, C. J. *The Anglican Church in Corea*. London: Livingstones, 1906.

Corwin, Charles E. *A Manual of the Reformed Church in America, 1628–1922*. 5th rev. ed. New York: Board of the Publication and Bible-Study Work of the Reformed Church in America, 1922.

Corwin, Edward Tanjore. *Manual of the Reformed Church in America*. 4th ed. New York: Board of the Publication of the Reformed Church in America, 1902.

Cox, Harvey. "Shamans and Entrepreneurs: Primal Spirituality on the Asian Rim." In *Fire from Heaven: The Rise of Pentecostal Spirituality and the Reshaping of Religion in the 21st Century*, 213–42. Cambridge: De Capo, 1995.

David, Ravi. *Mission Possible: Challenges for Indian Christian Mission Leaders in the 21st Century*. Bengalore: Brilliant, 2014.

Davis, Daniel M. "Henry G. Appenzeller: Pioneer Missionary and Reformer in Korea." *Methodist History* 30.4 (1992) 195–205.

———. *The Life and Thought of Henry Gerhard Appenzeller (1858–1902), Missionary to Korea*. Lewiston, NY: Mellon, 1988.

de Bary, Wm. Theodore. *Asian Values and Human Rights: A Confucian Communitarian Perspective*. Cambridge: Harvard University Press, 1998.

de Bary, Wm. Theodore. *Learning for One's Self: Essays on the Individual in Neo-Confucian Thought*. New York: Columbia University Press, 1991.

de Bary, Wm. Theodore. *The Liberal Tradition in China*. Hong Kong: Chinese University Press, 1983.

de Bary, Wm. Theodore, ed. *Sources of East Asian Tradition*. 2 vols. New York: Columbia University Press, 2008.

de Bary, Wm. Theodore, ed. *Sources of Japanese Tradition*. 2 vols. New York: Columbia University Press, 2005.

de Bary, Wm. Theodore, ed. *Sources of Korean Tradition*. 2 vols. New York: Columbia University Press, 1996–2000.

de Bary, Wm. Theodore, and Irene Bloom, eds. *Sources of Chinese Tradition*. 2 vols. New York: Columbia University Press, 1999–2000.

de Bary, Wm. Theodore, and John W. Chaffee, eds. *Neo-Confucian Education*. Los Angeles: University of California Press, 1989.

de Bary, Wm. Theodore, and JaHyun Kim Haboush, eds. *The Rise of Neo-Confucianism in Korea*. New York: Columbia University Press, 1985.

de Bary, Wm. Theodore, and Tu Weiming, eds. *Confucianism and Human Rights*. New York: Columbia University Press, 1998.

"Decennial Census Historical Facts." https://www.census.gov/programs-surveys/decennial-census/decade/decennial-facts.1880.html.

DeLombard, Jeannine M. "Sisters, Servants, or Saviors? National Baptist Women Missionaries in Liberia in the 1920s." *The International Journal of African Historical Studies* 24.2 (1991) 323–47.

Deuchler, Martina. *The Confucian Transformation of Korea: A Study of Society and Ideology*. Cambridge, MA: Harvard University Press, 1992.

Emsley, Clive, et al. "London History: A Population History of London." https://www.oldbaileyonline.org/static/Population-history-of-london.jsp.

Engler, George Nichols. "The Typewriter Industry: The Impact of a Significant Technological Revolution." PhD diss., University of California at Los Angeles, 1969.

Estep, William R. *Whole Gospel Whole World: The Foreign Mission Board of the Southern Baptist Convention 1845–1995*. Nashville: Broadman & Holman, 1994.

Faraday, Michael. *Experimental Researches in Chemistry and Physics*. London: Taylor and Francis, 1859.

Feldra. Robert. *History of Hudson County: Genealogies of Prominent Families*. Union, NJ: Michel & Rank, 1917.

Fenton, John Y., et al., eds. *Religion of Asia*. New York: St. Martin's, 1988.

Fenwick, M. C. *The Church of Christ in Corea*. New York: Hodder & Stoughton, 1911.

The Fiftieth Anniversary Celebration of the Korea Mission of the PCUSA (June 30–July 3, 1934). Seoul: John D. Wells School, 1934.

The Fifty-Second Annual Report of the Board of Foreign Missions of the Reformed Church in America. New York: Board of Publication of the Reformed Protestant Dutch Church, 1884.

Finney, Charles G. *Lectures on Revival*. Minneapolis: Bethany, 1988.

Fisher, James E. *Democracy and Mission Education in Korea*. New York: Columbia University Press, 1912.

Fisher, Miles Mark. "Lott Cary, the Colonizing Missionary." *The Journal of Negro History* 7.4 (1922) 380–418.

Foulk, George C. "Letter [to the Family] of August 18, 1885." In *America's Man in Korea: The Private Letters of George C. Foulk, 1884–1887*, by Samuel Hawley, 126–27. Lanham, MD: Lexington, 2008.

Gale, James Scarth. *A Korean-English Dictionary*. Yokohama: Kelly & Walsh, 1897.

Gale, James Scarth. *Korean in Transition*. New York: Young People's Missionary Movement of the United States and Canada, 1909.

Gale, James Scarth. *Korean Sketches*. New York: Revell, 1898.

Gale, James Scarth. "Tan-goon." *Korea Magazine* (1917) 404–5.

Gale, James Scarth. "The Korean's View of God." *Korea Mission Field* (1916) 66–70.

Gillard, Derek. *Education in England: A History*. http://www.educationengland.org.uk/history/index.html.

Graham, Billy. "Through Unexpected Doors: North Korea 1992 and 1994." In *Just as I Am*. New York: HarperCollins, 1997.

Granberg-Michaelson, Wesley. *From Times Square to Timbuktu: The Post-Christian West Meets the Non-Western Church*. Grand Rapids: Eerdmans, 2013.

Granberg-Michaelson, Wesley. "The Waters of Baptism and the Streams of Ecumenism." In *Concord Makes Strength: Essays in Reformed Ecumenism*, edited by John W. Coakley, 174–86. Grand Rapids: Eerdmans, 2002.

Graves, Dan. *Scientists of Faith: 48 Biographies of Historic Scientists and Their Christian Faith*. Grand Rapids: Kregel, 1996.

Grayson, James Huntley. "The Manchurian Connection: The Life and Work of the Rev. Dr. John Ross." *Korea Observer* 15.3 (1984) 345–60.

Griffis, William Elliot. *Corea, the Hermit Nation*. New York: Scribner, 1882.

———. "Corea: The Hermit Nation." *The Missionary Review* 6.6 (1883) 409–20.

———. *A Modern Pioneer in Korea: The Life Story of Henry G. Appenzeller*. New York: Revell, 1912.

Grubb, W. Barbrooke. *A Church in the Wilds*. London: Seeley, Service & Co., 1914.

Guder, Darrell L., et al., eds. *Missional Church: A Vision of the Sending of the Church in North America*. Grand Rapids: Eerdmans, 1998.

Gurney, Charles Edward. "History of the Colby Chapter." *Delta Upsilon Quarterly* 20.4 (1902) 200–204.

Gutierrez, Gustavo. "Hope of Liberation." In *Mission Trends No. 3: Third World Theologies*, edited by Gerald Anderson and Thomas F. Stransky, 64–69. New York: Paulist, 1976.

Gutzlaff, K. F. A. *Journal of Three Voyage along the Coast of China in 1831, 1832, & 1833 with the Notices of Siam, Corea and the Loo-Choo Island*. London: Fredrick Westley & A. H. Davis, 1834.

Handy, Robert T. *A Christian America: Protestant Hopes and Historical Realities*. New York: Oxford University Press, 1971.

Harding, William Henry. *The Life of George Müller*. London: Oliphants, 1914.

Harrington, F. H. *God, Mammom, and the Japanese: Dr. H. N. Allen and Korea-American Relations 1884–1905*. Madison: University of Wisconsin, 1944.

Hastings, Thomas John. *Seeing All Things Whole: The Scientific Mysticism and Art of Kagawa Toyohiko (1888–1960)*. Eugene, OR: Pickwick, 2015.

Hay, James, and Henry Belfrage. *Memoir of the Rev. Alexander Waugh, D.D., with Selections from His Epistolary Correspondence*. New York: R. Carter & Brothers, 1851.

Hesselgrave, David J. *Communicating Christ Cross-Culturally: An Introduction to Missionary Communication*. Grand Rapids: Zondervan, 1991.

Hick, John. "On Complementary Pluralism." In *The Second Christianity*, 82–87. London: SCM, 1983.

Hick, John, and Paul Knitter, eds. *The Myth of Christian Uniqueness: Toward a Pluralistic Theology of Religions*. New York: Wipf & Stock, 1987.

Hiebert, Paul G. *Anthropological Insights for Missionaries*. Grand Rapids: Baker, 1985.

Hirshfeld, Alan W. *The Electric Life of Michael Faraday*. New York: Walker & Co., 2006.

"History of Delta Upsilon." https://www.deltau.org/history.

Holtom, D. C., ed. *The Christian Movement in Japan, Korea and Formosa.* Kobe: Federation of Christian Missions Japan, 1924.

Hood, Robert E. *Must God Remain Greek? Afro Cultures and God-Talk.* Minneapolis: Fortress, 1990.

Hulbert, H. B. *History of Korea.* 2 vols. Seoul: Methodist Publishing House, 1905.

———. *The Passing of Korea.* New York: Doubleday, 1906.

Huntley, Martha. *Caring, Growing, Changing: A History of the Protestant Mission in Korea.* New York: Friendship, 1984.

Hutchison, William R. *Errand to the World: American Protestant Thought and Foreign Missions.* Chicago: University of Chicago Press, 1987.

Inter-Seminary Missionary Alliance. *Report of the Fifth Annual Convention of the American Inter-Seminary Missionary Alliance, Princeton New Jersey, Oct. 24th, 25th, and 26th, 1884.* Trenton, NJ: MacCrellish and Quigley, 1884.

Irvin, Dale T., and Scott W. Sunquist. *History of the World Christian Movement: Earliest Christianity to 1453.* Maryknoll, NY: Orbis, 2001.

———. *History of the World Christian Movement: Modern Christianity from 1454 to 1800.* Maryknoll, NY: Orbis, 2011.

James, Frank A. J. L., ed. *Correspondence of Michael Faraday: Vol. 1, 1811–1831: Letters 1–524.* London: Institution of Engineering & Technology, 1991.

———. "Faraday, Michael." https://doi.org/10.1093/ref:odnb/9153.

———. *Guides to the Royal Institution of Great Britain: History.* http://www.rigb.org/docs/brief_history_of_ri_1.pdf.

Jenkins, Philip. *The Next Christendom: The Coming of Global Christianity.* Oxford: Oxford University Press, 2002.

———. *The New Faces of Christianity: Believing the Bible in the Global South.* Oxford: Oxford University Press, 2006.

Jennings, Raymond P. *Jesus, Japan, and Kanzo Uchimura: A Brief Study of the Non-Church Movement and Its Appropriateness to Japan.* Tokyo: Christian Literature Society, 1958.

Johnstone, T. B., and D. Andrew Penny. "Müller, George Friedrich." https://doi.org/10.1093/ref:odnb/19513.

Jung, Woon-hyung. "Horace G. Underwood's Decision and Departure for the Mission Field: Emphasizing a Letter to His Sister on December 22, 1884." *The Journal of Korean Studies (Dongbang Hak-ji)* 175 (2016) 167–94.

Kane, J. Herbert. *A Concise History of the Christian World Mission.* Grand Rapids: Baker, 1978.

Karnoutsos, Carmela. "Jersey City Past and Present: Hasbrouck Institute." http://www.njcu.edu/programs/jchistory/Pages/H_Pages/Hasbrouck_Institute.htm.

Kim, Sebastian C. H., and Kirsteen Kim. *A History of Korean Christianity.* Cambridge: Cambridge University Press, 2015.

Kim, Stephen Cardinal. "Evangelization in the Asian Context." In *Mission Trends No. 2: Evangelization,* edited by Gerald Anderson and Thomas F. Stransky, 190–92. New York: Paulist, 1975.

Kim, Yong-Bok. *Minjung Theology: People as the Subjects of History.* Singapore: Christian Conference of Asia, 1981.

Knitter, Paul. *No Other Name? A Critical Survey of Christian Attitudes toward World Religions.* New York: Orbis, 1985.

The Korea World Missions Association. *Korea World Mission Association's 2013 Year-End Report.* https://kwma.org/cm_stats/34005.

Koryŏsa (*History of Koryŏ Dynasty*). Seoul: Yonsei University Press, 1955–56.

Koyama, Kosuke. "The Asian Approach to Christ." *Missiology* 12.4 (1984) 435–47.

———. "Christianity Suffers from 'Teacher Complex.'" In *Mission Trends No. 2: Evangelization,* edited by Gerald Anderson and Thomas F. Stransky, 70–75. New York: Paulist, 1975.

———. *Waterbuffalo Theology.* New York: Orbis, 1974.

———. "What Makes a Missionary?" In *Mission Trends No. 1: Crucial Issues in Mission Today,* edited by Gerald Anderson and Thomas F. Stransky, 117–32. New York: Paulist, 1974.

Kuhn, Thomas S. *The Structure of Scientific Revolutions.* Chicago: University of Chicago Press, 1962.

Ladd, George Trumbull. *In Korea with Marquis Ito.* New York: Scribners, 1908.

Lalitha, Jayachitra, and Mitzi J. Smith, eds. *Teaching All Nations: Interrogating the Matthean Great Commission.* Minneapolis: Fortress, 2014.

Lao Tzu. *Daodejing.* Translated by D. C. Lau. New York: Penguin, 1964.

Late Chosŏn Reference Compilation of Documents on Korea (*Chŭngbo munhŏn bigo*). Seoul: Tongguk munhwasa, 1957–59.

Latourette, Kenneth Scott. *A History of the Expansion of Christianity.* New York: Harper & Brothers, 1938.

Lee, Joseph Tse-Hei. *The Bible and the Gun: Christianity in South China, 1860–1900.* New York: Routledge, 2003.

Lee, Kun Sam. *The Christian Confrontation with Shinto Nationalism: A Historical and Critical Study of the Conflict of Christianity and Shinto in Japan in the Period between the Meiji Restoration and the End of War II (1868–1945).* Philadelphia: Presbyterian & Reformed, 1966.

Livingstone, David. *Missionary Correspondence, 1841–1856.* Edited by I. Schapera. Los Angeles: University of California Press, 1961.

Luzbetak, Louis J. *The Church and Cultures: New Perspectives in Missiological Anthropology.* Techny, IL: Divine Word, 1963.

M'Kerrow, John. *History of the Secession Church.* Rev. and enlarged ed. Glasgow: Fullarton & Co., 1841.

Marsden, George M. *Religions and American Culture.* San Diego: Harcourt, 1990.

Maruyama, Masao. "The Structure of *Matsurigoto*: The *Basso Ostinato* of Japanese Political Life." In *Themes and Theories in Modern Japanese History: Essays in Memory of Richard Storry,* edited by Sue Henny and Jean-Pierre Lehmann, 27–43. London: Athlone, 1988.

Mathieson, Alfred. *Judson of Burma: The Heroic Pioneer Missionary.* London: Pickering & Inglis, 1929.

May, Henry F. *Protestant Churches and Industrial America.* New York: Harper & Bros., 1949.

Mbiti, John S. *African Religions and Philosophy.* Portsmouth, NH: Heinemann, 1999.

———. "Theological Impotence and the Universality of the Church." In *Mission Trends No. 3: Third World Theologies,* edited by Gerald Anderson and Thomas F. Stransky, 6–18. New York: Paulist, 1976.

McFague, Sallie. "A Trial Run: Parable, Poem, and Autobiographical Story." In *Speaking in Parables: A Study in Metaphor and Theology*, 10–25. Philadelphia: Fortress, 1975.

McKenzie, F. A. *Korea's Fight for Freedom*. Seoul: Yonsei University Press, 1969.

———. *The Tragedy of Korea*. London: Hodder & Stoughton, 1908.

Mencius. *Mencius*. Translated by Irene Bloom. New York: Columbia University Press, 1987.

Merikoski, Ingrid A. "A Different Kind of Enlightenment." *Religion & Liberty* 11.6 (2001) 9–12.

Miguez-Bonino, Jose. "The Present Crisis in Missions." In *Mission Trends No. 1: Crucial Issues in Mission Today*, edited by Gerald Anderson and Thomas F. Stransky, 40–41. New York: Paulist, 1974.

Min, Kyoung-Bae. *A History of Christian Churches in Korea*. Seoul: Yonsei University Press, 2005.

Minamiki, George. *The Chinese Rites Controversy from Its Beginning to Modern Times*. Chicago: Loyola, 1985.

Moffett, Samuel Hugh. *The Christians of Korea*. New York: Friendship, 1962.

———. *History of Christianity in Asia*. 2 vols. Maryknoll, NY: Orbis, 1998.

———. "Mission to Korea." In *Korean American Ministry*, edited by Sang Hyun Lee and John V. Moore, 16–24. Louisville: PCUSA, 1987.

Moll, Rob. "Missions Incredible." *Christianity Today*, March 1, 2006. https://www.christianitytoday.com/ct/2006/march/16.28.html.

Moon, Baeklan, and Oak Sung-Deuk. "Articles on Korea in *The Missionary Review of the World*, 1882–1939." http://koreanchristianity.cdh.ucla.edu/images/stories/Articles_on_Korea_in_the_Missionary_Review_of_the_World.pdf.

Moore, George F. "Report of the Fourth Annual Convention of the American Inter-Seminary Missionary Alliance, Hartford Connecticut, October 25, 1883." *The Andover Review* (1884) 93.

Moore, Samuel F. "The Butchers of Korea." *Korean Repository* 5 (1898), 127–32.

———. "A Gospel Sermon Preached by a Korean Butcher." *Church at Home and Abroad* 12 (1898) 115–16.

Moreau, A. Scott, et al. *Introducing World Missions: A Biblical, Historical, and Practical Survey*. Grand Rapids: Baker Academic, 2004.

Mortensen, Viggo. "For All God's People: Being Church in Multireligious Societies." In *Theology and the Religions: A Dialogue*, edited by Viggo Mortensen, 465–79. Grand Rapids: Eerdmans, 2003.

Mott, John R. *The Decisive Hour of Christian Missions*. New York: PCUSA, 1910.

Müller, George. *The Autobiography of George Müller*. Shawnee, KS: Gideon, 2017.

———. *A Narrative of Some of the Lord's Dealings with George Müller*. Oxford: Benediction, 2009.

Mungello, David E. "Confucianism in the Enlightenment: Antagonism and Collaboration between the Jesuits and the Philosophers." In *China and Europe: Images and Influences in Sixteenth to Eighteenth Centuries*, edited by Thomas H. C. Lee, 99–128. Hong Kong: Chinese University Press, 1991.

———. *Curious Land: Jesuit Accommodation and the Origins of Sinology*. Honolulu: University of Hawaii Press, 1989.

———. *Leibniz and Confucianism: The Search for Accord*. Honolulu: University of Hawaii Press, 1977.

————. "The Reconciliation of Neo-Confucianism with Christianity in the Writings of Joseph de Premare, S. J." *Philosophy East and West* 26.4 (1976) 389–410.

Neibuhr, Richard. H. *Christ and Culture*. New York: Harper, 2001.

Neill, Stephen. *A History of Christian Missions*. New York: Penguin, 1964.

Neill, Stephen, et al., eds. *Concise Dictionary of the Christian World Mission*. London: Lutterworth, 1971.

Nevius, John. *The Planting and Development of Missionary Churches*. New York: Foreign Mission Library, 1899.

Newbigin, Lesslie. *The Gospel in a Pluralistic Society*. Grand Rapids: Eerdmans, 1989.

————. "Post-Enlightenment Culture as a Missionary Problem." In *Foolishness to the Greeks: The Gospel and Western Culture*, 1–20. Grand Rapids: Eerdmans, 1986.

Nicholls, Bruce J. *Contextualization: A Theology of Gospel and Culture*. Downers Grove, IL: InterVarsity, 1979.

Oak, Sung-Deuk. *The Making of Korean Christianity: Protestant Encounters with Korean Religions, 1876–1915*. Waco, TX: Baylor University Press, 2013.

————. "North American Missionaries' Understanding of the *Tan'gun* and *Kija* Myths of Korea, 1884–1934." *Acta Koreana* 5.1 (2002) 51–73.

————. "Periodicals, 1880–1940: Related to Korean Protestant Christianity." http://koreanchristianity.cdh.ucla.edu/images/stories/Periodicals.pdf.

Oduyoye, Mercy Amba. "The Future of Christianity in Sub-Saharan Africa." In *Christianity in Sub-Saharan Africa*, edited by Kenneth R. Ross et al., 461–77. Peabody, MA: Hendrickson, 2017.

O'Malley, John W. *Trent: What Happened at the Council*. Cambridge: Harvard University Press, 2013.

Ott, Craig, et al. *Encountering Theology of Mission: Biblical Foundations, Historical Developments, and Contemporary Issues*. Grand Rapids: Baker Academic, 2010.

Palmer, Spencer J. *Korea and Christianity*. Seoul: Royal Asiatic Society, 1986.

Park, Andrew S. *The Wounded Heart of God: The Asian Concept of Han and the Christian Doctrine of Sin*. Nashville: Abingdon, 1993.

Park, Timothy Kiho. "Korean Christian World Mission: The Missionary Movement of the Korean Church." Keynote Speech delivered at the 5th Annual Underwood Conference, New Brunswick Theological Seminary, 2006.

————. "The Missionary Movement of the Korean Church: A Model for Non-Western Mission." In *Korean Church, God's Mission, Global Christianity*, edited by Wonsuk Ma and Kyo Seong Ahn, 19–31. Oxford: Regnum, 2015.

Passenger Lists of Vessels Arriving at New York, 1820–1897. Washington, DC: National Archives and Records Service, 1958. https://archive.org/details/passengerlistsof0372unit/mode/2up.

Paul VI, Pope. *Nostra Aetate*. https://www.vatican.va/archive/hist_councils/ii_vatican_council/documents/vat-ii_decl_19651028_nostra-aetate_en.html.

Peterson, Willard J. "Why Did They Become Christians?" In *East Meets West: The Jesuits in China, 1582–1773*, edited by Charles Ronan and Bonnie B. C. Oh, 129–52. Chicago: Loyola University Press, 1988.

Pierson, Arthur Tappan. *George Muller of Bristol and His Witness to a Prayer-Hearing God*. New York: Revell, 1899.

Pierson, Delavan Leonard. *Arthur T. Pierson: A Spiritual Warrior, Mighty in the Scriptures*. New York: Revell, 1912.

The Proceedings of the 10th Annual Underwood International Symposium. Seoul: Saemunan Presbyterian Church, 2017.

"Professor Washington Hasbrouck." *New York Times*, February 26, 1895.

Rees, Jonathan. *Industrialization and the Transformation of American Life.* Armonk, NY: Sharpe, 2013.

Rhodes, Harry A., and Archibald Campbell. *History of the Korean Mission Presbyterian Church U.S.A.: Vol. 1, 1884–1934.* Seoul: Chosön Mission Presbyterian Church U.S.A., 1934.

———. *History of the Korean Mission Presbyterian Church U.S.A.: Vol. 2, 1935–1959.* New York: Commission on Ecumenical Mission and Relations, PCUSA, 1964.

Ricci, Matteo. *The True Meaning of the Lord of Heaven.* St. Louis: The Institute of Jesuit Sources, 1985.

Robert, Dana L. *Christian Mission: How Christianity Became a World Religion.* West Sussex: Wiley-Blackwell, 2009.

———, ed. *Converting Colonialism: Visions and Realities in Mission History, 1706–1914.* Grand Rapids: Eerdmans, 2008.

———. *Occupy until I Come: A. T. Pierson and the Evangelization of the World.* Grand Rapids: Eerdmans, 2003.

———. "The Origin of the Student Volunteer Watchword: 'The Evangelization of the World in This Generation.'" *International Bulletin of Missionary Research* (1986) 146–49.

Ronan, Charles, and Bonnie B. C. Oh, eds. *East Meets West: The Jesuits in China, 1582–1773.* Chicago: Loyola University Press, 1988.

Rosenwaike, Ira. *Population History of New York City.* Syracuse, NY: Syracuse University Press, 1972.

Ross, John. *History of Korea: Ancient and Modern with Description of Manners and Customs, Language and Geography.* London: Stock, 1891.

Ross, Kenneth R., et al. *Christianity in Sub-Saharan Africa.* Peabody, MA: Hendrickson, 2017.

Rule, Paul A. *K'ung-tzu or Confucius: The Jesuit Interpretation of Confucianism.* Sydney: Allen and Unwin, 1986.

Russell, Letty M. *Human Liberation in a Feminist Perspective—A Theology.* Philadelphia: Westminster, 1974.

Russell, Letty, et al., eds. *Inheriting Our Mothers' Gardens.* Louisville: Westminster, 1988.

Rutt, Richard A. *A Biography of James Sorath Gale and a New Edition of His History of the Korean People.* Seoul: Royal Asiatic Society, Korea Branch, 1972.

Sanneh, Lamin. "Secular Values in the Midst of Faith: A Critical Discourse on Dialogue and Difference." In *Theology and the Religions: A Dialogue,* edited by Viggo Mortensen, 137–52. Grand Rapids: Eerdmans, 2003.

Schineller, Peter. *A Handbook on Inculturation.* New York: Paulist, 1990.

Schreiter, Robert J. *Constructing Local Theologies.* New York: Orbis, 1985.

Schroeder, H. J., ed. and trans. *The Canons and Decrees of the Council of Trent.* Rockford, IL: TAN, 1978.

Sebes, Joseph. "The Precursors of Ricci." In *East Meets West: The Jesuits in China, 1582–1773,* edited by Charles Ronan and Bonnie B. C. Oh, 19–61. Chicago: Loyola University Press, 1988.

Seeger, Raymond J. "Faraday, Sandemanian." *The Journal of American Scientific Affiliation* 35 (1983) 101.

Shorter, Aylward. *Toward a Theology of Inculturation*. New York: Orbis, 1988.

Soltau, T. S. *Korea the Hermit Nation and Its Response to Christianity*. New York: World Dominion, 1932.

Song, Choan-Seng. *Theology from the Womb of Asia*. New York: SCM, 1988.

Song, Choan-Seng. "The Cross and the Lotus." In *Third-Eye Theology: Theology in Formation in Asian Settings*, 109–13. New York: Orbis, 1991.

Spence, Jonathan D. "Matteo Ricci and the Ascent to Peking." In *East Meets West: The Jesuits in China, 1582–1773*, edited by Charles Ronan and Bonnie B. C. Oh. 3–18. Chicago: Loyola University Press, 1988.

Steer, Roger. *George Müller: Delighted in God*. Tain: Christian Focus, 1997.

Steinfels, Peter. "Clash at Canberra: A Feminist Radical's Keynote." *New York Times*, March 16, 1991.

Sunquist, Scott W. *Explorations in Asian Christianity: History, Theology, and Mission*. Downers Grove, IL: InterVarsity, 2017.

———. *Unexpected Christian Century: The Reversal and Transformation of Global Christianity, 1900–2000*. Grand Rapids: Baker, 2015.

Tennent, Timothy C. *Invitation to World Missions: A Trinitarian Missiology for the Twenty-First Century*. Grand Rapids: Kregel, 2010.

"Theological Declaration by Christian Ministers in the Republic of Korea, 1973." In *Mission Trends No. 3: Third World Theologies*, edited by Gerald Anderson and Thomas F. Stransky, 227–32. New York: Paulist, 1976.

Thomas, M. M. "The Contribution of Christian Realism to the Idea of Indian Democracy." In *Ideological Quest within Christian Commitment*, 253–68. Madras: Christian Literature Society, 1983.

Thompson, Jack T. *Light on Darkness? Missionary Photography of Africa in the Nineteenth and Early Twentieth Centuries*. Grand Rapids: Eerdmans, 2012.

Tocqueville, Alexis de. *Democracy in America: And Two Essays on America*. Translated by Gerald E. Bevan. London: Penguin, 2003.

Tucker, Ruth A. *From Jerusalem to Irian Jaya: A Biographical History of Christian Missions*. Grand Rapids: Zondervan, 1983.

———. *Guardians of the Great Commission: The Story of Women in Modern Missions*. Grand Rapids: Zondervan, 1988.

Uhalley, Stephen, Jr., and Xiaoxin Wu, eds. *China and Christianity: Burdened Past, Hopeful Future*. New York: Sharpe, 2001.

Underwood, Elizabeth. *Challenged Identities: North American Missionaries in Korea, 1884–1934*. Seoul: Royal Asiatic Society, Korea Branch, 2003.

Underwood, Horace Grant, Jr. "A Foreigner's View of Korean Church: Present and Future." Lecture delivered at the 13th Pastoral Ministry Seminar, "The Future of the Korean Church—Challenge and Response," Yonsei University, 1993.

———. *Korea in War, Revolution and Peace: The Recollections of Horace G. Underwood*. Edited by Michael J. Devine. Seoul: Yonsei University Press, 2001.

Underwood, Horace Horton. *Modern Education in Korea*. New York: International, 1926.

———. *A Partial Bibliography of Occidental Literature on Korea to 1930*. Vol. 20. Seoul: Royal Asiatic Society, 1931.

———. *Tragedy and Faith in Korea*. New York: Friendship, 1951.

University of the City of New York. *Catalogue of the University of the City of New York, 1876–1877*. New York: Richard Handy, 1877.

————. *Class Merit Book, July 1835–June 1888*, Vol. 4.

————. *A General Catalogue of the University of the City of New York, Departments of Arts and Science*. New York: Crawford & Co., 1882.

————. *The Matriculation Books of the University of the City of New York, Student Records, 1832–1916: Vol. 2, 1853–93*.

————. *Union College 1795–1895: A Record of the Commemoration of the One Hundredth Anniversary of the Founding of the Union College*. New York, 1897.

van Winkle, Daniel. *Old Bergen*. https://www.cityofjerseycity.org/oldberg/.

Vinton, Cadwallader C. "Presbyterian Mission Work in Korea." *The Missionary Review of the World* 16.9 (1893) 665–71.

Volf, Miroslav. *A Public Faith: How Followers of Christ Should Serve the Common Good*. Grand Rapids: Brazos, 2011.

————. *Flourishing: Why We Need Religion in a Globalized World*. New Haven: Yale University Press, 2016.

————. "For the Life of the World: Theology that Makes Difference," *Proceedings of the 11th Horace G. Underwood International Symposium*. Seoul: Saemunan Church Press, 2018.

Walls, Andrew. "The Future of Missiology—Missiology as Vocation." In *Crossing Cultural Frontiers: Studies in the History of World Christianity*, 259–66. New York: Orbis, 2017.

————. *The Missionary Movement in Christian History: Studies in the Transmission of Faith*. New York: Orbis, 1996.

Walvin, James. *A Child's World: A Social History of English Childhood, 1800–1914*. London: Pelican, 1982.

Watson, Burton, trans. *The Analects of Confucius*. New York: Columbia University Press, 2007.

Wayland, Francis. *Memoir of the Life of the Rev. Adoniram Judson*. 2 vols. Boston: Philips, Samson & Co., 1853.

Wikisource. "Glasites." https://en.wikisource.org/wiki/Page:EB1911_-_Volume_12.djvu/99.

Williams, Raymond. *The Long Revolution*. London: Chatto and Windus, 1961.

Wilson, J. Christy, Jr. *Today's Tentmakers: Self Support: An Alternative Model for Worldwide Witness*. Wheaton, IL: Tyndale, 1987.

Wolterstorff, Nicholas. *Lament for a Son*. Grand Rapids: Eerdmans, 1987.

————. *The God We Worship: An Exploration of Liturgical Theology*. Grand Rapids: Eerdmans, 2015.

————. "Reformed Worship: Seven Questions on What Has It Been and Should It Continue So?," *Proceedings of the 7th Horace G. Underwood International Symposium*. Seoul: Saemuan Church Press, 2014.

World Missionary Conference, ed. *Report of Commission I: Carrying the Gospel to All the Non-Christian World*. New York: Revell, 1910.

Wright, Caroll Davidson, and Robert Percival Porter. *Compendium of the Eleventh Census, 1890: Population; Dwellings and Families; Statistics of Alaska*. U.S. Government Printing Office, 1892.

Yeh, Allen. *Polycentric Missiology: Twenty-First-Century Mission from Everyone to Everywhere*. Downers Grove, IL: InterVarsity, 2016.

Yi, Jong Yong. *An Emerging Theology in World Perspective: Commentary on Korean Minjung Theology*. Mystic, CT: Twenty-Third, 1988.

Yi, Mahnyol, ed. and trans. *Appenzeller*. Seoul: Yonsei University Press, 1985.

―――. Preface to *Underwood of Korea; Being an Intimate Record of the Life and Work of the Rev. H. G. Underwood*, by Lillias Underwood. Translated by Mahnyol Yi. 2nd ed. Seoul: IVP Korea, 2015.

Yi, Sujŏng. "A Christian Corean's Appeal." *Friend's Review: A Religious, Literary and Miscellaneous Journal* 37.26 (1884) 401–2.

Young, John D. *East-West Synthesis: Matteo Ricci and Confucianism*. Hong Kong: Centre of Asian Studies, University of Hong Kong, 1980.

Zwemer, Samuel M. *The Zwemer Diaries*. Edited by Matthew Garero. New Brunswick, NJ: Beardslee, 2018.